MAROULA JOANNOU

CONTEMPORARY WOMEN'S WRITING

From *The Golden Notebook* to *The Color Purple*

Manchester University Press

MANCHESTER AND NEW YORK

distributed exclusively in the USA by St. Martin's Press

Published by Manchester University Press
Oxford Road, Manchester M13 9NR, UK
and Room 400, 175 Fifth Avenue, New York, NY 10010, USA
http://www.manchesteruniversitypress.co.uk

Distributed exclusively in the USA by
St. Martin's Press, Inc., 175 Fifth Avenue, New York, NY 10010, USA

Distributed exclusively in Canada by
UBC Press, University of British Columbia, 2029 West Mall, Vancouver, BC, Canada V6T 1Z2

British Library Cataloguing-in-Publication Data
A catalogue record for this book is available from the British Library

Library of Congress Cataloging-in-Publication Data applied for

ISBN 0 7190 5338 2 *hardback*
     0 7190 5339 0 *paperback*

First published 2000

07 06 05 04 03 02 01 00   10 9 8 7 6 5 4 3 2 1

Typeset by Northern Phototypesetting Co Ltd, Bolton
Printed in Great Britain by Bell & Bain Ltd, Glasgow

Yes, yes, if you please no reference to examples in books. Men have had every advantage of us in telling their own story. Education has been theirs in so much higher a degree; the pen has been in their hands. I will not allow books to prove any thing.

Jane Austen, *Persuasion*

It has become a common feeling ... that our own small stone of activism, which might not seem to measure up to the rugged boulders of heroism we have so admired, is a paltry offering toward the building of an edifice of hope. Many who believe this choose to withhold their offerings out of shame. This is the tragedy of our world.

Alice Walker, *Anything We Love Can Be Saved*

For the Greeks, the hidden life demanded invisible ink. They wrote an ordinary letter and in between the lines, set out another letter written in milk. The document looked innocent enough until one who knew better sprinkled coal dust over it. What the letter had been no longer mattered; what mattered was the life flaring up undetected ... till now.

Jeanette Winterson, *Sexing the Cherry*

It seems to me that the best art is political and you ought to be able to make it unquestionably political and irrevocably beautiful at the same time.

Toni Morrison, 'Rootedness: The Ancestor as Foundation'

CONTENTS

ACKNOWLEDGEMENTS

I am indebted to the Arts and Humanities Research Board for generous funding under their Research Leave Scheme that allowed me time to bring this project to completion. Access to the Faculty of English Library and the Cambridge University Library made the use of other libraries unnecessary and I wish to express my warmest thanks to the staff of both institutions and especially to Rosemary Jones and John Reynolds at the borrowing desk, Morag Law in the West Room, Neil Hudson at the periodical desk, and Michael Fuller in the Reading Room. The prolonged absence of any full-time member of the teaching staff inevitably creates additional work for the remaining members of their department. I am deeply grateful to my colleagues in the English Department of Anglia Polytechnic University for their patience, support and understanding and in particular to those whose work-loads increased because mine became lighter. I regret that I cannot acknowledge every member of the department by name. I owe special thanks to Simon Featherstone who took on my MA teaching and administration while I was on leave. Elizabeth Maslen gave sensible advice on most of the typescript, much of this on a very convivial holiday in Norway which we enjoyed together. Her retirement from teaching will be a great loss to many of us. Simon Featherstone, Margaretta Jolly, Paulina Palmer, Anna Snaith and Nigel Wheale have all read and commented helpfully on particular sections of this book. I have enjoyed many discussions on contemporary women writers with my research student, Marion Treby. My colleagues in the Women's Studies team, especially Penelope Kenrick, Ros Minsky, Sarah Monk and Gina Wisker, have provided friendship and inspiration. My neighbour and friend Olga Grizopolou replenished me with excellent Greek home cooking, warmth and laughter during occasional bouts of sickness and she and Jack will be deeply missed when they move house.*

Avril Horner supplied the generous (and at that stage anonymous) reader's report on the proposal which I submitted to the Manchester University Press, without which I would not have received a contract. Matthew Frost and Pippa Kenyon oversaw the production of the book from the start with great efficiency and good humour. The sections on Nell Dunn and Anita Brookner have appeared in different but recognisable form in *Post-War Literatures in English*, 44, June 1999, and in Gina Wisker and Lynne Pearce (eds), *Fatal Attractions: Rescripting Romance in Contemporary Literature and Film*, Pluto Press, 1998. The tapestry, *Art Sleeps in Craft* on the front cover is reproduced by kind permission of the artist, Grace Erickson Wiant, and is taken from an original photograph by Tony Barney.

Finally, I wish to thank the friends (all of whom are now fifty something and most of whom are not academics) with whom I lived through the events

---

* Margaret Clark compiled the index.

of the 1960s and 1970s, especially Brenda Kirsch, from whom I have learned so much over the years. Their assessment of the immense importance of the two decades which we all remember in helping to shape us into the people we now are prompted me to write this book.

Mary Joannou
Cambridge

INTRODUCTION

'Truly, it Felt Like Year One'

I believe in yesterday.
John Lennon–Paul McCartney

IN FAY WELDON'S first novel, *The Fat Woman's Joke* (1967), the heroine, Esther complains that her husband pays lip-service to the idea of equality between the sexes but continues to act as though he were superior to her: 'You may *know* that I am equal, with your reason, but you certainly don't *feel* that I am.' To which her husband, Alan retorts, 'Quite the suffragette.' Such was the absence of feminist role models in 1967 that the term suffragette was still 'the worse term of abuse a man can think of to say to his wife'.[1]

This book is largely about the reinvention of rebellion in women's writing and society over a twenty-year period and will provide an analysis of the relationship between women's writing and social change in the 1960s and 1970s. I am concerned with literary texts in relation to what was a highly fruitful, vibrant and dynamic period in the history of literature and the history of women. The contours of my project are set by the twenty years between *The Golden Notebook* (1962) and *The Color Purple* (1982) My first chapter begins with *The Golden Notebook*, a text that prefigured the second wave of the organised feminist movement but expressed the discontents about sex and men that the movement would explore. The 'free women' in *The Golden Notebook* are supposedly independent, but in reality are locked into emotional dependency on men, and into a neo-Marxist analysis of society that does little to explain their discontents as women. Twenty years later, the certainties of the women's movement have been unsettled, in part by black women posing important questions to the ways in which women's oppression had been theorised, the experience of white women had been universalised, and black women's perspectives marginalised. My final chapter is concerned with *The Color Purple* as a flagship of the politics of difference and with Toni Morrison's powerful critique of whiteness in *The Bluest Eye* (1970). The latter exposes how the dominant assumptions about colour that guarantee the superiority of one racial group over others are perpetuated and their disastrous effects on the self-esteem of one young, black woman. My cut-off date of 1982, to which I have adhered in order to

reduce a potentially unwieldy project to manageable size, has unfortu-
nately meant the exclusion of much excellent fiction from both Britain
and America; for example, feminist detective fiction from the United
States which had its heyday later in the 1980s, and fiction by black British
writers which also comes into its own in that decade but outside my
parameters.[2]

There are a number of critical works which are wholly or largely
concerned with the same areas as my own study, of which the most
substantial are: Patricia Duncker, *Strangers and Sisters: An Introduction to
Contemporary Feminist Fiction*, Gayle Greene, *Changing the Story:
Feminist Fiction and the Tradition*, Molly Hite, *The Other Side of the Story:
Structures and Strategies of Contemporary Feminist Narrative*, Maggie
Humm, *Border Traffic: Strategies of Contemporary Women Writers*, Maria
Lauret, *Liberating Literature: Feminist Fiction in America*, and Paulina
Palmer, *Contemporary Women's Fiction: Narrative Practice and Feminist
Theory*.[3] Of these Palmer provides a welcome study of the relationship
between feminist theory and narrative and, like Duncker, writes from a
highly politicised and uncompromising lesbian radical feminist activist
position. Lauret is concerned exclusively with American writing and like
Humm makes important connections between the socially engaged
fiction of the 1930s and the later fiction she examines. Humm constructs
a sophisticated argument about how women use the contemporary
phenomenon of border journeys to adjust their writing to their experiential and historical sense of gender exclusion.[4] Lisa Maria Hogeland's
study of the consciousness-raising novel and the women's liberation
movement, *Feminism and its Fictions* I read after my book had gone to
press.[5]

Both Lauret and Greene make persuasive, theoretically informed,
and impassioned defences of feminist fiction. Greene argues that
'feminist fiction is the most revolutionary movement in contemporary
fiction – revolutionary both in that it is formally innovative and in that it
helped make a social revolution, playing a major role in the resurgence of
feminism in the sixties and seventies, the so-called second wave'. It is a
movement 'as significant as Modernism, producing texts that combine
the excitement and experimentation of Modernism with the social
critique of the great age of realism, though literary critics and historians
have scarcely recognised it as a movement – perhaps because it's recent,
perhaps because it comes from women'.[6] Lauret argues that 'feminist
realism, by virtue of its reliance upon extraliterary feminist discourses, is
then, indeed different from other realisms whether bourgeois or
socialist'. Moreover, 'as a subjective realism it further challenges and at
times erases the division between inside and outside, subjective psychic

life and objective social reality'.[7] My own work draws upon English and American fiction and has a more distanced relationship to feminist fiction than either Lauret or Greene. I also provide a historical context for the fiction, with which many students, some who were not born in the 1960s or 1970s, cannot be assumed to be familiar.

As Raymond Williams has put it, 'the structure of feeling which is tangible in a particular set of works is undoubtedly an articulation of an area of experience which lies beyond them. This is especially evident of those specific and historically definable moments when new work produces a sudden shock of *recognition.*' He adds that 'What must be happening on these occasions is that an experience which is really very wide suddenly finds a semantic figure which articulates it.'[8] Following Williams, what I have done in this study is to select women's responses to historically specific experiences, for example, the changing experience of motherhood, the feminine mystique, working-class life, etc. Such responses either differ from, prefigure, reflect, or mediate, the dominant structures of feeling of the time. I then show how a group of women writers, often with no ostensible connection between them, express common themes in their work, and how this articulation in its turn serves to shape the reader's awareness and understanding of the historical period in which they wrote.

Like the 1930s, the 1960s is a decade that invokes extraordinary passion from both ends of the political spectrum. At one end are those for whom the decade was synonymous with days of hope and liberation. At the other, those for whom the 'permissiveness' of the day laid the founda- tion of the country's subsequent ills. A famously vituperative indictment of the 1960s in Britain is contained in an interview with Margaret Thatcher conducted by David English for the *Daily Mail.* Thatcher told English that in the 1960s *'permissiveness, selfish and uncaring, proliferated under the guise of the new sexual freedom. Aggressive verbal hostility, presented as a refreshing lack of subservience, replaced courtesy and good manners. Instant gratification became the cult of the young and youth cultists'.* According to Thatcher, 'all individualism was despised, unless it was an arrogant and selfish individualism' and 'the country, under the control of Harold Wilson, had gone quite Socialist in its addiction to welfare, nationalisation and trade union dominance. But even more dramatically, Britain had become a world leader in the social and moral revolution of the "swinging sixties"'. Moreover, 'this business of breaking the rules began in universities, where most of the theoretical philosophies always start'.[9]

This is not a version of the 1960s that many who lived through it will recognise. In the words of Angela Carter, 'There is a tendency to underplay, even to completely devalue, the experience of the 1960s, especially for women, but towards the end of that decade there was a brief period of public philosophical awareness that occurs only very occasionally in human history; when truly it felt like Year One.'[10] Sara Maitland's anthology of women reflecting on the 1960s is entitled *Very Heaven*, borrowing from Wordsworth the reference to a revolutionary world in which it was 'bliss to be alive'. Many were conscious that, for perhaps the first time, Britain had acquired 'a full blooded, enquiring rootless urban intelligentsia', like the ones in Europe and the United States, and in both countries the 'sense of living on a demolition site' was widespread.[11] As Margaret Drabble later put it, 'we live in an unchartered world, as far as manners and morals are concerned, we are having to make up our morality as we go. Our subject matter is enormous, there are whole new patterns to create'.[12]

To write a study of a time which one can remember is in some respects to write an autobiographical study in which the past and present selves are involved in a critical and continuing dialogue. I write this book as someone who came to academic feminism after my experiences in the women's movement in the 1970s and whose ideas about politics, democracy and the possibilities of social change were largely shaped by discussions in and around the Communist Party. In 1968 I was the first person from my working-class, immigrant family to go to university. Like many of my contemporaries, I quickly became drawn into student politics and was one of a thousand or so students at Manchester University who occupied the university buildings and spent six weeks conducting the business of our 'alternative university' under a banner which declared to curious passers-by that the university had been proclaimed a 'liberated zone'. The situation was replicated in student sit-ins in universities all over the country.

Like the clothes in old photographs of the time, there are excesses from which many who took part in those heady days of student dissent would wish now to distance themselves. But there is also much that underpinned the intellectual formation of the generation who were politicised in 1968 for which little apology is needed: the commitment to peace and justice on a global scale, the perpetual questioning of received wisdom, the restless intellectual curiosity; the passionate alignment with the oppressed, the deep-rooted desire to democratise familiar institutions, the suspicion of anyone who appeared to be motivated largely by personal ambition, the rejection of elitism and the determination to break down hierarchy, the belief in the efficacy of co-operation rather than competition, and, above all, the belief in the power of collective action to change whatever needed changing. Impossibly idealistic or wildly utopian though this might now seem, it still appears vastly preferable to what came afterwards; the election in 1979 of Margaret Thatcher who was later to advocate that Britain return to the socially divisive 'Victorian values' and the attitudes of the far right publicly espoused by Ronald Reagan after his election 1981.

For conservatives, the universities in the sixties and early seventies were not 'fortresses of democratic idealism but forerunners of a shameless politicization at odds with the pursuit of truth'.[13] Social abundance and personal affluence were the prerequisites of the campus-based radicalism. Britain was a country in which food and wages were relatively low and taxes relatively high. Student grants were, in the main, sufficient for students to live on, and good jobs were plentiful for graduates. University education was still largely the privilege of a few. Even with the creation of the six new universities of East Anglia, Essex, Sussex, Kent, York and Warwick, the percentage of the population in the United Kingdom who went on to higher education was minute compared to that in the United States.

The emergence of a mass student movement was informed and galvanised by the anti-imperialist struggle particularly directed around the war in Vietnam. It was the strength of the anti-war opinion in the United States that brought American soldiers back home, and the victory of the Vietnamese people against the richest nation in the world which had been thought to be invincible was a trauma from which it would take the United States long to recover. One by one the nations of the Commonwealth achieved their independence and immigration to Britain from the Commonwealth, and in particular from the Caribbean and the Indian sub-continent, grew rapidly in the 1950s. My chapter on the narratives of empire deals with some of these changes in the fiction of Jean Rhys, Buchi Emecheta and Ruth Prawer Jhabvala. Britain narrowly voted for the end of thirteen years of Conservative rule with the election of Harold Wilson's Labour government of 1964, which was returned with a sizeable majority in 1966. Although their foreign policy was a disappointment to many radicals at the time, Labour was more liberal at home than its predecessors, and instigated a number of important social reforms, including the abolition of capital punishment, the reform of the antiquated divorce laws (1969), and the legalisation of abortion (1967), and of homosexual acts between consenting adults in private (1967). The gay and lesbian liberation movements in Britain and the United States were inspired by the successful attempt to resist police harassment in the Stonewall bar in New York in 1969.

In the United States, the most lasting achievement of the decade was the development of a movement dedicated to civil rights and the dismantling of the legal edifice of racial discrimination. The young Alice Walker summarised the lasting achievements of that movement in an essay written in 1967, 'The Civil Rights Movement. What Good Was It?'. Walker argues that

> If the Civil Rights Movement is 'dead', and if it gave us nothing else, it gave us each other forever. It gave some of us bread, some of us shelter, some of us knowledge and pride, all of us comfort. It gave us our children, our husbands, our brothers, our fathers, as men reborn and with a purpose for living. It broke the pattern of black servitude in this country. It shattered the phoney 'promise' of white soap operas that sucked away so many pitiful lives. It gave us history and men far greater than Presidents. It gave us heroes, selfless men of courage, and strength for our little boys and girls to follow. It gave us hope for tomorrow. It called us to life. Because we live, it can never die.[14]

If the 1960s was the decade of youth, the 1970s was the decade of women. The women's movement was born out of a climate of left political struggle in Britain and in its early days many women described themselves as socialist feminists. The United States did not have the same socialist tradition but, as Sara Evans argues, there the women's movement was initiated by women in the civil rights movement and the new left who dared to test the old assumptions and myths about female nature against their own experience and discovered that something was seriously wrong: 'They had to dare because within the same movement that gave them so much they were simultaneously thrust into subservient roles – as secretary, sex object, housekeeper, "dumb chick"'.[15] While the notion of sisterhood was later to become problematic, as women became painfully aware of the differences which separated them across lines of sexuality, age, class, religion, disability and generation, it resonated with meaning in the early days of the movement, as countless women discovered the joy of support from other women for the first time, and acquired a new sense of their own worth, potential and importance.

The full impact of the women's liberation movement can be understood with reference to what Rita Felski has termed the feminist public sphere. By this Felski means the creation of a discursive space in which the shared experience of gender-based oppression provides the impetus for the development of a self-consciously oppositional identity among women. Externally, the movement sought to challenge existing power structures through political activity and theoretical critique. Internally, it generated a supportive sense of community and solidarity which empowered women individually and collectively.[16] To do justice to the ways in which the lives of women were enriched by the feminist renaissance of the 1970s is impossible. For the first time, large numbers of women, who often had no connection with the organised women's movement, began to look critically at their own lives and expectations and to recognise that their feelings of depression, entrapment and lack of fulfilment could, at least in part, be laid at the door of the society which did not recognise them as fully equal human beings. Acceptance of their situations gave way to demands for agency, justice, equality, autonomy and freedom, in the workplace and at home. Dissent found expression less often in 'outrageous acts' than in what Gloria Steinem, the co-founder of *Ms*, has termed 'everyday rebellions' on the part of women.[17]

A list of initiatives which would never have come into being had it not been for the influence of feminist ideas would include women's health centres, credit unions, rape crisis centres, refuges for battered women, feminist therapy centres, consciousness raising groups, commercial businesses, and women's co-operatives. Feminist caucuses proliferated within the professions, along with access courses and women's studies programmes in adult and higher education, and the provision of work-based creches and nurseries. Campaigns were launched against sexual harassment in the workplace, to highlight the feminisation of poverty, and in support of poorly paid women who went on strike for better pay and conditions. Others were directed against pornography, sexism in the media, and in attempts to 'reclaim the night'.

By the end of the 1970s, the day-to-day realities and expectations of women's lives had been changed beyond recognition. The majority of women no longer expected to marry young and to spend the rest of their lives as housewives with no paid employment. In place of the 'feminine mystique' which had bound middle-class women to the home in the decade after the Second World War, women had asserted their right to go out to work as well as to have children. 'In contrast to the baby boom of the 1950s, the population birthrate fell to a simple population replacement level in the 1970s.'[18] While marriage still remained popular, more couples were cohabiting, women were choosing to have children outside marriage, to divorce, to live with same-sex partners, or to bring up children on their own. I provide a short summary of changes affecting motherhood, divorce, contraception and workplace legislation in my second chapter. Here I also look at changing attitudes to motherhood in fiction, and in particular at the representation of the unmarried mother, with reference to the writing of Margaret Atwood, Lynne Reid Banks, Margaret Forster, Penelope Mortimer, Margaret Drabble and Fay Weldon.

The question which hangs over the sexual revolution of the 1960s and 1970s is, Was it a woman's revolution? It is certainly true that women continued to be treated as sex objects and that the availability of contraception meant that they often felt under pressure from men to have sex that they did not want. Radical feminists sometimes complained that sexual freedom 'includes no freedom to decline sex, to refuse to be defined at every turn by sex'.[19] Although it took considerable time for the feminist case that women had the same sexual rights as men to become widely accepted, the period was also characterised by a more widespread understanding of women's sexual needs and, after the publication of the Hite Report in 1976, by a greater understanding of the nature and importance of woman's sexual pleasure. What Bea Campbell has often termed 'women's sexual misery' was much in evidence. But to argue that the sexual revolution was a revolution on men's terms is to deny the revolutionary importance of the sexual choices which became possible for women when contraceptives became freely available, and sex became separated from marriage and the fear of pregnancy, for many women for the first time. As Anthony Giddens observes in *The Transformation of Intimacy*, 'for most women, in most cultures, and through most periods of history sexual pleasure, where possible, was intrinsically bound up with fear – of repetitive pregnancies, and therefore of death, given the substantial proportion of women who perished in childbirth and the very high rates of infant mortality which prevailed'.[20]

The women's movement made a lasting impact in the cultural arena with the establishment of feminist book shops, theatre groups and art galleries. The large numbers of women wishing to read and purchase works that were being discussed in feminist circles and outside them constituted a substantial market not only for the well-known titles like *The Female Eunuch* (1970) and *Sexual Politics* (1969)[21] that became hallmarks of feminist identity but also for new works of fiction like *Fear of Flying* (1973) *Kinflicks* (1976) and *The Women's Room* (1977). These bore an obvious relationship to the concerns of the movement and reached widely beyond it, to became blockbusters selling hundreds of thousands of copies across the world. Many independent and radical bookshops stocking feminist books, some like Sisterwrite in London run by women's collectives, were started in cities all over Britain and the United States.

A major success story of the 1970s was the establishment of the long-running feminist magazine *Spare Rib*, which was widely recognised as the central forum for debate among British feminists. In the United States, *Ms* combined a commitment to a popular, non-threatening mode of feminism which aspired to reach as many women as possible with the project of establishing a dialogue with men and a space for feminism within the political mainstream. A number of radical feminist publications also thrived such as *Trouble and Strife* in Britain and *off our backs* in the United States. Feminist interdisciplinary journals like the socialist-feminist *Feminist Review* in Britain and *Signs* in the United States made a sizeable impact upon academia. The most successful of the feminist publishing houses, Virago and the Women's Press in Britain, and the Feminist Press in the United States, became internationally known and respected, bringing forgotten and neglected titles of fiction by women back into print as well as publishing new authors. Several of the best-known figures of the movement in the early days had a strong interest in English literature: Kate Millett in *Sexual Politics* (1969), which pinpointed the masculinist assumptions of established writers like Lawrence, Mailer and Miller; Germaine Greer in *The Female Eunuch* (1970), which ransacked the literary tradition for examples of misogyny; and Mary Ellmann in *Thinking about Women* (1968), which exposed the absurdity of the notion that woman's biology determined her way of thinking. All combined a feminist critique of the English literary tradition with a commitment to feminist change.[22] Adrienne Rich's influential essay 'When We Dead Awaken: Writing as Re-Vision' (1971) was followed by a number of important feminist studies, including Judith Fetterley's *The Resisting Reader: A Feminist Approach to American Literature* (1978), which helped to establish the feminist practice of reading 'against the grain' of the literary tradition.[23]

The question preoccupying many feminists and other radicals at this time was, to borrow Audre Lorde's words, whether or not it was possible 'to use the master's tools to dismantle the master's house?'[24] Were realist forms so tarnished by bourgeois ideology that it was impossible to appropriate them for radical purposes? While feminist writers like Angela Carter were to fashion new modes of experimental fiction, emphasising the lexical surface of the text and inventively parodying existing modes such as the Gothic or the fairy tale, the desire to represent a world in flux as faithfully as possible often took the form of attempts to revitalise realism rather than to reject it. The relationship between realism, social commitment and literary form was memorably explored in Doris Lessing's monumental novel, *The Golden Notebook* (1962). But despite Lessing's own pessimism about the capacity of realist modes of fiction to represent the fragmented nature of modern reality, much writing by women in this period illustrates that the uses of omniscient narration, the socially expressive novel, and the traditions of moral realism were far from exhausted. Moreover, in a context in which Margaret Thatcher declaimed that there was 'no such thing as society'[25] but 'only individuals and their families' – a statement made in 1988 but preceded by a number of similar utterances – the socially engaged novel acquired a new political dimension. As Molly Hite has noted, 'the writing perceived as the avant-garde at a particular moment tends to define that moment in literary history'.[26] Other practices do not usually elicit the same critical attention.

The fact that women writers, with honourable exceptions such as Angela Carter and, in her very different way, Joanna Russ, do not readily come to mind in connection with the innovative postmodern novel, and are not to be found in any significant numbers at the forefront of stylistic experimentation during this period, should not distract from the importance of the attempts of individual women to articulate an '"other side" to the dominant stories of a given culture', to devise strategies of opposition 'to a narrative tradition that works to inscribe her within its own ideological codes'.[27]

One way in which feminist ideas found a wide readership in this time was through the subversion of popular genres: for example, science fiction with its ability to explore 'what could be' rather than 'what is', and detective fiction which provided a space for feminist fantasy and questioned stereotypical notions of what was suitable work for woman. My chapter on popular fictions deals with Ursula Le Guin, Marge Piercy and Joanna Russ as writers of science fiction and with examples of detective fiction by P.D. James and Valerie Miner. The questions raised for women by romantic fiction receive attention separately in my discussion of Anita Brookner.

This book is concerned with woman-centred writing rather than with 'feminist fiction'. This is in part because the term 'feminist' is more problematic in relation to fiction than is sometimes supposed. Is a feminist novel one written by a feminist?; one in which the subject matter is of feminist interest?; one which offers a feminist vision?; one which appears to have affinities with specific types of feminist theory or makes use of the *écriture feminine* associated with writers like Luce Irigaray and Hélène Cixous? And who is to decide? But it is also because it is a term which many women writers have said that they do not wish to use. In the case of black women this is usually because of the part that middle-class feminists have played in marginalising black women's experience. But for many others it is often because 'feminist fiction' has become synonymous with 'bad fiction', that is to say fiction which is the antithesis of the subtle, questioning and allusive fiction which they wish to write, and which is perceived as a procrustean bed in which they do not wish to lie. Whether or not women choose to write as feminists they have no choice but to write as women.

The changes in the perception of what it was to be a woman which occurred in the course of the twenty-year period with which I am concerned were of monumental significance. Thus the fiction written at a time when feminist ideas were hegemonic is likely to reflect and mediate the impact of a culture which was radically altered by feminism whether this is desired by the author or not. As Virginia Woolf had pointed out in *A Room of One's Own*, works of art 'are not single and solitary births; they are the outcome of many years of thinking in common, of thinking by the body of the people, so that the experience of the mass is behind the common voice'.[28]

Although they might appear to have nothing in common, Marilyn French's *The Women's Room* and Anita Brookner's *Hotel du Lac* are good examples of woman-centred texts which have been read by countless women who have turned to them, usually with a realistic expectation of what to expect, and often very largely because they know that such texts will offer the reader the satisfaction of heroines with whose predicaments and feelings they can identify. This is equally true of a heroine whose situation confirms the importance of woman's desire to feel loved, as in *Hotel du Lac* – the question then becomes, Why is the kind of love for which so many women crave elusive? – as it is of a heroine who desires to break away from suburban life, to use higher education as a route to personal emancipation, and to build a life of her own as in *The Women's Room*.

Woman-centred fictions, then, whether of the feminine or feminist variety, address women about issues of primary concern to women. In practice, even the most unpromising of woman-centred texts is capable of producing a reading that is of interest to feminism, as I shall argue in relation to the fiction of Anita Brookner and A.S. Byatt. Rather than constituting their readers as naive or unquestioning, it is important to understand the variety of reading positions for women inscribed within them, and the ways in which the changes rung on familiar themes disclose to the reader how the heroine is constrained by factors not of her choosing. As I have argued elsewhere, the fact that substantial numbers of women read woman-centred fictions underwrites their importance for those who wish to bring about feminist change.[29] This, is of course, precisely why the 'feminist confessionals' of the 1970s were written. The fact that feminist fictions are frequently didactic, eschew artifice and distanciation, and set out to politicise the reader does not mean that the woman reader is thereby passively situated and undiscriminating. The road to the happiness in such novels is often paved with good intentions and strewn with patriarchal obstacles, and, if the heroine does succeed in getting there, it is often by circuitous routes that involve finding the courage to change at the same time as experiencing doubt, crisis of identify and fragmentation. As Patricia Waugh has put it, 'What many of the texts suggest is that it is possible to experience oneself as a strong and coherent agent in the world *at the same time* as understanding the extent to which identity and genre are socially constructed and represented.'[30]

Like much polemical writing, the feminist confessionals at which I look closely in this book, *The Women's Room*, *Fear of Flying* and *Rubyfruit Jungle* were engendered by the controversies of a particular historical moment and have arguably not survived the moment of controversy well. Their importance for women today lies in their reinsertion into history and social relations which is largely what this study attempts to do. I agree with Ellen Cronan Rose that 'the task confronting feminist scholars of contemporary women's fiction at this time is to theorize and historicize today's novels rather than to memorialize a feminist high renaissance of the 1970s'.[31] It is in recovering, historicising and relating to literature the very real improvements in women's lives, for which feminism was responsible, that my energies as a feminist critic are most productively engaged, rather than in the defence *per se* of the feminist realist fiction in which many women, myself included, may once have been fascinated, but for which we may now feel complete indifference.

The distinction between women's writing and feminist writing on which Rosalind Coward has famously insisted[32] is simplistic, if only because it is difficult to see what useful purpose is served by the use of feminist fiction as a yardstick whereby other types of women's writing is judged and found wanting. If the key questions to be asked of feminist realism (as of *all* realist texts) are, Do they generate new knowledge rather than reiterate that which we already know? and, if so, How?, the questions to be asked of *all* writing by women (including woman-centred texts) might include, Are they intelligent?, emancipatory?, irreverent?, inventive?, funny? How do they employ strategies of parodic transformation probing beyond the limits of the known and familiar? How do they image new worlds or interrogate reality and suggest other possibilities? The feminist confessionals of the 1970s were largely concerned with women's suffering and reflected the anger and frustration to which the women's movement gave expression and on which their success was predicated. Twenty years later 'notions of "woman as a unified category", of "feminism", of "women's writing", and of "feminist criticism" itself have been effectively deconstructed, thereby undermining the possibility of a feminist reading of feminist fiction without the use of inverted comas.'[33] The feminist confessionals may ironically be now of more interest to a rather different constituency, those who are hostile to feminism in the academy and outside it, and to post-feminists for whom such novels are merely examples of feminism's history of preoccupations with the arcane and irrelevant.

In *No More Sex Wars: The Failures of Feminism*, Neil Lyndon denies the existence of systemic and institutional discrimination against women in Britain today. Moreover, he contends that all that feminism has produced is sex wars and any freedom that women may have achieved is the result of access to abortion and reliable contraception.[34] Post-feminists like Natasha Walter and Naomi Wulf are stylish and articulate proponents of new varieties of 'power feminism'. They believe strongly in individual equality but are highly critical of earlier feminists; happy to enjoy what has been won for them but disowning those whose struggles made such gains and opportunities possible. Works like Wulf's *Fire with Fire* and Walter's *The New Feminism* have pinpointed with acuity some of the more obvious failings of the women's movement,[35] for example, its alienation of innumerable women who felt powerless to express their love of individual men without sensing disapproval or hostility, and its obsession with regulating the minutiae of dress and behaviour (good examples are the antipathy to the wearing of feminine clothes and make-up that was common in feminist circles) which now appears curiously puritanical and oppressive.

But, as Nicci Gerrard argues, the position of such women 'is not political but anti-political – they have discarded the collective spirit for a liberated individualism. They would fight from their own rights and against manifest sexual prejudice, but they would not organise to fight for the rights of all women.'[36] As Alice Echols has put it, feminism has been the victim of its own successes. Its lack of appeal to younger women is witness of the extent to which its language has become part of the mainstream and its demands either acknowledged or recuperated: 'Equality is presented as a fait accompli, and feminism, as a consequence, rendered an anachronism.'[37] The willingness of those in power to exploit women's issues (often with no reference to feminism) points to the tremendous gains that have been made over the past twenty years, especially for those white middle-class women who have traditionally provided most of its support. The chapters which follow examine some of the transformations that women experienced during these twenty years and the ways in which this is reflected and mediated in their fiction.

NOTES

1 Fay Weldon, *The Fat Woman's Joke* (London: Hodder and Stoughton, 1967), p. 69.
2 The exceptions I have made are for Anita Brookner's *Hotel du Lac* (1984), Margaret Atwood's *The Handmaid's Tale* (1985) and Jan Clausen's *Sinking, Stealing* (1984), none of which are considered at any length.
3 Patricia Duncker, *Strangers and Sisters: An Introduction to Contemporary Feminist Fiction* (Oxford: Blackwell, 1992); Gayle Greene, *Changing the Story: Feminist Fiction and the Tradition* (Bloomington: Indiana University Press, 1991); Molly Hite, *The Other Side of the Story: Structures and Strategies of Contemporary Feminist Narrative* (Ithaca and London: Cornell University Press, 1989); Maggie Humm, *Border Traffic: Strategies of Contemporary Women Writers* (Manchester: Manchester

University Press, 1991); Maria Lauret, *Liberating Literature: Feminist Fiction in America* (London: Routledge, 1994), and Paulina Palmer, *Contemporary Women's Fiction: Narrative Practice and Theory* (Hemel Hempstead: Harvester, 1989).

4 Humm, *Border Traffic*, p. 1.

5 Lisa Maria Hogeland, *Feminism and its Fictions: The Consciousness-Raising Novel and the Women's Liberation Movement* (Philadadelphia: University of Pennysylvania Press, 1998).

6 Greene, *Changing the Story*, p. 2.

7 Lauret, *Liberating Literature*, p. 104, p. 105.

8 Raymond Williams, *Politics and Letters: Interview with New Left Review* (London: NLB, 1979), p. 164.

9 David English, interview with Margaret Thatcher, *Daily Mail*, 29 April 1988, pp. 6–7, p. 6, p. 7.

10 Angela Carter, 'Notes From the Front Line', in Micheline Wandor (ed.), *Gender and Writing* (London: Pandora, 1985), pp. 69–77, p. 70.

11 Angela Carter, 'Truly it Felt Like Year One', in Sara Maitland (ed.), *Very Heaven: Looking Back at the 1960s* (London: Virago, 1988), pp. 209–16, p. 210, p. 213.

12 Margaret Drabble, 'A Woman Writer', *Books*, 11, Spring 1973, p. 6.

13 Steven Macedo (ed.), *Reassessing the Sixties: Debating the Political and Cultural Legacy* (New York: Norton, 1997), p. 14.

14 'The Civil Rights Movement: What Good Was It?', 1967, in Alice Walker, *In Search of our Mother's Gardens: Womanist Prose* (London: The Women's Press, 1984), pp. 119–29, pp. 128–9.

15 Sara Evans, *Personal Politics: The Roots of Women's Liberation in The Civil Rights Movement and the New Left* (New York: Vintage Books, 1980), p. 213.

16 Rita Felski, *Beyond Feminist Aesthetics: Feminist Literature and Social Change* (London: Hutchinson Radius, 1989), pp. 166–7.

17 Gloria Steinem, *Outrageous Acts and Everyday Rebellions* (New York: Holt, Rinehart and Winston, 1983).

18 Felski, *Beyond Feminist Aesthetics*, p. 226.

19 Dana Densmore, 'Independence from The Sexual Revolution,' in Anne Koedt, Ellen Levine and Anita Rapone (eds), *Radical Feminism* (New York, Quadrangle, 1973), pp. 107–18, p. 111.

20 Anthony Giddens, *The Transformation of Intimacy: Sexuality, Love and Eroticism in Modern Societies* (Oxford: Polity/Blackwell, 1992), p. 27.

21 Kate Millett, *Sexual Politics* (London: Hart-Davis, 1969), Germaine Greer, *The Female Eunuch* (London: MacGibbon and Kee, 1970).

22 Mary Ellman, *Thinking About Women* (New York: Harcourt Brace Jovanovich, 1968).

23 Adrienne Rich, 'When We Dead Awaken: Writing as Re-Vision' (1971), reprinted in *On Lies, Secrets and Silence* (New York: Norton, 1979), pp. 33–49. Judith Fetterley, *The Resisting Reader: A Feminist Approach to American Literature* (Bloomington: Indiana University Press, 1978).

24 Audre Lorde, 'The Master's Tools Will Never Dismantle the Master's House', in Cherry Moraga and Gloria Anzaldua (eds), *This Bridge Called My Back: Writings by Radical Women of Color* (New York: Women of Color Press, 1991), pp. 98–101, p. 99.

25 Margaret Thatcher, as reported in the *Sunday Times*, 10 July 1988, p. 1.

26 Hite, *The Other Side of the Story*, p. 3.

27 Ibid.

28 Virginia Woolf, *A Room of One's Own* (London: Hogarth Press, 1929), p. 85.

29 Maroula Joannou, *'Ladies, Please Don't Smash These Windows': Women's Writing, Feminist Consciousness and Social Change 1918–1938* (Oxford: Berg, 1995), p. 158.

30 Patricia Waugh, *Feminine Fictions: Revisiting the Postmodern* (London: Routledge, 1989), p. 13.

31 Ellen Cronan Rose, 'Review Essay: American Feminist Criticism of Contemporary Women's Fiction', *Signs*, 18(2), 1993, pp. 346–75, p. 375.

32 Rosalind Coward, '"This Novel Changes Lives": Are Women's Novels Feminist Novels? A Response to Rebecca O' Rourke's Article "Summer Reading"', *Feminist Review*, 5, 1980, pp. 53–64.

33 Maria Lauret, 'Seizing Time and Making New Feminist Criticism, Politics and Contemporary Feminist Fiction', *Feminist Review*, 31, Spring 1989, pp. 94–106, p. 97.

34 Neil Lyndon: *No More Sex Wars: The Failures of Feminism* (London: Sinclair-Stevenson, 1992).

35 Naomi Wulf, *Fire with Fire: The New Female Power and How it Will Change the 21st Century* (London: Chatto and Windus, 1993), Natasha Walter, *The New Feminism* (London: Little Brown, 1998).

36 Nicci Gerrard, *Into the Mainstream: How Feminism Has Changed Women's Lives* (London: Pandora, 1989), p. 7.

37 Alice Echols, *Daring to be BAD: Radical Feminism in America 1967–1975* (Minneapolis: University of Minneapolis Press, 1989), p. 294.

1

From *The Golden Notebook*

This country's full of women going mad all by themselves.
Doris Lessing, *The Golden Notebook*

WHEN ANNA WULF in *The Golden Notebook* is canvassing for votes, she encounters 'five lonely women going mad quietly by themselves, inspite of husband and children or rather because of them. The quality they all had: self doubt. A guilt because they were not happy. The phrase they all used: "There must be something wrong with me."' A woman to whom Anna tells this story retorts, 'This country's full of women going mad all by themselves.'¹

Like the mad woman in the attic in the nineteenth-century novel, the figure of the isolated woman going mad 'inspite of husband and children or rather because of them' is an arresting image which prompts questions about the links between the society in which the woman lives and her precarious state of mental health. Anna eventually goes mad herself, and is perhaps the most well known of all the women suffering from mental illness who occur in a variety of guises in the literature of the 1960s and 1970s, from Penelope Mortimer's Mrs Armitage in *The Pumpkin Eater* (1962), who dreams of having more babies but is sterilised against her will, to Fay Weldon's gargantuan compulsive eater, Esther Sussman in *The Fat Woman's Joke* (1967), who is disappointed by her expectations of marriage, to Sylvia Plath's Esther Greenwood in *The Bell Jar* (1963), who is let down by unattainable dreams of metropolitan glamour.²

The Golden Notebook and *The Bell Jar* were both published in the 1960s but deal with events in the previous (and far more conformist) decade. What Lessing and Plath resist is any notion that madness is a purely individual phenomenon rather than an involuntary response to the pressures which *all* women experience. Breakdown, in these novels and others, has a complicated relationship to femininity. What the fiction illuminates are the metonymic links between mental illness and the post-war feminine mystique. To understand why femininity is a straitjacket in which women are so often imprisoned in the fiction of the post-war period, it is necessary to establish the historical context in which a specific and highly restrictive set of ideas about femininity became hegemonic in the 1950s.

Both Britain and the United States after the Second World War were deeply traditional and conservative societies. The post-war settlement involved a strong desire on the part of women to return to the home on a full-time basis, which Denise Riley has attributed to their concern about the disturbing experience of children and women in wartime, and to ideological pressures to vacate jobs for returning servicemen.[3] There was a vogue for large families in the United States, of a kind which had not been seen since before 1914, and a widespread belief that the role of women was to concentrate on raising the next generation: 'The United States population increased by twenty-eight million in ten years at a rate even faster than India's'. Half of the brides in the United States were married by the time they were twenty, and three-quarters of English women by the time they were twenty-five.[4]

The idea of the 'happy housewife' was integral to the affluent society of the 1950s. Full employment transformed the lives of those whose parents' lives had been blighted by unemployment and poverty before the war. The revolution in the production of consumer goods, such as washing machines, refrigerators and vacuum cleaners, removed much of the difference between middle-class women who had enjoyed paid domestic help before the war and were now expected to do their own housework and working-class women who had always done so. Elizabeth Wilson refers to this levelling process as 'the equalization of drudgery'.[5]

The hallmarks of both British and American society in the 1950s were affluence and conformity. Although *The Lonely Crowd* (1953),[6] a book which Sylvia Plath had read,[7] warned of the dangers of Americans abdicating their individuality and moral judgement in order to be accepted by their peers, 'the bomb, communist spies, and Sputnik all scared Americans. And fear bred repression both of the blatant McCarthyite type and the more subtle, pervasive, and personal daily pressures to conform'.[8] As Elaine Tyler May put it, the home was a refuge from 'a world gone amok'.[9] In *The Paradox of Change: American Women in the Twentieth Century*, William Chafe has suggested that the anxiety generated by the cold war made the United States determined to safeguard its most cherished institutions: 'Where better to start than with the family, the oldest and most important institution of all?' Thus in some respects 'the new focus on conforming to traditional sex roles represented an act of "domestic containment" that paralleled the act of "international containment" whereby the Free World said no to the spread of Communism'.[10]

The values of middle America were respectability, security and affluence. These were enthusiastically promoted through women's magazines, advertising, and in the trim, neat vision of comfortable suburban life, promulgated by Hollywood in such films as the melodramas of Douglas Sirk, and on television by situation comedies like *Father Knows Best*.[11]

As Betty Friedan pointed out, the mass-circulation magazines for women, such as the *Ladies' Home Journal* and *McCall's*, carried hundreds of articles on political topics in the 1930s and 1940s, but by the 1950s 'they printed virtually no articles except those that serviced women as housewives, or described women as housewives or permitted a purely feminine identification'.[12] This remained the case until late into the 1960s. In 1970, the premises of the *Ladies' Home Journal*, among the most conservative of all the women's magazines in its unwavering support for traditional ideas about femininity and domesticity, was chosen for a 'sit-in' by feminists as a result of which the journal reluctantly agreed to produce a special supplement on feminism.[13] Radical women did not establish their own journals in the 1950s as they had done in the 1920s, although a number of gifted women including Margaret Mead, Eleanor Roosevelt, Mari Sandox and Mary McCarthy did manage to reach large popular audiences by writing for magazines like *Harper's* and the *Reader's Digest*. Sylvia Plath, who had been seduced by fashion, style and beauty during her time as young trainee on *Mademoiselle*, and whose ambition had at one time been to write for the *Ladies' Home Journal*, became increasingly scathing about the dreams of glamour and contentment which the popular magazines purveyed to women. She wrote that it is much better for her to 'know that people are divorced and go through hell,' than to hear about happy marriages, 'Let the *Ladies' Home Journal* blither about *those*.'[14] The heroine of *The Bell Jar* (1963) is confronted with a series of unhelpful images from popular magazines from the *Reader's Digest* strictures 'in Defence of Chastity' (*BJ*, p. 84) to *Baby Talk* with its beaming 'Eisenhower faced' babies. (*BJ*, p. 34). In *The Golden Notebook*, Ella is employed by a woman's magazine, *Women at Home*, which successfully purveys idealised images of domestic bliss to women. It is Ella's responsibility to attend to the correspondence from women readers detailing the realities of their misery and frustration.

The extent to which women colluded with men in rejecting the gains of earlier feminists is open to dispute. Women's organisations were instrumental in bringing about equal pay legislation in the civil service and teaching professions in Britain and also in many states in America. In *Happily Ever After?* Niamh Baker has questioned 'the myth that women were universally happy in the role ascribed to them in the postwar period, that they passively accepted, or were deceived into accepting, this narrow view of their potential'.[15] Baker argues that the 'persistence of the image of the happy housewife–mother during the 1950s' obscured the fact that 'conformism to this narrow ideal of womanhood was not as widespread as had been imagined'.[16] But quiet dissatisfaction was more common than open dissent. Fay Weldon recalls how intelligent women routinely internalised their misery: 'We women thought if we were unhappy it could only be our fault. We were in some way neurotic, badly adjusted – it was our task to change ourselves to fit the world. We read Freud, Helene Deutsch, Melanie Klein (these last two at least being moderately relevant to our female condition), bow our heads in shame in the face of our penis envy, and teach ourselves docility and acceptance'.[17]

In France, the publication of the first part of Simone de Beauvoir's influential autobiography *Memoirs of a Dutiful Daughter* (1958) offered the woman reader a role model, of the author living an independent intellectual existence, freely exercising existential and sexual choices, and pursuing a life dedicated to work and politics, all without the ties of marriage or children. But such role models for English and American women were few and far between, although women were choosing to go out to work and ignore the received wisdom that this was bad for their children. Viola Klein and Alva Myrdal's *Women's Two Roles* (1956)[18] argued that women had a permanent role to play in the workplace and that everything should be done to facilitate their return to work as their children grew up. Ten years later, Hannah Gavron's survey of mothers in the St Pancras and Hampstead areas of London, published as *The Captive Wife* (1966),[19] asked the question as to whether women's employment threatened the stability of the family or the welfare of children and found no conclusive evidence to support either proposition.

In her survey of her classmates who had graduated from Radcliffe in 1951, carried out for the *Ladies' Home Journal* in 1981, Rona Jaffe discovered that very many of her highly educated contemporaries had expected to find their identity through their husbands and had no expectation of developing separate selves.[20] The book which is generally credited with raising the consciousness of middle-class women such as these was Betty Friedan's *The Feminine Mystique* (1963). In this path-breaking volume, Friedan appears to have gone to great lengths to present herself as an 'ordinary' homebound mother of three living in a prosperous suburb and able to speak authoritatively about the plight of women from her own experience as a trapped suburban housewife.[21] The reality, as Daniel Horowitz has recently pointed out, was somewhat different. Friedan had an impressive political track record, first as a student and then as a labour journalist working for left-wing and trade union publications, and had sustained an interest in issues such as childcare, equal pay, and women taking positions of leadership as a labour movement activist between 1943 and 1952.

Horowitz argues that, although she was never a member, Friedan moved within the orbit of the Communist Party, and that it was the fear of 'redbaiting', of McCarthyist witch-hunts in the 1950s, and later of having the women's movement tainted with associations with communism, that led the mature Betty Friedman to be less than open about her radical history.[22] Friedan's subjects in *The Feminine Mystique* are the generation of women who had received higher education, but who had voluntarily given up their careers to pursue marriage, children and home-making. The 'problem without a name' identified in *The Feminine Mystique*, is the intelligent middle-class housewife's unfocused sense of restlessness and discontent because she had failed to fulfil her potential. Friedan argued that the feminine mystique was so powerful 'that women grew up no longer knowing that they have the desires and capacities that the mystique forbids' and she found the use of tranquillisers, hospitalisation, alcohol abuse, and depression lay under the veneer of contentment.[23] She concludes that 'we can no longer ignore that voice within women that says '"I want something more than my husband and my children and my home"'.[24] As Melissa Benn has pointed out, *The Feminine Mystique* was addressed to the affluent women of suburban America and not to the millions of poor women who worked out of economic necessity. Although Friedan wanted women to get out of the house, what she appears to have envisaged for them was the voluntary or socially committed work which women had done *en masse* in the nineteenth century.[25]

Fay Weldon pinpoints the misery of the English suburban housewife in her first novel, *The Fat Woman's Joke* (1966), a novel which makes the connections between femininity and eating disorders, later to be popularised through the publication of Susie Orbach's *Fat Is a Feminist Issue* (1978). For Esther, the first of a long line of female grotesques in Weldon's fiction, the reality of marriage is 'altogether too heavy and powerful'. She experiences marriage as a 'single steady crushing weight, on top of which bore down the entire human edifice of city and state, learning and religion, commerce and law; pomp, passion and reproduction besides'.[26] Consumption of junk food is Esther's way of coping with her husband's serial adultery, and she becomes a compulsive eater after her children have left home. Anorexia is for Marion in *The Edible Woman* what compulsive eating is for Esther in *The Fat Woman's Joke*.[27] Marion instinctively turns away from meat, which is a trope for marriage and the ritual exchanges of women, at the same time as she turns away sexually from her fiancé. The novel finishes with her baking a pink cake in the shape of a woman, which she devours as a symbolic victory over the feminine body-shape, which has been held up for her consumption by the marketing firm for which she works.

In *The Golden Notebook* Ella, the 'smart, gay, sexy mistress' is the antithesis of the 'sober respectable little wife' who likes watching television and reading *Women at Home* (*GN*, p. 227). In *The Bell Jar*, Esther Greenwood tries to envisage life as a suburban wife: 'This seemed a dreary and wasted life for a girl with fifteen years of straight 'A's.' Esther knew what marriage was like, 'because cook and clean and wash was just what Buddy Willard's mother did from morning till night, and she was the wife of a university professor and had been a private school teacher herself' (*BJ*, p. 88).

In *Changing the Story: Feminist Fiction and the Tradition*, Gayle Greene has discussed a number of 'mad housewife novels' which provide powerful accounts of women's entrapment in this period.[28] In these books, 'the protagonist suffers alone and imagines that her misery is unrelated to anything outside; lacking the literary and critical powers of writer protagonists and with no way of connecting personal to political, she ends up reaffirming the domestic ideology that has been driving her "mad".'[29] Greene argues that 'even those writers who do glimpse the connections between their protagonists' individual experiences and their social and historical contexts fail to incorporate this understanding into their narratives'.[30]

Not all women exhibiting the symptoms of psychic disorder are, of course, 'housewives'. To Greene's selection should be added Jennifer Dawson's *The Ha-Ha* (1961), a novel which provides unusual insights into the institutional regime to which her heroine is committed. Josephine Traughton is a gifted but socially awkward student with a penchant for abstruse medieval scholarship whom the glittering prizes at Oxford University have eluded. A troubled relationship to her mother lies at the root of her mental disorder as is the case for Esther in *The Bell Jar*.

Far from being a place of safety, the mental asylum is a place where Josephine is first seduced and then abandoned by a fellow patient. Josephine's electric shock treatment appears to be a punishment for sexual activity – until the 1950s women in Britain could be consigned to mental hospitals merely for having a baby outside marriage. She adapts the stratagem of appearing to become a model patient – i.e. a patient who reflects the traditional feminine virtues, passive, pliant, docile, unquestioning, eager to please, and showing no signs of spirit or resistance – in order to persuade the authorities to release her. Josephine finally engineers her own freedom more effectively by running away: 'I knew for certain that I had not after all been extinguished, and that my existence had been saved.'[31]

The Golden Notebook and *The Bell Jar* deal with politicised women who experience nervous breakdowns from which they eventually emerge. In Anna's case, nervous breakdown is largely but not entirely a response to the horrors of the contemporary world. In the case of Esther in *The Bell Jar*, it is largely due to the feminine mystique which, as we have seen, weighed heavily on women in the 1950s.

As Richard Ohmann has put it, 'in the illness story deep social contradictions are transformed into an individual crisis, and the resolution – usually a hesitant one – involves the disordered person "coming to terms" through some personal therapy with social reality'.[32] But this is 'the reality that initially discomposed them, and it remains as untransformed, is imagined as untransformable'.[33] In *The Bell Jar*, Esther emerges from her ordeal in hospital like an automobile which has been serviced after an accident, 'patched, retreaded and approved for the road' (*BJ*, p. 257). But as the social contradictions of her existence remain unaltered she has no guarantee that 'someday – at college, in Europe, somewhere, anywhere – the bell jar, with its stifling distortions, wouldn't descend again' (*BJ*, p. 254). In *The Golden Notebook*, Anna falls apart because the world around her appears to be doing so and she sees her reactions as a perfectly rational response to its horrors. When it dawns on her that she is 'cracking up' and living through the 'breakdown', she had foreseen, it does not strike her that she was even slightly mad; 'but rather that people who were not as obsessed as she was with the inchoate world mirrored in the newspapers were out of touch with an awful necessity' (*GN*, p. 624).

Like her precursor, the nineteenth-century writer Olive Schreiner, Doris Lessing was a white, southern African radical who sought refuge abroad from the troubled situation of her own country. Lessing moved to England in 1949. She remained emotionally involved with the progressive forces within her native Rhodesia, and drew upon her formative experiences of anti-racist struggle there to inform her early fiction, including *The Grass Is Singing*, and the *Martha Quest* series written in the 1950s. The subject matter of *The Golden Notebook* is the experience of Anna Wulf, an active member of the Communist Party just after the Suez invasion, the Russian invasion of Hungary, and the other cataclysmic political events of 1956. Anna Wulf is a thirty-year-old divorcee with a small daughter who is living on the money earned from a novel set in southern Africa, which was praised by the critics, and depicts resistance to its racist regimes. *The Golden Notebook* is strikingly different from many other novels of the time. As Margot Heinemann has put it, 'most political novels, at least in English, have dealt with people concerned with politics only to the exent that seems "average" ... the people don't *want* to be involved in politics, it happens to them.'[34] In this respect, *The Golden Notebook* resembles *Burger's Daughter* (1978), a much later novel written by a fellow southern African writer, Nadine Gordimer.

Like *Burger's Daughter*, which explores the consciousness of Rosa, the daughter of two members of the South African Communist Party, who must decide whether or not to follow in her parents' footsteps, *The Golden Notebook* is concerned with the lives of political activists, and with the debates that were preoccupying the international Communist movement which are seen from 'the inside'. Lessing explains that the novel is set among socialists and Marxists 'because it has been inside the various chapters of socialism that the great debates of our time have gone on; the movements, the wars, the revolutions, have been seen by their participants as movements of various kinds of socialism, or Marxism, in advance, containment, or retreat'.[35] *The Golden Notebook* is essential reading for anyone who is curious about the crisis which was confronting the left in Britain in the 1950s and wishes to understand the culture in which Communists worked and thought. It is particularly strong in its depiction of 'a certain kind of atmosphere where it is taken for granted that their lives must be related to a certain philosophy' (*GN*, p. 338). It also evokes with acuity what Raphael Samuel has described in the 'Lost World of British Communism': the sense of the Communist Party as a particular kind of 'moral community' with a shared sense of purpose and values.[36]

Like Lessing herself, Anna Wulf who works in London headquarters in King Street, is the only writer with a national reputation to have joined the Communist Party since the cold war. The decision to join the party is prompted largely by her respect for the party's record of opposition to racism and imperialism: 'There is no group of people or type of intellectual I have met outside the Party which isn't ill-informed, frivolous, parochial, compared with certain types of intellectuals inside the Party' (*GN*, p. 338). Anna's decision to leave the Communist Party coincides with the onset of her monthly menstrual period. Lessing dwells upon the physical discomfort which Anna experiences during her period thus reminding the reader that the workings of the body and the mind are sometimes connected for women in ways that are different for men. The openness with which the subject of menstruation is treated in *The Golden Notebook* was highly unusual and excited much interest at the time.

Although intellectuals like Lessing might sometimes be assigned work for the party that made use of their particular skills, they were not exempt from attendance at branch meetings, or from routine work like distributing leaflets and selling newspapers on street corners. The description of Anna's futile quest for Communist votes in the local elections is the outcome of the party's electoral policy, requiring its members to canvass in opposition to Labour Party candidates, whom they often knew and respected, and which was deeply resented by many activists at the time.[37]

As Michael Kenny has pointed out, most former members of the Communist Party remained 'sympathetic to the liberal–left culture and political commitments, and many have held on to aspects of their political past, retaining a "habit of sharpness and intensity of argument, a seriousness about ideas, a tone that differed from the tone of the dominant liberal"'.[38] Thousands of disenchanted members left the Communist Party in the 1950s, often to join the Labour Party, or to become part of the New Left, a loose socialist grouping free of the restraints of party membership and discipline. Where Anna differs from them is in the decisiveness of her break with the political culture which she has inhabited and with the optimism of the past. Anna unequivocally rejects the idea of political change through collective action, much as Lessing was to do herself: 'I must have been mad – I'm not just talking about being a Communist; I mean thinking that politics comes up with answers to social problems, which it manifestly doesn't do.'[39]

Through the character of Anna, Lessing is able to question the appropriateness of realist forms to represent the fragmented nature of modern reality (which she had come to believe was unrepresentable), and the crises of belief with which intellectuals on the New Left were having to grapple. In abandoning conventional narrative, *The Golden Notebook* also explores the relationship between language and ideology and the possibility of a new revolutionary literary form. In an essay entitled 'The Small Personal Voice',[40] Lessing had praised the nineteenth-century novel because it excelled in ethical judgement and in the language of moral debate. But the realist novel, to which Marxist critics like Georg Lukács had traditionally attached so much importance, no longer performs the functions which it did. The worst examples of realism, which Anna has to read are the socialist realist novels which purport to deal with situations in 'everyday life'. Most of the writing that comes her way is on 'a curiously jolly note even when dealing with suffering and war' (*GN*, p. 343). 'The writing is bad, the story lifeless, but what is frightening about this book is that it is totally inside the current myth' (*GN*, p. 341). It is, moreover, formulaic and repetitive: she has read it in about fifty different guises in the last year.

As Andrzej Gasiorek has summarised Anna's predicament, 'her socialism, however tenuous it has become, has left her with a politicised view of aesthetics. But her continuing belief in committed art is at odds with her loss of faith in politics'.[41] *The Golden Notebook* has a strongly self-reflexive relationship to Marxist aesthetics. Anna observes that the novel in the twentieth century has become an outpost of journalism and a 'function of a fragmented society, the fragmented consciousness' (*GN*, p. 79). *The Frontiers of War*, her own bestselling novel is an interracial romance, the success of which is to some extent predicated on racist curiosity and sexual voyeurism.

But it is a thoughtful and serious novel, and Anna persists in believing that it is a good one and is determined to prevent its misappropriation. She thus turns down requests for permission to make it into a popular musical, resists financial inducements to 'change the story', and to remove all references to race in order to make it more commercially successful. The irony is that the only kind of novel which Anna still believes to be worthwhile is 'a book powered with an intellectual or moral passion strong enough to create order, to create a new way of looking at life' (*GN*, p. 80). But she is no longer capable of writing it because she has lost her socialist convictions. She writes the 'free woman' section of the novel in an attempt to resolve her writer's block.

As Lorna Sage has put it, *The Golden Notebook* was a 'book of its moment, opened up to subconscious and subcultural imperatives which the realist perspective had structured and suppressed'.[42] The structure of *The Golden Notebook* rejects linear narrative and requires the reader to piece together Anna Wulf's fragmented experience in ways which duplicate her own reconstruction of what had happened. The novel's evocation of the turbulent inner life is emblematic of alienation and disintegration. The formal organisation of *The Golden Notebook* reinforces the subject matter and reflects a particularly acute awareness of the relationship between ideology and literary form. Lessing's was convoked that the form of the novel required to be revitalised by self conscious experimentation. As Molly Hite puts it, 'the notion that the truth has become alien to the forms originally created to express it is analogous to the notion, also pervasive to this novel, that history no longer admits of a Marxist interpretation'.[43]

The novel is set in 1957 and is narrated to cover events going back to 1950. Anna attempts to take control over her life, by writing in a set of different notebooks keeping 'four, and not one because, as she recognises, she has to separate things off from each other, out of fear of chaos, of formlessness – of breakdown'.[44] Her notebooks consist of the black notebook which is set in Africa in the 1940s, the red notebook which is about politics, a yellow notebook, in which Ella becomes an alter-ego for Anna, and Michael an alter-ego for Paul, a blue notebook which attempts to be a diary. The notebook entitled 'Free Women' has been written by Anna to resolve her writer's block and only covers events in 1957. There is also 'The Golden Notebook' with which the novel ends.

In her study of women in the Communist Party, Tricia Davis concludes that there was little convergence between socialism and feminism in the Communist Party of Great Britain between 1941 and 1955, the years leading up to the climactic events in *The Golden Notebook*. Such connections as there are were operated as in *The Golden Notebook* beneath the surface of the party's formal politics. Not only were gender issues relegated to a position of minor importance within the party, but there was considerable hostility to feminism which was regarded as a bourgeoise movement. Moreover, while Communist women were sometimes able to create a space for themselves and issues of concern to women, 'the questions they raised were ultimately contained and diffused and limited in their political impact'.[45]

Anna is one of a growing number of single, sexually experienced women living on their own (whether unmarried or divorced) who became more visible in the 1960s and 1970s. From being dismissed as frustrated, joyless and undesirable, the young, unattached woman became someone whose lifestyle was to be sought after. The rise in the numbers of sexually active and financially independent single woman dealt a blow to the idea that sex was only for procreation and to the notion that marriage was the only acceptable site of sexual pleasure for women. Helen Gurley Brown's *Sex and the Single Girl*[46] was published in 1962 in the United States, the same year as *The Golden Notebook*. In 1965 Gurley Brown moved to the magazine *Cosmopolitan* which popularised the image of the single woman with time and money to spend on herself.

The 'free women' in *The Golden Notebook* are without husbands after marital breakdown. However, while they believe themselves to be free – and for many of the novel's first readers Anna Wulf was associated with the *Zeitgeist* – they are not the liberated women who were to emerge in the feminist literature of the 1970s. In their structures of sensibility they are much closer to the new 'artist-women' of the turn of the century like the artistic heroine of Kate Chopin's *The Awakening* (1899). The novel starts with a conversation between two 'artistic' women, Anna, a writer and Molly, an actress, both of whom are divorcees. Divorce was still unusual in the early 1960s and divorcees often felt stigmatised. Molly says, 'I've decided that we're a completely new type of woman' (*GN*, p. 26). Asked to say how she believes herself to be different – 'Are you saying there haven't been artist–women, before. There haven't been women, who were independent?' (*GN*, p. 459) – Anna replies that 'they didn't look at themselves as I do. They didn't feel as I do. How could they?' (p. 459). Anna is convinced that there is a part of her which is made by the 'kind of experience women haven't had before' (*GN*, p. 458). Anna does not 'want to be told when I suddenly have a vision ... of a life that isn't full of hatred and fear and envy and competition every minute of the night and day that this is simply the old dream of a golden age brought up to date' (*GN*, p. 458).

In so far as they live outside the traditional family unit, in which the woman remains in the home, and the man is the breadwinner, Molly and Anna are indeed 'free' women. But they are only free of the traditional family obligations and of the domestic responsibilities that are expected of wives. Because Anna is exiled from her native country and living in the metropolis with no family, 'the fabric of security' for her daughter Janet is woven, 'not of grandparents, cousins, a settled home; but that friends telephone every day, and certain words are spoken' (*GN*, p. 257). The attitude to motherhood in *The Golden Notebook* is essentialist. Elsewhere in the novel, Lessing subscribes to the view that human identity is unstable and fragmented, but she makes an exception in relation to the identity of the mother, which is presented as fixed and unchanging. While Anna's somewhat casual attitude to mothering is clearly a protest against the devotion to full-time mothering advocated by such influential figures as Winnicott and Bowlby in the 1950s (whose work I discuss in the next chapter) it is her acceptance of her role as Janet's mother that keeps Anna anchored to reality.

What saves Anna from total collapse is her knowledge that when her daughter comes home again her obsessive behaviour will cease. Her nervous breakdown coincides with the absence of her daughter at boarding school: 'She knew that Janet's mother being sane and responsible was far more important than the necessity of understanding the world; and one thing depended on the other. The world would never get itself understood, be ordered, be "named", unless Janet's mother remained a woman who was able to be responsible' (*GN*, p. 624). At the end of the novel, Anna decides to become a marriage guidance counsellor, thus effectively abandoning any feminist opposition to the idea of marriage and actively endorsing the very institution against which she had formerly rebelled. This move prefigures the massive interest in the counselling and personal-growth industries which were to flourish later in the 1960s.

Anna and Molly do not lead lives which are psychically independent of men. Relationships with women are always secondary for both of them. Sex and love are still indivisible. Aroused by a man who means nothing to her emotionally, Anna is disgusted by the physical manifestations of her own sexual response. Lessing's 'free woman' may enjoy her sexual freedom but she is not liberated from the conventions of romantic love which assume a reparative psychic communion with another as a result of which the flawed individual is made whole.

Once she has fallen in love, Anna becomes mesmerised; emotionally dependent, passive, obsessive and possessive: 'The truth is that I don't care a damn about philosophy or politics or anything else; all I care about is that Michael should turn in the dark and put his face against my breasts' (GN, p. 298). When Anna's alter-ego, Ella, makes love to Paul what sets the seal on the fact that she loves him is her orgasm. There is 'only one real female orgasm and that is when a man, from the whole of his need and desire takes a woman and wants all her response. Everything else is a substitute and a fake, and the most inexperienced woman feels this instinctively' (GN, p. 220).[47]

Men use women for their own purposes dividing women into the categories of wife and mistress and playing one against the other, 'every one of them, even the best of them, have the old idea of good women and bad women.' Although there is some ironic awareness of gendered inequality – 'Free,' says Julia. 'Free! What is the use of us being free if they aren't?' (GN, p. 446) – there is also a resignation to the existing dynamics of sexual repulsion and attraction, rather than any desire to confront and change oppressive power relations. Where The Golden Notebook disappoints those women interested in emancipatory sexual politics is in its lack of interest in what E.P. Thompson has usefully termed the 'education of desire'.[48] What this entails is the willingness to understand the ideological character of that which one takes for granted as 'natural' and to move from that position to the difficult but necessary business of learning from experience and changing the way one feels and behaves.

As Lessing commented in the introduction written in 1972, The Golden Notebook described many emotions of aggression, hostility and resentment that women were experiencing. It put them into print: 'Apparently, what many women were thinking, feeling, experiencing, came as a great surprise.'[49] The book identified problems which women recognised in their own sexual relationships with an extraordinary degree of accuracy. It also contained hints of revolutionary changes to come. Paul asks Ella what she thinks is the 'great revolution of our time?' and tells her that 'The Russian revolution, the Chinese revolution – they're nothing at all. The real revolution is, women against men' (GN, pp. 217–18). But the book did not offer its readers any way out of the impasse in communications between the two sexes. What Anna nurtures is a deep sense of resentment because a man cannot love her in the romanticised way that she would wish. What she does not do is to probe into the nature of masculinity, or to ask herself why this should be.

As Elizabeth Wilson has pointed out, much of *The Golden Notebook* was 'the antithesis of women's liberation' because it supported many of the attitudes that 1960s feminists 'were in revolt *against*'.[50] For example, the thousands of consciousness-raising groups which women were later to form were predicated on disclosure, honesty about intimate experience, and emotional openness. But Lessing's *soi disant* radicals do not discuss their emotional and physical needs honestly in *The Golden Notebook*. Flying in the face of the new sexual honesty, Anna still believes that 'the difficulty about writing about sex, for women, is that sex is best when not thought about, not analysed' (*GN*, p. 219). Instead, the two sexes define each other according to vastly different needs and shape reality imaginatively to fit their desires. Because women depend emotionally on men for their happiness, they collude with them in denying their shortcomings, while harbouring a deep and often unvoiced inner resentment at the breakdown in communication between the sexes: 'And yet there's always a point even with the most perceptive and intelligent man, when a woman looks at him across a gulf: he hasn't understood' (*GN*, p. 219).

Though there is an unfocused sense of unhappiness at sexual relationships, it remains inchoate. Through Anna's attraction to a 'real man' (*GN*, p. 383), as opposed to men who do not parade their aggressiveness and chauvinism, the novel partakes in the protest against the 'feminisation' of post-war society, which is characteristic of the 1950s, and was expressed by the 'angry' young men. In *The Golden Notebook*, as in the work of John Osborne, Alan Sillitoe and John Braine, the expression of masculinity is often imperilled by the presence of women and the enveloping blanket of femininity which suffocates manliness. The sexual relationships between men and women with which Anna appears comfortable are those characterised by submission and domination. She thinks, 'By God, there are a few real men left, and I'm going to see she [Janet] gets one of them. I'm going to see she grows up to recognise a real one when she meets one' (*GN*, p. 395).

Thirty years before *The Golden Notebook*, Virginia Woolf had cautioned against the dangers of women boosting the male ego and acting as a mirror in which man could see himself reflected at twice his size.[51] But in *The Golden Notebook*, Anna is able to note that 'the truth is, women have this deep instinctive need to build a man up as a man ... I suppose this is because real men become fewer and fewer, and we are frightened trying to create men' (*GN*, p. 470). Ella is confident 'that when she loved a man again she would turn to normal: a woman that is whose sexuality would ebb and flow in response to his. A woman's sexuality is, so to speak, contained by a man. If he is a real man; she is, in a sense put to sleep by him. She does not think about sex' (*GN*, p. 441).

The *Golden Notebook*'s homophobia has been capably discussed elsewhere.[52] Here it suffices to note that Lessing has a particular distaste for any sign of effeminate behaviour in a man, and that this is manifested in her representation of Anna's lodger, Ivan, a homosexual, who is dutifully attentive to both mother and daughter, but earns Anna's withering contempt for not being a 'real man'. The phrase 'real man' is deployed without irony: 'With a real man there would be a whole area of tension, of wry understanding that there can't be with Ivor' (*GN*, p. 383). There is no attempt in the novel to engineer a critical awareness of existing sexual relationships in order to transform them, but rather an unquestioning endorsement of discriminatory attitudes that were to come under scrutiny with the formation of the gay liberation movement at the end of the decade. The widely discussed Wolfenden Report which drew attention to the victimisation of homosexuals and recommended a measure of decriminalisation was published in 1957, and is a structuring absence in the novel.

Like many on the New Left with which Lessing was associated in its early days, Anna is attracted to the ideas of psychoanalysis and Marxism which in their very different ways appear to provide frames of reference whereby psychic disorder and social fragmentation can be understood. Somewhere at the back of Anna's mind when she joined the Communist Party was a need 'for wholeness, for an end to the split, divided, unsatisfactory way we all live'. Yet the irony is that 'joining the Party intensified the split – not the business of belonging to an organisation whose every tenet, on paper, anyway, contradicts the ideas of the society we live in; but something much deeper than that' (*GN*, p. 171). The disillusionment with the Communist Party, precipitated by the Soviet invasion of Hungary, Kruschev's devastating revelations in 1956, and Anna's rejection of the authority which the party had hitherto exercised over her, prompts her to consult a Jungian analyst, Mrs Marks (the saccharine, 'Mother Sugar' as she and Molly call her) in a quest for solutions to problems which she is conscious of sharing with millions across the world.

The understanding of mental disorder which underpins the account of Anna's breakdown in *The Golden Notebook* reflects Lessing's extensive knowledge of mental illness, 'first through various brands of analysts and therapists and psychiatrists, and then through people who were "mad" in various ways and with whom I had very close contact'.[53] The basis of Anna's unsatisfactory experiences with psychoanalysis is Mother Sugar's determination to situate a personal self within the Jungian framework of mythological archetypes, which are themselves outside history. This is at odds with what Anna considers to be the social and historical context in which her illness must be understood. Mother Sugar undermines Anna's political judgement by addressing problems she knows to be symptomatic of a global crisis of belief as if they were of a purely individual nature, and by dehistoricising and depoliticising her interpretation of events.

The impossibility of achieving the psychic wholeness for which she aspires is reflected in Anna's nervous breakdown with which the book ends. In her later preface to the novel Lessing explained that breakdown was the most important theme of the novel but 'nobody so much as noticed this central theme' because the book was taken to be about the sex war.[54] The ideas about psychic division in *The Golden Notebook* resemble those in R.D. Laing's influential study *The Divided Self* (1960). Laing controversially argued that the experience of a mental breakdown can sometimes be a prerequisite for reconstituting and healing the damaged self, and Lessing has situated Anna's nervous breakdown at the interface of the political and the psychoanalytical.

There appear to be two contending personalities within the central protagonist each at war with the other. The self at war is Anna (the woman) and Anna (the Communist). The Communist self is rational, purposeful, disciplined. When Anna mentions the five women 'going quietly mad by themselves' to another woman in the party, her confidante replies that she used to be the same 'until I joined the Party and got myself a purpose in life' (*GN*, p. 176). Thus a sense of purpose in life is constituted as that which keeps life's horrors at bay. The nightmares which Anna (the woman) experiences are the price to be paid for excessive preoccupation with her feelings, which her training in the Communist Party has taught her to distrust and reject. But what was to come clear, with the formulation of socialist–feminist critiques of the masculinist nature of socialist groupings some years after the publication of *The Golden Notebook*, was that what Anna perceives here as an individual problem was in fact representative of the split between their reason and their emotions that women on the left frequently experienced, but which they lacked the language, support and confidence to express. Anna's predicament is a response to a masculinist political culture and to the misogyny which was endemic to both the old and the new left. She resolves this inner split by leaving the Communist Party.

The person who is preventing the disintegration of Anna (the woman) is the Communist self: 'Anna you are betraying everything you believe in; you are sunk in subjectivity, yourself, your own needs.' There is also a Freudian death wish in the novel: the 'Anna who wanted to slip under the dark water would not answer' (*GN*, p. 592). It is clear to Anna that she remains the person she is because of a particular kind of rational, methodical, questioning intelligence which she is in danger of losing. It is this loss which frightens her more than anything else.

Anna sees her mental illness as a response to a particular historical moment: after Suez, Hungary, Algeria, Cuba. She obsessively reads masses of newsprint which she cuts out and pastes on her walls. When she breaks down she sees a succession of flickering images, the soldier in Cuba, the soldier in Algeria, the Chinese peasant, one of millions, the British conscript, the Communist detained in a communist gaol. These images invoke liberation struggles, decolonisation, destalinisation, the dream of freedom, and the reality of oppression shared by millions of people. She wakes 'changed by the experience of being other people' (*GN*, p. 580). Her nervous breakdown is an analogue of collective insanity.

In both *The Golden Notebook* and *The Bell Jar* schizophrenia is a temporary condition from which the central figure eventually recovers, but which renders her momentarily incapable of acting purposefully and imbues her with feelings of powerlessness. As Shoshana Felman has put it, madness is 'quite the opposite of rebellion. Madness is the impasse confronting those whom cultural conditioning has deprived of the very means of protest or self-affirmation.'[55] Schizophrenia has sometimes been taken as the literary analogue *par excellence* for the feminine condition, powerfully expressive of infantilisation, dependency and a split between irreconcileable perceptions of the self as it is experienced by the subject.

In her influential *Women and Madness* Phyllis Chessler argues that 'mad' behaviour represents a socially powerless individual's attempt to unite body and feeling: '*What we consider "madness", whether it appears in women or in men, is either the acting out of the devalued female role or the total or partial rejection of one's sex-role stereotype.*'[56] Chessler warns against the dangers of valorising madness simply because it is the antithesis of resignation to a woman's lot or romanticising that which should properly be recognised as an expression of desperation. Madness does not offer any privileged insights into the human condition: 'Most weeping, depressed women, most anxious and terrified women are neither about to seize the means of production and reproduction, nor are they any more creatively involved with problems of cosmic powerlessness, evil and love than is the rest of the human race.'[57] If femininity is taken to be synonymous with madness, and madness the label attached to women who are in a psychic revolt against patriarchy, such rebellion is doomed to fail because it has no social dimension, and the rebels cannot be taken seriously by society precisely because they are deemed to be mad.

Although she was not a political activist in the sense that Lessing was, Sylvia Plath thought of herself as 'rather a political person'.[58] She was highly critical of the American witch-hunts of the 1950s, distressed by the bombing of Hiroshima and the Holocaust, and felt a strong distaste for cold war politics:' people don't seem to see that this negative Anti-Communist attitude is destroying all the freedom of thought we've ever had ... Everything they don't agree with is Communist.'⁵⁹ Before her offer of a place at Cambridge she was tempted to teach abroad as a gesture against McCarthyism ('I do believe I can counteract McCarthy and much adverse opinion about the US by living a life of honesty and love').⁶⁰ The peace movement was especially close to her heart. A letter to her mother in 1960 urges her not to vote for Nixon and describes 'an immensely moving' experience watching the arrival of the anti-nuclear marchers in Trafalgar Square, London. She felt proud that the baby's first real adventure should be as a protest against the insanity of world-annihilation.⁶¹ She later protests at the 'ghastly H-bomb sermon' delivered by the rector of her parish and 'felt it was a sin to support such insanity even by my presence'.⁶² *The Bell Jar* reflects and mediates some of Plath's unhappiness about the values of middle America.

As I have suggested, acceptance of the dominant ideas about femininity depends on a rigid distinction between the public and private spheres. The separation was strictly maintained and perpetuated by the mass-circulation women's magazines of the 1950s, like *McCall's* and *The Ladies' Home Journal*, in which the woman reader is deemed to have no role to play outside the home and little or no interest in public affairs. It is this separation which Sylvia Plath's *The Bell Jar* contravenes. Like Anna in *The Golden Notebook*, Esther is sickened by the fate of Ethel and Julius Rosenberg, with whose execution as spies for the Soviet Union *The Bell Jar* begins: 'All I could think about was the Rosenbergs How stupid I'd been to buy all those uncomfortable, expensive clothes' (*BJ*, p. 2). Esther's desire for approval and acceptance in college, the world of fashion, and the Boston of the 1950s, depends on maintaining the pretence (effective because it is to some extent internalised) that she shares the values and attitudes of those around her.

Esther's aversion to the execution of the two reviled outsiders – the Rosenbergs were Communists and Jews – is contrasted with a glamorous friend who is more comfortable with her role as a trainee at the fashion magazine. Hilda confidently asserts that 'it's awful such people should be alive' (*BJ*, p. 105). As the Rosenbergs' political dissidence is recognised by those from whom it has been carefully hidden and is punished by the electric chair, so Esther's dissident femininity will be recognised and punished through the electric shock treatment which is administered to her. Esther is working for a month in New York, as one of twelve guest editors at a fashion magazine, *Ladies' Day* at the beginning of the novel.

The others are young women of her own age, with wealthy parents who wanted to be sure their daughters would be living where men couldn't get at them and deceive them, and they are all going to superior secretarial schools (*BJ*, p. 4).

Femininity is, of course, a contradictory and complex phenomenon and debates about its significance still resonate in feminist circles today. In their willingness to embrace the outward signifiers of femininity, such as the use of hair colorants and lipstick, young feminists often differ radically from their older counterparts. But while the women's movement in the 1970s rebelled against the sexual objectification of women, rebellion against femininity has not always been a part of the history of organised feminism. Emmeline Pankhurst and many of her followers among the militant suffragettes in Britain, for example, prided themselves on their keen fashion sense; on wearing up-to-date garments and expensive millinery while committing outrageous acts of civil disobedience. Although a disapproval of the advertising and fashion industries inspired Betty Friedan to write *The Feminine Mystique*, other women of her day, including many sympathetic to feminist ideas, continued to relish the expression of their sexuality, through dress, style, ornamentation and parading of the body. This was especially during their teenage years and twenties, when women's bodies are most widely admired, and the sense of their bodies giving women power is often the strongest.

The Bell Jar starts with Esther contemplating a photograph of herself drinking martinis in a 'skimpy, imitation silver-lamé bodice stuck on to a big fat cloud of white tulle', in the company of 'several anonymous young men with all-American bone structures hired or loaned for the occasion' (*BJ*, p. 2). This is the zenith of her success as a desirable woman and appears on the cover of the magazine for which she works. The impressionable Esther is seduced by the dazzling images of women, and the unattainable mirages of metropolitan glamour, style and sexual attractiveness, which she actively creates, and therefore knows to be illusory. The photograph returns to haunt her in the mental hospital where its initial glamour has faded. What has changed is not the image of herself which Esther contemplates but the context in which it acquires new meanings. The photograph of a desirable Esther exercising her power over men is viewed by an older, more experienced Esther who feels herself to be undesirable and powerless. Her response is embarrassment. She denies that the photograph is of her and says that it is someone else.

Esther is anxious to succeed, and when she is not selected to work permanently for the magazine (the fictional equivalent of *Mademoiselle*), which promulgates the feminine ideal to young women across the continent of America, her identity as a woman is thrown into crisis. She goes home where her problems are compounded by her troubled relationship with her mother and her dislike of the courtship rituals and values of small-town America. In a conversation with the medical student of whom her mother approves, Buddy Willard, Esther confesses that 'if neurotic is wanting two mutually exclusive things at one and the same time, then I am neurotic as hell. I'll be flying back and forth between one mutually exclusive thing and another for the rest of my days' (*BJ*, p. 98). The 'two mutually exclusive things' that Esther desires throughout the novel are conformity and dissidence. She copes with some of the unwelcome overtures from men by playing games, for example, adopting the imaginary persona of Elly Higgingbottom from Chicago, telling another potential suitor that she is about to marry a childhood sweetheart, and joking repeatedly about her desire to be seduced by a simultaneous interpreter from New York.

Esther's discomfiture in all this closely resembles Plath's. A diary entry describes the 'barren, desperate days of dating, experimenting, hearing of mother warning me I was too critical, that I set my sights too high and would be an old maid'.[63] The diary entries also testify to Plath's emotional vulnerability: 'I am, at bottom, simple, credulous, feminine and loving to be mastered, cared for.'[64] The satisfactory resolution of her marriage quest – the discovery of the man whom at that time she thought of as her ideal man in the shape of Ted Hughes – is one that does not materialise in the novel.

Like Anna in *The Golden Notebook* Esther becomes painfully aware of the iniquity of the sexual double standard. She discovers that Buddy Willard – 'coming from such a fine, clean family' (*BJ*, p. 71) – is not a virgin and has had an affair with a waitress: 'I couldn't stand the idea of a woman having to have a single pure life and a man being able to have a double life, one pure and one not' (*BJ*, p. 85). A quiet rebellion against conventional marriage patterns and domesticity is registered in this section of the novel as Esther rejects the advice which she is offered: 'The last thing she wanted was intimate security and to be the place the arrow shoots from'. She wants 'change and excitement and to shoot off in all directions myself' (*BJ*, p. 87). The trouble is that she hates 'the idea of serving men in any way' (*BJ*, p. 79). Marriage and children was 'like being brainwashed, and afterwards you went about numb as a slave in some private, totalitarian state' (*BJ*, p. 89).

As Elaine Tyler May has pointed out, 'Postwar America was the era of the expert.' Moreover, 'when the experts spoke, postwar America listened'.[65] What the response of the psychiatric profession to Esther's mental breakdown highlights is the ethical problems raised by the pressures exerted on patients to conform, and the social control of women by the psychiatric profession. It is not clear why Esther needs to be institutionalised – many of those who attempt suicide are not. It is even less clear why electro-convulsive therapy (ECT) is thought to be necessary although Esther herself construes it as a punishment for some unspecified transgression to which she has no choice but to submit. The excruciatingly painful description of her first electric shock ('a great jolt drubbed me till I thought my bones would break and the sap fly out of me like a split plant', *BJ*, p. 151) concludes with the question, 'I wondered what terrible thing it was that I had done.' (*BJ*, p. 152)

In *The Body in Pain*,[66] Elaine Scarry has argued persuasively that pain – and this would include the kind of pain that Esther experiences in electric shock therapy – is inherently resistant to language. Scarry's argument that authoritative pronouncements on the nature of pain by the medical experts have mystified pain and silenced the voices of those who are suffering it are certainly compelling. But her model allows too little space for the spirited resistance of pain sufferers whose written and oral accounts of their experiences – including their experiences of pain directly related to their treatment in the hands of the medical and psychiatric professionals – have provided an experiential account of pain, successfully alerting others to the power imbalances which have helped to bring their suffering about. In *The Bell Jar* Esther's willing submission to electric shocks both represents a form of self-hatred on the woman's part – a tacit concession that the punishment is somehow deserved – and illustrates the social control of women by the psychiatric profession.

Sylvia Plath herself underwent a course of insulin treatment and ECT. Any journals that may once have existed for the two years after Plath's breakdown in the summer of 1953 have since disappeared. But according to Ted Hughes, perhaps the most important element in her recovery was 'her relationship with Dr. Ruth Beuscher, an extraordinary therapist who played an important role in Plath's life, both at the time and for years afterward'.[67] Plath was later to write with great warmth of her therapist that 'she is for me "a permissive mother figure". I can tell her anything, and she won't turn a hair or scold or withhold her listening.'[68]

By contrast, Esther's mother in *The Bell Jar* is a victim of the socially conformist outlook of the 1950s, and because she cannot see beyond the platitudes of suburban America, the communication between mother and daughter is severely strained: 'My mother kept telling me that nobody wanted a plain English major. But an English major who knew shorthand was something else again. Everybody would want her' (*BJ*, p. 79). Mrs Greenwood quite literally delivers her daughter into the hands of her institutional inquisitors. This is not because she is a 'bad', negligent or uncaring mother, but because she has no understanding of how she herself is trapped by a combination of her femininity and her unquestioning respect for patriarchal authority. Esther's recovery takes place when she acquires a mother substitute who is able to widen her horizon of expectations instead of restricting them. Her therapist, Doctor Nolan recognises Esther's right to have sex safely and refers her to a clinic for contraceptive advice. She also permits her to express her real feelings about her mother and not those which are socially sanctioned: '"I hate her," I said, and waited for the blow to fall.' But Doctor Nolan replies, 'I suppose you do' (*BJ*, p. 215).

The wave of revulsion against ECT, associated with the anti-psychiatry movement, gathered momentum in the 1960s and 1970s and was popularised by films like *One Flew over the Cuckoo's Nest*, *Edna the Inebriate Woman* and *Family Life*, and in novels such as Marge Piercy's *Woman on the Edge of Time*, which I shall discuss in my chapter on science fiction. Yet Plath appears to have been convinced of the efficacy of ECT and to have voiced none of the questions and objections that were being expressed in progressive circles at the time. Elaine Showalter has suggested that Plath may have identified electric shock treatment with the act of purgation and rebirth, 'because it has the trappings of a powerful religious ritual conducted by a priestly masculine figure' and for the patient it represents a 'rite of passage in which the doctor kills off the "bad" crazy self, and resurrects the "good" self so that the patients feel that in a sense they have died and been born again, with the hated parts of the self annihilated – literally, electrocuted'[69] It might be argued that it is her feminine self that Plath wishes to be extinguished since this has demonstrably caused her the most trouble.

A far more questioning and critical account of electric shock treatment is provided by the New Zealand writer Janet Frame. In her autobiography, *An Angel at my Table*, Frame recounts her discharge from a mental hospital in New Zealand after having received over two hundred applications of unmodified ECT, 'each the equivalent, in degree of fear, to an execution, and in the process having my memory shredded and in some aspects weakened permanently or destroyed'. It was also proposed that she should have herself changed 'by a physical operation into a more acceptable, amenable, normal person'. By this time, Frame says that she had 'seen enough of schizophrenia to know that I had never suffered from it'.[70] Against this she had 'the weight of the "experts" and the "world"' and was in no state to assert herself.[71] She is literally saved from a leucotomy by the timely award of a national prize for her prose writing. In a later autobiographical volume, *The Envoy from Mirror City* Frame relates how she is admitted to the Maudsley Hospital in London in the late 1950s where she is officially told that she had never suffered from schizophrenia, that she should never have been admitted to a mental hospital in the first place, and that any problems she later experienced were a direct result of her stay there.[72]

There is, of course, an inherent contradiction in any writer's attempt to present the experience of nervous breakdown, a time in which the self is experienced at its most distressingly confused, depressed and incoherent, with clarity and precision. Both *The Bell Jar* and *The Golden Notebook* have exceptionally intelligent and lucid writer protagonists. It is their ability to communicate the contradictory experiences of femininity, in ways which make clear that they understand the problematic imbalances of power with which they are faced as women, and which also show that they can negotiate their way around some of the tensions that the lived experience of femininity produces for them, which guarantees the survival of the protagonists as writers and as women.

NOTES

1 Doris Lessing, *The Golden Notebook* (1962), reprinted with a new preface (1971) by the author (St Albans: Granada, 1972), pp. 175–6. All quotations are from this edition and given parenthetically – (*GN*).

2 Fay Weldon, *The Fat Woman's Joke* (London: Hodder and Stoughton, 1967), Penelope Mortimer, *The Pumpkin Eater* (London: Hutchinson, 1962), Sylvia Plath, *The Bell Jar* (London: Faber and Faber, 1963). All quotations are from this edition and given parenthetically – (*BJ*).

3 Denise Riley, *War in the Nursery: Theories of the Child and Mother* (London: Virago, 1983).

4 Peter Lewis, *The Fifties* (London: Heinemann, 1978), p. 42.

5 Elizabeth Wilson, *Only Halfway to Paradise: Women in Postwar Britain 1945–1968* (London: Tavistock, 1980), p. 13.

6 David Reisman, Nathan Glazer and Ruel Denny, *The Lonely Crowd* (New Haven: Yale University Press, 1950).

7 Ted Hughes and Frances McCullough (eds), *The Journals of Sylvia Plath 1950–1962* (New York: The Dial Press, 1982), p. 306.

8 Douglas T. Miller and Marion Nowak, *The Fifties: The Way We Really Were* (New York: Doubleday, 1977), p. 6.

9 Elaine Tyler May, *Homeward Bound: American Families in the Cold War* (New York: Basic Books, 1988), p. 24.

10 William Chafe, *The Paradox of Change: American Women in the Twentieth Century* (New York and Oxford: Oxford University Press, 1991), p. 187

11 Marty Jezer, *The Dark Ages: Life in the United States 1945–1960* (Boston: South End Press, 1982), p. 196.

12 Betty Friedan, *The Feminine Mystique* (1963) (Harmondsworth: Penguin Books, 1965), p. 45.

13 Flora Davis, *Moving the Mountain: The Women's Movement in America Since 1960* (New York: Simon and Schuster, 1991), pp. 111–14.

14 Sylvia Plath, *Letters Home: Correspondence 1950–61*, ed. Amelia Schober Plath (London: Faber and Faber, 1975), p. 473.

15 Niamh Baker, *Happily Ever After? Women's Fiction in Postwar Britain 1945–60* (Basingstoke: Macmillan, 1989), p. 3.

16 Ibid., p. 4.

17 Fay Weldon, 'The Changing Face of Fiction' (1990), in Regina Barreca (ed.), *Fay Weldon's Wicked Fictions* (Hanover: University of New England Press, 1994), pp. 189–97, p. 193.

18 Alva Myrdal and Viola Klein, *Women's Two Roles* (London: Routledge, Kegan and Paul, 1956).

19 Hannah Gavron, *The Captive Wife: Conflicts of Housebound Mothers* (London: Routledge and Kegan Paul, 1966).

20 Cited in Eugenia Kaledin, *American Women in the 1950s: Mothers and More* (Boston: Twayne, 1984), p. 43.

21 *The Feminine Mystique*, p. 45.

22 Daniel Horowitz, *Betty Friedan and the Making of the Feminine Mystique: The American Left, the Cold War and Modern Feminism* (Amherst: Massachusetts University Press, 1999).

23 *The Feminine Mystique*, p. 60.

24 Ibid., p. 29.

25 Melissa Benn, *Madonna and Child: Towards a New Politics of Motherhood* (London: Jonathan Cape, 1998), p. 208.

26 Fay Weldon, *The Fat Woman's Joke* (1967) (London: Sceptre, 1982), p. 9.

27 Margaret Atwood, *The Edible Woman* (New York: Fawcett, 1969).

28 Gayle Greene, *Changing the Story: Feminist Fiction and the Tradition* (Bloomington: Indiana University Press, 1991), pp. 58–85. The novels which Greene explores are Fay Weldon, *The Fat Woman's Joke* (1966); Penelope Mortimer, *The Pumpkin Eater* (1963); Alix Kates Shulman, *Memoirs of an Ex-Prom Queen* (1969); Anne Richardson Roiphe, *Up the Sandbox* (1970); Dorothy Bryant, *Ella Price's Journal* (1982); Johanna Davis, *Life Signs* (1972); Barbara Raskin, *Loose Ends* (1973); Sheila Ballantyre, *Norma Jean the Termite Queen* (1975).

29 Ibid., p. 26.

30 Ibid., p. 66.

31 Jennifer Dawson, *The Ha-Ha* (London: Anthony Blond, 1961), p. 176.

32 Richard Ohmann, *Politics of Letters* (Middletown, CT: Wesleyan University Press, 1987), pp. 210–19, quoted in Alan Sinfield, *Literature, Politics and Culture in Postwar Britain* (Berkeley: University of California Press, 1989), p. 209.

33 Ibid., p. 210.

34 Margot Heinemann, '*Burger's Daughter*: The Synthesis of Revelation', in Douglas Jefferson and Graham Martin (eds), *The Uses of Fiction: Essays on the Modern Novel in Honour of Arnold Kettle* (Milton Keynes: Open University Press, 1982), pp. 181–97, p. 183.

35 Lessing, preface to *The Golden Notebook*, p. 11.

36 Raphael Samuel, 'The Lost World of British Communism', parts 1–3, *New Left Review*, 154, 155, 156. 1985–87.

37 See Eric Hobsbawm, 'Address at the Funeral of Margot Heinemann, 19 June 1992', in David Margolies and Maroula Joannou (eds), *Heart of the Heartless World: Essays in Memory of Margot Heinemann* (London: Pluto, 1995), pp. 216–19, p. 218.

38 Michael Kenny, 'Communism and the New Left', in Geoff Andrews, Nina Fishman and Kevin Morgan (eds), *Opening the Books: Essays on the Social and Cultural History of the British Communist Party* (London: Pluto Press, 1995), p. 195–209, pp. 196–7.

39 Doris Lessing, 'Profile', *New Review*, 1, (8), November 1974, pp. 17–23, p. 20.

40 Doris Lessing, 'The Small Personal Voice', in *A Small Personal Voice: Essays,*

Reviews Interviews, ed. Paul Schlueter (New York: Alfred A. Knopf, 1974).

41 Andrzej Gasiorek, *Post-War British Fiction* (London: Edward Arnold, 1995), p. 89.

42 Lorna Sage, *Women in the House of Fiction: Postwar Women Novelists* (London: Routledge, 1992).

43 Molly Hite, *The Other Side of the Story: Structures and Strategies of Contemporary Feminist Narrative* (Ithaca: Cornell University Press, 1989), p. 68.

44 Lessing, preface to *The Golden Notebook*, p. 7.

45 Tricia Davis, 'What Kind of a Woman Is She? Women and Communist Party Politics, 1941–1955', in Roslind Brunt and Caroline Rowan (eds), *Feminism, Culture and Politics* (London: Lawrence and Wishart, 1982), pp. 85–107, p. 87.

46 Helen Gurley Brown, *Sex and the Single Girl* (New York: Cardinal, 1962).

47 Anne Koedt was later to popularise the findings of the sexologists Masters and Johnson who had established that the clitoris had no other function than sexual pleasure while the vagina was largely devoid of sensitivity and was therefore not a source of orgasm and sexual pleasure. Anne Koedt, 'The Myth of the Vaginal Orgasm', in Anne Koedt, Ellen Levine and Anita Rapone (eds), *Radical Feminism* (New York: Quadrangle, The New York Times Book Company, 1973), pp. 198–207.

48 E.P. Thompson, *William Morris: Romantic to Revolutionary* (1961) (London: The Merlin Press, 1977), p. 806.

49 Lessing, preface to *The Golden Notebook*, p. 9.

50 Elizabeth Wilson, 'Yesterday's Heroines: On Rereading Lessing and de Beauvoir', in Jenny Taylor (ed.), *Notebooks/Memoirs/Archives, Reading and Rereading Doris Lessing* (London: Routledge and Kegan Paul, 1982), pp. 57–75, p. 71, p. 72.

51 Virginia Woolf, *A Room of One's Own* (London: Hogarth, 1929), p. 54.

52 See Joseph Allen Boone, *Libidinal Currents: Sexuality and the Shaping of Modernism* (Chicago: University of Chicago Press, 1998), pp. 389–418.

53 Quoted in Roberta Rubenstein, *The Novelistic Vision of Doris Lessing* (Urbana, University of Illinois Press, 1979), p. 197.

54 Lessing, preface to *The Golden Notebook*, p. 8.

55 Shoshana Felman, 'Women and Madness: The Critical Fallacy', *Diacritics*, 5 (4), winter 1975, pp. 2–10, p. 2.

56 Phyllis Chessler, *Women and Madness* (New York: Avon Books, 1972), p. 56.

57 Ibid., p. xxiii.

58 Peter Orr, *The Poet Speaks* (London: Routledge and Kegan Paul, 1966), p. 169.

59 Linda W. Wagner-Martin, *Sylvia Plath* (London: Chatto and Windus, 1988), p. 59.

60 Plath, *Letters Home*, p. 36.

61 Ibid., p. 378.

62 Ibid., p. 449.

63 *Journals of Sylvia Plath*, p. 213.

64 Ibid.

65 Elaine Tyler May, 'Explosive Issues: Sex, Woman and the Bomb', in Lary May (ed.), *Recasting America: Culture and Politics in the Age of the Cold War* (Chicago: University of Chicago Press, 1988), pp. 154–70, pp. 155–6.

66 Elaine Scarry, *The Body in Pain: The Making and Unmaking of the World* (Oxford: Oxford University Press, 1985), pp. 4–6.

67 Ibid., p. 88.

68 Ibid., p. 266–7.

69 Elaine Showalter, *The Female Malady: Women, Madness and English Culture, 1830–1980* (London: Virago, 1987), p. 217.

70 Janet Frame, *An Angel at my Table: An Autobiography*, vol. 2 (London: The Women's Press, 1984), p. 112.

71 Ibid., p. 113.
72 Janet Frame, *The Envoy from Mirror City: An Autobiography* (1984), vol. 3 (London: The Women's Press, 1985), p. 103.

2

Motherhood

Mother had outfaced a junkful of Chinese pirates, nursed a village through a visitation of the plague, shot a man-eating tiger with her own hand and all before she was as old as I?

Angela Carter, *The Bloody Chamber*

THIS CHAPTER will explore some literary representations of mother-hood with particular reference to the contemporary 'unmarried-mother narrative' and to accounts of women immediately before and after giving birth. The marginal position of the unmarried mother provides a good perspective from which to consider changing gender roles, and the values and institutions in society. Before that, I shall touch briefly on some of the key changes in the position of women and the family which occurred in the 1960s and 1970s and are reflected and mediated in women's fiction. The two decades with which I am concerned are characterised by far-reaching changes in family structure and organisation; increasing divorce and abortion rates, many more couples cohabiting and babies conceived outside marriage, and more people choosing to move out of the parental home and live on their own, or to bring up children in non-traditional families. Attitudes to roles within the nuclear family also altered radically, often as a direct result of women's contact with feminist ideas, and their investment in sexual politics which made their relationship to their male partners difficult, and the bringing up of sons a troubled experience.

The start of the modern women's liberation movement in the United States is usually dated from the foundation of the National Organisation of Women, a broadly based grouping of women committed to a defence of women's rights in 1966. The movement in Britain is usually dated from a conference in Ruskin College, Oxford, in 1970. The women's liberation movement (which in the United States extended far beyond those women who identified with NOW) sought liberation rather than equality with men and became associated with permissiveness because of the emphasis it placed on personal autonomy and its analysis of women's subordination within the family.[1] From its early days the movement was highly critical of marriage as a bourgeois institution, and mounted a vigorous challenge to the conventional nuclear family as an oppressive, male-dominated institution; a critique which it shared with large sections of the revolutionary left in the 1960s: '"Liberation" itself was, to a large extent, defined in terms of emancipation from this kind of family form. This gave rise simultaneously to a new kind of individualism and to the search for new forms of collective living.'[2]

From the 1960s onward there were many experimental modes of living as an alternative to the conventional nuclear family including the establishment of thousands of communal and collective households in which childcare arrangements were shared. The YBA Wife campaign was launched in Britain in 1977. By the end of the 1970s some feminist hostility to the family had abated. While many feminists still viewed the traditional nuclear family with suspicion as an oppressive patriarchal institution, there was a greater willingness to concede that it did meet some women's needs and that the idealistic attempts to construct alternatives had been fraught with difficulties. A number of sociological studies showed that the modern and most desirable form of marriage was widely considered to be the companionate marriage which was becoming more common and filtering down from middle- to working-class families.[3]

But in working-class communities where women had more limited career choices, motherhood continued to be an attractive option for women, compensating for poorly paid, low-status jobs and providing them with approval and respect in their communities. In black communities many women regarded the family as their main refuge against a hostile, racist society and a way of continuing important traditions which might otherwise be lost. The failure of white middle-class feminists to take into account the different perspectives of black women on motherhood and the family was one crucial reason why black women often felt alienated by feminism. As bel hooks put it, 'early feminist attacks on motherhood alienated masses of women from the movement, especially poor and/or non-white women, who find parenting one of the few interpersonal relationships where they are affirmed and appreciated'.[4]

Underlying the sexual permissiveness of the 1960s lay the belief that sexual behaviour should be the concern of the individual and that the state should not attempt to regulate this through the imposition of religious and moral precepts enshrined in the law. In Britain the National Health Services (Family Planning) Act of 1967 authorised local authorities to provide free contraceptive aids and advice on the basis of need alone. The legislation which made contraceptives available under the National Health Service contained no reference to marriage. The number of abortions, illegitimate births and divorces increased substantially during the 1960s and 1970s, and particularly steeply after the passing of the 1967 Abortion Act, which provided for abortion up to twenty-eight weeks if the mother's health or life was at risk, or if the baby was likely to be handicapped, and the 1969 Divorce Act which abolished the concept of the matrimonial offence, and with it the attribution of blame for the breakdown of marriage to one or other of the parties. But, as Jane Lewis has pointed out, evidence of changing marital and sexual behaviour in Britain in the form of a falling age of marriage, more premarital conceptions, increasing numbers of divorces and rising illegitimacy rates were all present before the major legislative change took place.[5]

Changes in the law relating to women's rights in the workplace also affected women's decisions about whether or not to have children. In 1974 the Employment Protection Act gave women in Britain the right to paid maternity leave, protection from dismissal during pregnancy, and the right to return to work up to twenty-nine weeks after having a baby. Equal-pay legislation was enacted much earlier in the United States, in 1963, although there were problems in the way of its practical enforcement. The Equal Pay Act which came into force in Britain in 1975 gave women the same pay as men if they were doing work that was 'the same or broadly similar'. The Sex Discrimination Act of that same year made it illegal to discriminate against women in any sphere of employment with a few exceptions, for example in businesses which employed less than six people or where issues of decency were involved. In the United States feminists became involved in a bitter and protracted battle over the Equal Rights Amendment which was finally passed in 1972 but subject to ratification by individual states.

In the United States higher college attendance, more women in paid employment, later marriage, and higher abortion rates were all found among middle-class and working-class women, both black and white throughout the 1970s – but not among the very poor.[6] Between 1967 and 1970 twelve American states had reformed their abortion laws. There was a major victory for women in 1973 when the Supreme Court ruled that a woman's right to privacy precluded state interference with abortion during the first twelve weeks of pregnancy and that only limited state interference was permissible in the twelve weeks after that.[7]

Because many of the younger women attracted to the movement were anxious to avoid having babies – many did choose to become mothers at a later date – discussion of motherhood was often less fashionable than of contraception and abortion. Sheila Rowbottom has described the gap between 'those of us who had children and those of us who had not' and the way she listened to mothers talking about childcare problems, while secretly wanting to 'pass on to more exciting stuff like the domestic labour debate'.[8] As Vicky Randall has put it, in Britain 'abortion emerged in the early 1970s as almost the definitive issue of contemporary feminism'.[9] The National Abortion Campaign (NAC) formed in the mid-1970s and campaigning under the slogan, 'a woman's right to choose', mobilised massive demonstrations against two unsuccessful attempts to change the 1967 legislation in anti-abortion bills introduced by two backbench MPs, White in 1975 and Corrie in 1979.[10]

The issue of abortion was always less contentious in Britain than in the United States where the Catholic anti-abortion lobby was particularly strong. The Women's Equity Action League (WEAL) broke away from NOW after it espoused abortion law reform in 1968. There was a backlash against the liberalisation of the abortion laws in the Hyde Amendment passed by Congress in 1978 which prohibited federal Medicaid funding for abortion. The abortion 'speak-outs' in the late 1960s in the United States in which women were encouraged to speak honestly about their experiences of abortion are vividly dramatised in Alix Kates Shulman's novel, *Burning Questions* (1979)[11]

In *The Mother/Daughter Plot: Narrative, Psychoanalysis and Feminism* Marianne Hirsch objects to the absence of the 'maternal narrative' in the literary tradition which she sees as symptomatic of the lack of importance which society has attached to motherhood. Her study elucidates formal connections between specific types of narratives centred on reproduction and birth and feminist appropriations of psychoanalysis.[12] In *Women Writing Childbirth*, Tess Cosslett notes that accounts of women giving birth are rare until the twentieth century and are usually depicted from the spectator's point of view rather than the mothers, perhaps from the father's or someone in attendance. Cosslett is concerned with 'the recovery of maternal subjectivity in the birth story'. She argues that all too often the story has been taken away from the mother and that childbirth needs to be made visible from a woman's point of view.[13] The experiences of pregnancy, childbirth and motherhood, on which the fictional representations depend, are, of course, the *only* major areas in which women have exclusive first-hand knowledge which is not available to men. This does not mean that men cannot write sensitively about these things, as, for example, Lewis Grassic Gibbon does in his account of Chris Guthrie's pregnancy and childbirth in *A Scots Quair*. But it does prompt us to ask why such accounts are few and far between. The exclusions of pregnancy and childbirth as proper subject matter for the novel until the twentieth century again pinpoints the extent to which a mode of writing which has been claimed as universal has historically functioned as an expression of men's descriptions of men's lives.

Sara Maitland's first novel, *Daughters of Jerusalem* (1978) is centrally concerned with the issue of a woman's right to choose whether or not to have a baby. Its heroine, Liz, is a feminist, who is part of a group of women campaigning to protect abortion rights for other women. At the same time, she is in receipt of treatment for infertility, and is trying hard to become pregnant but with little success. Some of her friends appear to conceive effortlessly, and, in comparing their situations and histories to those of Liz and her partner, this undeservedly neglected novel provides perceptive insights into the social and psychological reasons why both women and men feel the need to invest so much of themselves in becoming parents.[14]

Paddy Kitchen's *Lying-In* begins arrestingly in *media res*, in a labour ward of a London hospital, in which Vanessa Talisend, an architect about to have her first baby, is being cajoled by the nurses to push harder as she is giving birth. Vanessa's personal life has hitherto been unconventional although last-minute concessions to outward respectability have been made. The father of her baby has been killed in an accident and a pregnant Vanessa has married another man who is prepared to accept her child as his own. The nine chapters of the novel represent her nine days in the hospital.

Lying-In describes the mechanics of giving birth from the mother's point of view and provides gynaecological detail in place of the usual decorous literary silence. Although she is educated, middle class and articulate, Vanessa is 'virtually ignorant about the whole process of contraception, pregnancy, abortion and birth' (*LI*, p. 79). Like many young professional women, her decision not to continue with an untimely pregnancy is not prompted by economic necessity but is a rational choice to delay motherhood to a more propitious moment in her career. At a moment when legal abortion was still often extremely costly, and had to be justified by two doctors, and on the grounds that pregnancy constituted a serious threat to the mother's health, Vanessa's operation in a private nursing home is defended in an earnest moral tone: 'I had brought an extension to my untrammelled freeedom, and it must be brought to learn and expand. Now it was freedom in order to make myself truly capable of designing and building for people, not just freedom for frittering'[15] (*LI*, p. 88). Ella Price in *Ella Price's Journal*[16] is a married woman who opts for an abortion in order to be free to leave an unsatisfying marriage and to exercise greater control over her own life. The Catholic anti-abortion position is forcefully expressed by her mother-in-law and Ella is lied to by a psychiatrist who insists that his permission for an abortion is necessary legally although this is not the case.

The 1960s and 1970s saw a resurgence of interest in natural childbirth, which was frequently linked to a distrust of the male-dominated medical profession, resented for monopolising childbirth as a medical event, making hospitalisation almost universal, and removing control of delivery from the mother. Women frequently give birth in Fay Weldon's fiction, and she has speculated on the relationship between birth and fiction, contesting the notion that 'women have babies ... and men have art', and suggesting that she may have had her own children because she found that she wrote best just before their births.[17] *Puffball*, written after the birth of her fourth and final child, is an elaborate spoof on the current vogue for natural childbirth which was supported by women of radically different political persuasions. The protagonist Liffey retires to the countryside to have her first baby in peace and tranquillity. Her neighbour, Mabs, is a malevolent witch (Queen Mab), whom Liffey has been persuaded to trust, but who plots to destroy Liffey's baby because she mistakenly believes her own husband to be the father. The elements of the playfulness and treachery which are defining characteristics of the postmodern novel are much in evidence in *Puffball*, in which the unborn baby takes on a life of its own and begins to talk in a chapter teasingly entitled 'Annunciation'.[18]

What makes *Puffball* unusual is the frequent interruption of Weldon's narrative by paratextual insertions about the menstrual cycle, pregnancy and labour in clinical language reminiscent of a medical textbook. The longest insertion is the chapter entitled 'Labour' in which there are thirty-eight lines of technical explanation about the contractions of the uterus. There is artistry in this – thirty-eight weeks is also the length of the heroine's pregnancy – and the medical information about women's bodies Weldon supplies has a compelling narrative logic of its own. But, more to the point, there is no attempt to mystify the reader with scientific information, but rather to wrest this from its usual home of the medical textbooks, where it remains an abstraction, to restore knowledge of their bodily functions to women, and, above all, to point to its useful-ness. Liffey's innocence in relation to what is happening inside her own body, which is endangered by the unusual development of the foetus and the placenta, is juxtaposed to her innocence about the machinations of her husband and her neighbour which also jeopardise her health.

Weldon ridicules both those feminists who have principled objec-tions to institutionalised medicine and traditional women who delight in their fecundity and wish to revert to a state of nature when giving birth. A group of Liffey's friends have abandoned doctors as an 'essential part of the male conspiracy against women' and are intent on avoiding 'enemas, shaving, epidurals, and all the ritual humiliations, women in childbirth were subjected to' (*PB*, p. 94). Although Weldon caricatures the representatives of orthodox medicine, she makes it clear that it is medical science which is able to deal with the complications of a difficult pregnancy and ultimately to save both the baby and the mother's life.

Margaret Atwood appears to share some of Weldon's misgivings about the possible abuses of natural childbirth. Throughout her futuristic novel, *The Handmaid's Tale* (1986) displays an ambivalent attitude to natural childbirth which is the only state-approved form of reproduction in her dystopian totalitarian state. The state has institutionalised surrogacy and adopted prenatal policies which require women to give birth 'naturally' without men present or scientific or technological intervention. However, as the same time as motherhood is publicly venerated the state forbids women to read and write and denies them the normal rights of citizenship. One of the disturbing facets of Atwood's dystopia is the ease with which radical feminist demands in relation to reproduction, pornography and rape appear to have been incorporated into a male supremacist, anti-feminist agenda. Atwood cautions women against political agendas which are too narrow. The demand for reproductive rights must always be linked to a defence of women's rights in all other areas or else such rights quickly become meaningless. In an imaginary dialogue with her lost mother, who had been an active feminist in the 1970s, the handmaid declaims, 'you wanted a women's culture. Well, now there is one. It isn't what you meant, but it exists.'[19]

As *The Handmaid's Tale* illustrates, motherhood has never been a universal condition but has always been socially constructed and regulated. In her influential *Of Woman Born*, Adrienne Rich differentiates between the institution and the experience of motherhood.[20] She argues that under patriarchal modes of social organisation, the institution of motherhood functions as a mode of social control of women by infantilising them and encouraging economic and emotional dependency. A mother's will to power over her children is therefore the correlative of her powerlessness in the world. The distinction which Rich makes between motherhood as experience and institution is an important one in reflecting on the literature of period. The first-hand experience of pregnancy in the fiction is one which usually serves to bring the mother-to-be closer to others and make her more receptive to the needs and situations of women of other backgrounds. Whereas most fictional heroines find acquiring babies a fulfulling experience, a few, including Weldon and Atwood, appear to be critical of motherhood as an institution. Dissatisfaction with the institution tends to be expressed not in those novels which I discuss that are largely concerned with pregnancy – the woman has usually opted to have her baby or is at least reconciled to this – but in other novels concerned with family relationships in which the mother's unhappiness with what society or her family expects of her is expressed.

Although many of the better-known theorists in the early days of the movement including Germaine Greer, Kate Millett and Betty Friedan were deeply suspicious of Freudian psychoanalysis – penis envy was a particular *bête noir* – Juliet Mitchell's path-breaking *Women and Psychoanalysis* (1974) allayed the anxieties of many feminists. Feminist understandings of motherhood became more theoretically sophisticated during the 1970s as more women began to look to psychoanalysis for explanation of their behaviour and feelings that could not be satisfactorily accounted for by social factors alone. Feminist therapists interested in helping women with problems such as child abuse and eating disorders often drew upon the work of Melanie Klein, Nancy Chodorow and other representatives of the object-relations school of psychoanalysis.

Some influential studies which helped to explain the intensity of the relationship between parent and child and the troubled reaction of adolescent girls to their mothers were Jessie Bernard's *The Future of Motherhood* (1974), Dorothy Dinnerstein's *The Mermaid and the Minotaur: Sexual Arrangements and the Human Malaise* (1977), Jean Baker Miller's *Towards a New Psychology of Women* (1976), and Nancy Chodorow's *The Reproduction of Mothering* (1978). Chodorow explains maternal unhappiness by arguing that the dissolution of boundaries between self and others characteristic of mothering makes it difficult for women to achieve autonomy. The primary attachment of both girls and boys is to the mother, but boys find separation and individuation easier. Chodorow argues that 'Girls cannot and do not "reject" their mother and women in favor of their father and men but remain in a bisexual triangle throughout childhood and into puberty.'[21] Moreover, girls 'usually make a sexual resolution in favor of men and their fathers, [they] retain an internal emotional triangle'[22] and an attachment to their mother throughout their life.

Chodorow advocates an increased involvement of the father in parenting as one solution to the mother's predicament. Julia Kristeva argues that women have privileged access to the semiotic and the Imaginary through their experience of giving birth. In her essay 'Women's Time' (1979), Kristeva also considers the consequences for girls of an intense attachment to the mother and affirms the maternal dream as the symbolic basis for a counter-society 'imagined as harmonious, without prohibition, free and fulfilling'[23] as a utopian alternative to patriarchal society as it is constituted. Kristeva argues that the arrival of a child 'leads the mother into the labyrinths of an experience that, without the child, she would only rarely encounter: love for another ... the slow, difficult and delightful apprenticeship in attentiveness, gentleness, forgetting oneself ... without annihilating one's affective, intellectual and professional personality – such would seem to be the stakes to be won through guiltless maternity.'[24]

How motherhood is understood and women come to regard themselves as mothers is very much part of the historical period and the ideological circumstances in which specific ideas about motherhood are constructed. For example, a number of important studies in the 1950s had insisted on the crucial role of the mother in her child's development and had been instrumental in persuading women to devote themselves to full-time mothering at the expense of their own careers. They included John Bowlby's *Child Care and the Growth of Love* (1953) and David Winnicott's *The Child and the Family* (1957). What Niamh Baker has described as a 'composite Wife/Mother' figure[25] was common in the fiction of the 1950s and the 'invisibility of women who were not attached to a husband is remarkable'.[26]

In literature as in life, motherhood has been romanticised and idealised as every woman's supreme physical and emotional achievement. Elaine Aston has provided a useful resume of how contemporary feminist drama has challenged such notions through stage productions which included the Women's Theatre Group's *My Mother Says I Never Should* (1975), Pam Gem's *Dusa, Fish, Stas and Vi* (1976), Caryl Churchill's *Top Girls* (1982) and David Edgar and Susan Todd's *Teendreams* (1979).[27] Incorporated within the term mothering is the intensity and emotional closeness of the idealised mother–child relationship. Penelope Mortimer's *The Pumpkin Eater* centres on a woman who finds mothering totally fulfilling and whose psychiatric problems begin only when others no longer permit her to perform that role. It is certainly possible to read *The Pumpkin Eater* as a study in the disillusionment experienced by those women in the post-war period who uncritically embraced motherhood only to find that it denied them the wider nexus of adult relationships they need. But Mortimer's fiction displays little interest in emancipated women and suggests no alternatives for those women who do not wish to travel to the usual destinations of marriage and motherhood. Mrs Armitage's nervous breakdown is clearly symptomatic of a more general breakdown in family values, and of the disjunction between her own conventional beliefs and those of her family and friends who try to wean her away from them.

The novel makes an attempt, albeit less than convincing, to reassert traditional values about a woman's biology being her destiny, but the dialogic interaction of its characters forces it to concede that such attitudes will not suffice in the modern world. It elicits sympathy for its protagonist's uncritical affirmation of motherhood at the same time as it undercuts this by dwelling on her sense of isolation and increasingly volatile state of mind. What many readers of *The Pumpkin Eater* remember best is Mrs Armitage's breakdown in the linen department of Harrods department store after her abortion. She is an attractive woman and has 'everything any woman could want'[28] including a nanny whom she later discovers has been having an affair with her husband. Her husband is at a loss to understand why his wife wants more children: 'Why doesn't she go abroad, or make some friends or ... make a life for herself?' (*PE*, p. 52). He is an incorrigible philanderer who craves the excitement his marriage does not provide: 'But what joy do you think *I* get out of this god-awful boring family life of yours? Where do *I* come in?' (*PE*, p. 40). He is sick of living in a 'bloody nursery' (*PE*, p. 51) and resents the children's incursions on his freedom.

At the heart of Mrs Armitage's predicament lies the realisation that she is bereft of any identity other than that of wife and mother. Her analyst even suggests that she dislikes sex for its own sake and that it must be sanctified by constant reproduction. (*PE*, p. 64) Her privileged position is contrasted with that of a working-class woman worn out by years of child-bearing and poverty. A letter from this unknown woman contains 'the only evidence I had in the world that I was not alone' (*PE*, p. 150).

Mrs Armitage's idealisation of motherhood is quasi-mystical: 'A womb isn't all that important. It's only the seat of life, something that drags the moon down from the sky like a kite and draws the sea in and out, in and out, the world's breathing' (*PE*, p. 148). She is obsessed with the experience of pregnancy to a degree which raises questions about her mental balance. The doctors not only terminate the pregnancy but also subject her to the trauma of sterilisation – an operation that was far more common for black women and working-class women than middle-class women at this time. Moreover, she suspects that she has been persuaded to have an abortion because her husband's mistress would have left him and the mistress's pregnancy subsequently becomes a visible reproach to her own sterility. *The Pumpkin Eater* dramatises a state of mind which came to be recognised as the 'empty nest' syndrome. When her children leave home there is nothing to put in their place: 'Over-indulgence in sexual and family life had left us, as far as other relationships were concerned, virginal; we said we had friends much as schoolchildren, busy with notes and hearts and keepsakes, say they have lovers. In a packed address book there was not one person to whom I could speak or write' (*PE*, p. 172). Despite its curiously old-fashioned structures of feeling, *The Pumpkin Eater* was in 1964 made into a successful film by Harold Pinter with an acclaimed performance by Anne Bancroft in the leading role.

The ideological project of Margaret Forster's *Georgy Girl* (1965) is to sever the relationship between maternal feelings and motherhood by showing that not all women who give birth love children and that many women who have never given birth love them passionately. Maternal behaviour in this novel is learned rather than 'natural'. Meredith, who is baby Sara's biological mother, has no attachment to her daughter whom she regards as a nuisance, and happily gives her away to be adopted. Georgy, who has had a temporary relationship with the child's father, becomes besotted with the baby and determined to keep her ('What's so marvellous about being married?' yelled Georgy. 'You'd think only married people were human, or had a prerogative on decency. Meredith was married and she didn't even want her baby. There are some lousy married mothers and some wonderful unmarried ones').[29]

It is Georgy's infatuation with the baby that ruins her relationship with its father with whom she cohabits. In the end, they separate, the father's indifference to his daughter contrasting sharply with Georgy's devotion: 'He had no feelings for the baby. No pride, no excitement in her, no devotion to the mere fact of her existence. She didn't think he'd foreseen how Sara would become an extension of her, how she would adore and think and live and breathe this baby daughter of his. He'd thought she would look after her through a sense of duty, that she would come between them in the sense that she was a burden' (*GG*, pp. 194–5). Like *The Lying-In*, this novel ends with reluctant concessions to respectability. Georgy agrees to marry an older man who will adopt Sara.

Because what is accepted as good mothering is socially constructed, changes in family structure such as increases in the number of unmarried mothers are invariably identified as a threat to the status quo and a cause for official concern. The social construction of motherhood entails a model of 'normal' motherhood against which to compare the experience of 'deviant' mothers, for example unmarried mothers, lesbian mothers, or very young mothers.[30] The struggle against dominant constructions of mothering also involves racial, class and heterosexual privilege because the ability of black, lesbian and working-class mothers to provide emotionally and materially for their children is often constrained by poverty, racism and homophobia.

Lesbian mothers have had a long struggle to establish their identities as mothers when society has construed lesbian mothering as something of a contradiction. *In Rocking the Cradle: Lesbian Mothers, A Challenge to Family Living* (1981) Gillian Hanscombe and Jackie Forster assembled evidence, much of it from research conducted in the United States, to show that there are no medical or psychological reasons why lesbians should not be mothers, and to disprove many of the common myths, i.e.

that children brought up by homosexual parents are more likely to become homosexually orientated than those brought up by heterosexuals: 'The problem is not with the relationship between predominantly homosexual parents and their children, but with a society which has misunderstood and denied human sexuality and most particularly that of persons whose orientation differs from the majority's'.[31]

A spirited attempt to pinpoint the emotional, economic and legal problems lesbian mothers face was made by Michèle Roberts in *A Piece of the Night* (1978).[32] When Julie Fanchot leaves her husband to live in a feminist communal household he threatens to evict the women from the house which he owns in the knowledge that his estranged wife cannot afford to buy a house herself. He also demands custody of their daughter, knowing that Julie would stand no chance of obtaining this through the courts if her sexual orientation were to be made public. Jan Clausen, herself a non-biological parent in a lesbian partnership, discusses issues of lesbian motherhood, for example, the use of artificial insemination by donor, in her collection of short stories, *Mother, Sister, Daughter, Lover* (1981). A much later novel *Sinking, Stealing* (1985) is a subversion of the 'on-the-road' novel which reflects the lesbian custody battles of the 1970s and 1980s. When Erica's biological mother dies in a car accident custody is given to the child's father. But Josie, her mother's lover, has looked after ten-year-old Erica for much of her life, and, rather than be separated, the two run away together on a greyhound bus in a desperate attempt to maintain the parent–child relationship which society refuses to condone. In Britain, Section 28 of the Local Government Act (1988) made it illegal for local authorities to encourage homosexuality or for children in schools to be taught that 'pretended', i.e. homosexual, family relationships were acceptable.

In the United States the infamous Moynihan Report (1965) attributed the blame for the social problems experienced disproportionately by many African-Americans to the matriarchal structure of the family headed by a single mother, rather than to factors such as poor schooling, unemployment, economic disadvantage and racial prejudice.[33] In 1981 over 47 per cent of black families with children present were headed by women, an increase from 31 per cent in 1970.[34] In *The Women of Brewster Place* (1982) Gloria Naylor provides a sympathetic portrait of a young black woman, Cora Lee, who loves baby dolls, becomes accidentally pregnant in her Sophomore year, and then a single parent with six unruly children 'growing wild-eyed and dumb, coming home filthy from the streets with rough corduroy, khaki, and denim that tattered faster than she could mend, and with mouthfuls of rotten teeth, and scraped limbs, and torn school books, and those damned truant notices in her mailbox'.[35]

In Alice Walker's short story, 'Strong Horse Tea', Rannie Toomer's baby is critically ill from double pneumonia and whooping cough: 'She was not married. Was not pretty.Was not anybody much. And he was all she had.'[36] The story hinges on Rannie's belief in modern medicine and her initial rejection of Aunt Sarah's traditional folk remedies, to which she has always had a strong antipathy. Rannie, who is illiterate, has pleaded with the white mailman who calls at her door to summon a doctor from the nearest town. He has simply made reassuring noises and departed at speed. In desperation, Rannie turns to the old woman's 'home remedies' obeying instructions to go out in the night and collect warm horse urine which she administers in vain to the dying child. The story's tension depends on the non-arrival of the doctor who is confidently expected. Walker movingly depicts the depths of maternal love in the lengths to which Rannie is prepared to go, grasping at any straw to save her baby. She also evokes the hopelessness of a situation in which the baby's life is lost because of the misunderstandings which have ensued from a combination of Rannie's race and appearance – the mailman finds her physically repulsive and does not understand why she is agitated or the urgent need to summon help – and from her poverty which is the root cause of her child's ill health.

The social and psychological construction of 'normal' mothers runs counter to the reality of motherhood which many mothers experience. Some have been unable or unwilling to conform to that construction, for example unmarried mothers. As a consequence, many mothers, particularly those who have been very young, very poor, or have opted to bring up their children without a husband, have been construed as pathological. There has also been a tension between the social construction of mothering as an essentially private activity, and statutory intervention which has countered the notion that bringing up children is an entirely private function.

It is this tension which Zoe Fairbairns explores in her dystopian novel, *Benefits* (1979).[37] The novel is set in the 1970s, but moves to an imaginary future in which the social trends discernible in contemporary Britain, including the moral panics about the growing number of unmarried mothers, have taken on a far more sinister aspect. Like *The Handmaid's Tale*, *Benefits* dramatises what happens when feminist demands are implemented by a right wing, anti-feminist, authoritarian state. The demand which has been conceded in *Benefits* is for payment of 'wages for housework'. This is essentially a modern variant of the 'endowment of motherhood', which feminists like Eleanor Rathbone had supported earlier in the century, but which was canvassed in a much more radical form in the 1970s by Selma James and others. In *Benefits*, wages for housework, far from enhancing the status of domestic labour, motherhood, and childcare, and removing women's dependency on individual men, as its advocates had hoped, merely augment the powers of the state, consolidate the feminisation of poverty, and produce an increase in domestic violence.

A number of well-known nineteenth-century novelists including Nathaniel Hawthorne, Elizabeth Gaskell, Margaret Harkness, George Moore, Thomas Hardy, and Margaret Harkness in *The Scarlet Letter*, (1850), *Ruth* (1853), *A City Girl* (1887), *Esther Waters* (1894), and *Tess of the D'Urbervilles* (1891), had depicted the unmarried mother sympathetically. Ostracised because of the sexual double standard, marginalised in society because she had no man to support her, the unmarried mother served these and other novelists as an icon of the ways in which *all* women suffered under patriarchal ideology. Many of their novels depict her as a loving woman struggling to do the best for her child, and some like *Tess of the D'Urbervilles*, subtitled 'a pure woman', insist that virtue has nothing to do with virginity. Until late into the twentieth century, illegitimate birth was a condition to which shame was automatically attached.

After the Second World War the image of the unmarried mother altered from someone who represented a moral danger to society to someone who was psychologically troubled but had the potential to be redeemed: 'In the 1950s and most of the 1960s it was possible to treat unmarried mothers as "abnormal", either in terms of their immature personalities, or, more traditionally in terms of their "waywardness"'.[38] Until the last quarter of the twentieth century the vast majority of unmarried mothers were 'hidden away' or 'found refuge refuge with kin'.[39] Only since the 1970s have the 'majority of never-married mothers joined the dramatically increasing number of divorced women living autonomously in the community, often in social housing and often drawing state benefits'.[40] In Britain the Social Security Act of 1966 deprived unmarried mothers who were suspected of cohabiting of their right to claim social security payments. During the 1970s, the 'problem' of unmarried motherhood was overtaken by the 'problem' of divorce. There was a brief period of public sympathy for the single mother in the middle of the 1970s when more liberal changes in welfare benefits were introduced. But as the number of women bringing up children alone rose, and with them the benefits bill, that tide of sympathy ebbed.

The emotional and economic toll which the decision to remain single could extract from a pregnant woman from a respectable background was enormous. A 'shotgun wedding' was until comparatively recently a common answer to an unplanned pregnancy in many working-class communities, In a later preface to her semi-autobiographical account of a working-class childhood, *That's How It Was* (1962), Maureen Duffy describes fear of pregnancy as 'the terror that kept so many chaste, not moral qualms or a lack of adolescent lust'. Duffy adds that 'Pregnancy was the great trap and once in there was no way out except by abortion. It's important to remember how this problem obsessed women in the pre-contraception era.'[41] Paddy, the heroine of *That's How It Was* is illegitimate: 'Lucky for me I was born at all really, I mean that she could have decided not to bother. Like she told me, she was tempted, head in the gas oven, in front of a bus, oh a thousand ways.'[42] Her mother, who has been abandoned by her feckless Irish lover, was born into a large, impoverished East London family, 'number nine of a batch of ten, alternatively boy, girl with eighteen months between' (*THIW*, p. 22). She is sterilised when she becomes pregnant and Paddy's step-sister has an illegitimate baby who is given away for adoption. The book describes the troubled relationship between the two women, culminating in Paddy's sense of shock and loss when her mother who has developed tuberculosis, a killer disease in working-class communities, dies without warning.

The heroines of the last two novels I shall consider, *The Millstone* (1965) and *The L-Shaped Room* (1960) live outside marriage enabling their authors to create narratives which function as critiques of the ideological foundations upon which the dominant narratives of courtship and marriage have been erected. Margaret Drabble has often written about motherhood and was married and in her third pregnancy when she wrote *The Millstone*. As Elaine Showalter has put it, 'Drabble is the novelist of maternity, as Charlotte Bronte is the novelist of the school-room.'[43]

It is to avoid social disapprobation that Jane Graham in *The L-Shaped Room*, briefly masquerades as a widow. But the situation of the unmarried mother has historically been mitigated by a number of factors, the most important of which have been money and social class. In *The L-Shaped Room* Jane receives an unexpected legacy which gives her a cottage to live in and a private income to bring up her son. She is also conveniently reconciled with her erstwhile angry but now forgiving father. In *The Millstone*, Rosamund Stacey has free use of her parents' flat and an income of five hundred pounds a year – the sum that Virginia Woolf specified was necessary for a woman writer to be independent. In the liberal academic world in which she moves – she verges on a caricature of the middle-class liberal intellectual – sexual peccadilloes excite very little interest. Moroever, she secures a job in a new university and her academic qualifications shield both herself and her daughter from the opprobrium of illegitimacy: 'Her name would be Dr Rosamund Stacey, a form of address which would go a long way towards obviating the anomaly of Octavia's existence'[44] (*M*, p. 155).

The pregnancies in both novels are not planned but accidental. They continue by default because the heroines are too indecisive to terminate them. In *The L-Shaped Room*, Jane reacts angrily to an unctuous doctor who is prepared to countersign an affidavit stating that she is psychologically unfit to have a child and to arrange a legal abortion in exchange for one hundred guineas – the literary prototype for the plausible, money-grubbing abortionist in an earlier novel, Rosamund Lehmann's *The Weather in the Street* (1936). In *The Millstone*, Rosamund and her friends drink the bottle of gin which she has purchased for a half-hearted attempt at abortion. The attempt at do-it-yourself abortion which was common before the reform of the abortion law often features in fiction and perhaps nowhere more chillingly than in Marge Piercy's *Braided Lives* (1982).[45] There is a well-meaning woman friend in Jane's lodging-house who makes her a gift of a bottle of gin ('Mother's ruin. Now you know why they call it that – one reason, anyway. Of course, you have to drink lots of it – "lots and lots, no tiny tots", as they say').[46]

Until relatively recently, the only grounds on which it was permissible for a respectable unmarried woman to have sex with a man was love or the promise of marriage. For much of literary history the story of the unmarried mother has been conjoined with the romance plot, in which the heroine has been loved by a man, but has been separated from love by some accident, personal tragedy, misplaced trust, broken promise, or act of deception by the father of her child. A love child in literature has very often been quite literally that.

The self-realisation or place in society with which heroines have traditionally been conferred in fiction is frequently predicated upon romantic love and marital union. The story of the unmarried mother is a rebellion against the dominance of romance and marriage plots, which show marriage as the conclusion of the heroine's quest for self-knowledge and also as the closure of the novel. In formulating how best to live a life outside marriage the contemporary 'unmarried mother' narratives question the conventions of the novel as well as the social order.

The babies in *The L-Shaped Room* and *The Millstone* are not conceived in passion, neither are their mothers strongly libidinous, but, on the contrary, are characterised by English emotional reserve. The moment of conception in *The Millstone* and *The L-Shaped Room* is joyless and takes place with men for whom the protagonists feel very little. Virginity is an encumbrance which, like Esther in *The Bell Jar*, Rosamund is determined to shake off. She has the bad luck to conceive the first time she has sexual intercourse. Jane's son is the product of a chance encounter with a distant acquaintance. It is not only love which is missing. Sex hardly features in either novel. But what is perhaps more puzzzling is the absence of sexual need. For women to admit to sexual needs is a troubling break both with sexual morality and literary convention. To suggest that sex is a desirable aspect of a woman's life, whether she is married or not, prevents a significant challenge to traditional morality.

Like Rosamund in *The Millstone*, Jane has chosen not to accept help from the man who made her pregnant. Unlike Rosamund, who suspects that Octavia's father is really a homosexual, Jane discloses to her lover that her son is his, but turns down his offer of marriage because he admits that he thought of her as 'that kind of girl' (*LR*, p. 253). The division of women into madonnas and magdalenes made here is one that Jane has also internalised.

Their situations may indeed constitute a rebellion against gender norms and social conventions, but neither Jane nor Rosamund are rebellious by temperament or conviction. Though Rosamund is a feminist ('My mother, you know was a great feminist. She brought me up to be equal. She made there be no questions, no difference. I was equal. I am equal' *M*, pp. 28–9), her rebellion pales into significance compared to the spirited defence of nineteenth-century unmarried motherhood in Olive Schreiner's *The Story of an African Farm* (1883). But Rosamund does draw analogies between herself and the heroines of didactic novels: 'I'm one of those Bernard Shaw women who wants children but no husband' (*M*, p. 106). Her baby, Octavia, is called after the Victorian social reformer, Octavia Hill.

Like Penelope Mortimer, Drabble has overwhelmingly powerful feelings about motherhood which is for her 'the greatest joy in the world'.[47] Although neither Drabble's heroines nor Reid Banks's actively seek motherhood they are radically changed by it. In both novels, motherhood is experienced as a great leveller. Like an errant Victorian daughter, Jane has been expelled from her comfortable suburban family home for being 'no better than a street-woman' (*LR*, p. 36). Her response to an authoritarian father is one of defiance: she'll prove to herself that she can manage alone. She finds refuge in 'one of those "gone-to-seed houses"' (*LR*, p. 1) infested with bedbugs in the worst part of Fulham, with one bathroom for a whole house, an ogre of a landlady, and two prostitutes in the basement, one of whom is ominously also called Jane. The house has been specifically chosen to safeguard her anonymity.

In *The L-Shaped Room* (1960) the nuclear family is depicted as an oppressive institution whereas friends and neighbours are a reliable source of support. *The L-Shaped Room* traces Jane's transition from emotionally inhibited middle-class respectability to enjoyment of bohemian life. As in *The Millstone*, motherhood is a passport to forming new relationships with those of a different race and class. It is Jane's friendship with her fellow tenants who are also socially ostracised, John, an affable black musician and Toby, an impoverished Jewish writer, which rescues her from her emotional isolation. Jane learns how to ask for support like Rosamund whose parents 'had drummed the idea of self-reliance into me so thoroughly that I believed dependence to be a fatal sin' (M, p. 9) and who realises that she 'was going to have to ask for help, and from strangers too' (M, p. 72). The life-denying obsession with respectability which characterises her own family is entirely absent in the lodging-house – a maiden aunt even proposed that Jane should pretend that her own baby had been adopted in order to preserve outward appearances. In a manner reminiscent of Shelagh Delaney's *A Taste of Honey* (1958) in which a pregnant teenager, Jo, is cared for by a young homosexual who, unlike her own mother, is shown to have her best interests at heart, John and Toby see Jane through her pregnancy and are both present in the hospital when she gives birth.

Jane makes a last visit to the L-shaped room. The new tenant comments only on the room's shabbiness and reveals that she has turned down all overtures of friendship from the other tenants. She is at once a reminder of Jane's former self and an indicator of how much she has been changed for the better by the experience of pregnancy. *The L-Shaped Room* was filmed by Bryan Forbes in 1962 with the actress Lesley Caron in the leading role. The change of the heroine's nationality – she is depicted as a French woman who is impervious to subtle nuances of behaviour which an English person would notice – eliminates the critiques of the English class system which are present in the book.

The Millstone, like *The L-Shaped Room*, is largely a study of the positive changes in a woman which maternity brings about: the protagonist confesses to, 'a vague and complicated sense that this pregnancy had been sent to me in order to reveal to me a scheme of things totally different from the scheme which I inhabited, totally removed from academic enthusiasms, social consciousness, etiolated, undefined emotional connexions, and the exercise of free will' (M, p. 67).

Rosamund has hitherto prided herself in her difference from other women: 'I could not recall a single other instance in my life when I had felt what all other women feel' (M, p. 103). Her primary allegiance has been to what Susan Spitzer describes as her 'intellectual (in her view) masculine self'.[48] At first, she refuses to let her pregnancy act as a distraction from her academic work, but the rational self gives way to the feeling self as she is overwhelmed by love of her daughter: 'Love, I suppose one might call it, and the first of my life' (M, p. 102). As Drabble puts it, 'the emotional life, even though it may be more tragic, is more satisfying than the conscious intellectual life. The conscious intellectual life is very dry. This is one of the things that Rosamund suffers from.'[49]

'Having children gives you an access to an enormous common store of otherness about other people.' Drabble has admitted that 'this is how I learned that other people existed'.[50] Rosamund's pregnancy exposes her directly to the suffering of others. The women in the waiting room are 'representatives of a population whose existence I had hardly noticed' (*M*, p. 37). Anaemia and exhaustion were written on most countenances: the clothes were 'dreadful, the legs swollen' (*M*, p. 57). At first, she believes that they have nothing in common but 'birth, pain, fear and hope, these were the subjects that drew us together in gloomy awe, and so strong was the bond that even I, doubly, trebly outcast by my unmarried status, my education, and my class, even I was drawn in from time to time, and compelled to offer some anecdote of my own' (*M*, p. 60).

The novel contains a pointed critique of hospital management which subordinates the needs of mothers to the smooth running of the institution. A turning point is when Rosamund is refused access to her baby daughter who is ill. She realises that a lifetime's conditioning in considerate, self-effacing behaviour must be abandoned and embarks on an angry tearful confrontation with two nurses until her request is finally acceded. Uncontrolled anger produces results where politeness and courtesy did not.

That women should chose to live outside patriarchal arrangements is, of course, deeply threatening to those who believed such arrangements to be essential to the stability of the social order. But the threat is compounded if the women who eschew marriage are articulate, educated and middle class. The rebellion in both *The L-Shaped Room* and *The Millstone* is qualified and decorous. In many respects their heroines are disappointingly more conservative and *less* adventurous than women in the late nineteenth-century 'new woman' novels of Olive Schreiner, George Egerton and Sarah Grand.[51] These later novels show how unmarried motherhood represents a move for the better for the protagonists who become more assertive, emotionally aware, and responsive to other people. They interestingly update earlier literary representations and narrativise a dream of motherhood in which its pleasures are possible with the minimum of sex, the complications of men, and the burdens of marriage.

NOTES

1 Jane Lewis, *Women in Britain Since 1945: Women, Family, Work and the State in the Post-War Years* (Oxford: Blackwell, 1992), p. 42.

2 Joni Lovenduski and Vicky Randall, *Contemporary Feminist Politics: Women and Power in Britain* (Oxford: Oxford University Press, 1993), p. 269.

3 Lewis, *Women in Britain Since 1945*, p. 47. See also Janet Finch and Penny Summerfield, 'Social Reconstruction and the Emergence of Companionate Marriage, 1945–59', in David Clarke (ed.), *Marriage, Domestic Life and Social Change* (London: Routledge, 1991), pp. 7–32.

4 bel hooks, *Feminist Theory: From Margin to Centre* (Boston: South End Press, 1984), pp. 134–5.

5 Lewis, *Women in Britain Since 1945*, p. 41.

6 Rochelle Gatlin, *American Women Since 1945* (London: Macmillan, 1987), p. 181.

7 Ibid., p. 137.

8 Sheila Rowbottom, 'To Be or Not To Be: The Dilemma of Mothering', *Feminist Review*, 31, 1989, pp. 82–93, p. 83.

9 Vicky Randall, *Women and Politics* (London: Macmillan, 1987), p. 263.

10 In 1971 Simone de Beauvoir was one of the eminent women who stated that they had undergone abortions and signed the *Manifeste des 343* which called for a liberalisation of French abortion law and appeared in *Le Nouvel Observateur*.

11 Alix Kates Shulman, *Burning Questions* (New York: Bantam Books, 1978).

12 Marianne Hirsch, *The Mother/Daughter Plot: Narrative, Psychoanalysis, Feminism* (Bloomington: Indiana University Press, 1989).

13 Tess Cosslett, *Women Writing Childbirth: Modern Discourses of Motherhood* (Manchester: Manchester University Press, 1994), p. 2.

14 Sara Maitland, *Daughters of Jerusalem* (London: Blond and Biggs, 1978).

15 Paddy Kitchen, *Lying-In* (London: Arthur Barker, 1965). All quotations are from the first edition and are given parenthetically – (*LI*).

16 Dorothy Bryant, *Ella Price's Journal* (Philadelphia: Lippincote, 1972).

17 Fay Weldon, 'Of Birth and Fiction', in Regina Barecca (ed.), *Fay Weldon's Wicked Fictions* (Hanover: University Press of New England, 1994), pp. 198–208, p. 199.

18 Fay Weldon, *Puffball* (London: Hodder and Stoughton, 1980), p. 92.

20 Margaret Atwood, *The Handmaid's Tale* (London: Jonathan Cape, 1986), p. 137.

20 Adrienne Rich, *Of Woman Born: Motherhood as Experience and Institution* (1976) (London: Virago, 1977).

21 Nancy Chodorow, *The Reproduction of Mothering* (Berkeley: University of California Press, 1978), p. 140.

22 Ibid.

23 Julia Kristeva, 'Women's Time' (1979), trans. 1981, in Toril Moi (ed.), *The Kristeva Reader* (Oxford: Basil Blackwell, 1986), pp. 187–213, p. 202.

24 Ibid., p. 16.

25 Niamh Baker, *Happily Ever After? Women's Fiction in Postwar Britain 1945–60* (London: Macmillan, 1989), p. viii.

26 Ibid.

27 Elaine Aston, 'Home Alone: Re-thinking Motherhood in Contemporary Feminist Theatre', in John Lucas (ed.), *Writing and Radicalism* (London: Longman, 1996), pp. 281–300.

28 Penelope Mortimer, *The Pumpkin Eater* (London: Hutchinson, 1962), p. 52. All quotations are from this edition and are given parenthetically – (*PE*).

29 Margaret Forster, *Georgy Girl* (London: Secker and Warburg, 1965), p. 201. Further quotations are given parenthetically – (*GG*).

30 Ann Phoenix, Anne Woollett and Eva Lloyd (eds), *Motherhood: Meanings, Practices and Ideologies* (London: Sage, 1991), p. 14.

31 Judd Marmor, quoted in Gillian E. Hanscombe and Jackie Forster, *Rocking the Cradle: Lesbian Mothers, A Challenge to Family Living* (London: Peter Owen, 1981), p. 147.

32 Michèle Roberts, *A Piece of the Night* (London: The Women's Press, 1978).

33 Aminata Forma, *Mother of all Myths: How Society Moulds and Constrains Mothers* (London: HarperCollins, 1998), p. 221.

34 Gatlin, *American Women Since 1945*, p. 180.

35 Gloria Nayor, *The Women of Brewster Place* (New York: Viking, 1982), pp. 112–13.

36 Alice Walker, 'Strong Horse Tea', *In Love and Trouble* (1967) (London: The Women's Press, 1983), pp. 88–98, p. 88.

37 Zoe Fairbairns, *Benefits* (London: Virago, 1979).

38 Kathleen Kiernan, Hilary Land and Jane Lewis, *Lone Motherhood in Twentieth-Century Britain* (Oxford: Clarendon Press, 1998), p. 122.

39 Ibid., p. 9.

40 Ibid., p. 5.

41 Maureen Duffy, preface to *That's How It Was* (1962) (London: Virago, 1983), p. v–xi, p. ix.

42 Maureen Duffy, *That's How It Was* (London: Hutchinson, 1962), p. 13. All quotations are from the first edition and given parenthetically – (*THIW*).

43 Elaine Showalter, *A Literature of Their Own: British Women Writers from Charlotte Brontë to Doris Lessing* (London: Virago, 1998), p. 305.

44 Margaret Drabble, *The Millstone* (London: Weidenfeld and Nicolson, 1965; reprinted Harmondsworth: Penguin, 1968). All quotations are from the 1968 edition and are given parenthetically – (*M*).

45 Marge Piercy, *Braided Lives* (New York: Fawcett, 1982).

46 Lynne Reid Banks, *The L-Shaped Room* (London: Chatto and Windus, 1960), p. 140. All quotations are from this edition and are given parenthetically – (*LR*).

47 Interview with Diana Cooper-Clark, 'Margaret Drabble: Cautious Feminist', *Atlantic Monthly*, 246, November 1980, pp. 69–75, p. 74.

48 Susan Spitzer, 'Fantasy and Femaleness in Margaret Drabble's *The Millstone*', *Novel*, 11, Spring, 1978, pp. 227–45, p. 239.

49 Diana Cooper-Clark, 'Margaret Drabble: Cautious Feminist', in Ellen Cronan Rose (ed.), *Critical Essays on Margaret Drabble* (Boston: G.K. Hall, 1985), pp. 19–30, p. 25.

50 Dee Preussner, 'Talking with Margaret Drabble', *Modern Fiction Studies*, 25, 1979–80, pp. 563–77, p. 575.

51 See Olive Schreiner, *The Story of an African Farm*, (1883), George Egerton, *Keynotes* (1894), Sarah Grand, *The Heavenly Twins* (1893).

3

Working-class women's experi

> We were born, and had no choice in the matter; but we were burdens, expensive, never grateful enough. There was nothing we could do to pay back the debt of our existence. 'Never have children, dear,' she said; 'they ruin your life.'
>
> Carolyn Steedman, *Landscape for a Good Woman*

THE RELATIONSHIP between writing and social class is a vexed one because it is always complicated by variations between metropolitan and regional experience, and by age, race, gender, sexuality and sexual orientation. Moreover, social class signifies very different things in Britain from what it does in the United States. In the novels of Jeanette Winterson and Maureen Duffy, set in working-class communities in Lancashire and the south-east of England, the open expression of sexual desire in working-class communities where there is a premium on respectability and conformity is often dangerous for women, and is especially dangerous for very young women. Jeanette Winterson's first novel, *Oranges Are Not the Only Fruit* (1985), and Maureen Duffy's two novels written in the 1960s, *That's How It Was* (1962) and *The Microcosm* (1966),[1] all deal with the formation of working-class and lesbian subjectivities. If a working-class community perceives women's sexual desires as transgressive, and a threat to its dominant sexual norms, it will react by closing ranks and with punitive or repressive measures to indicate its disapproval. Thus the sentimental pieties of working-class life, the famed 'warmth', 'supportiveness', and 'generosity' are exposed in the community's treatment of women who will not conform. As Francis Mulhern has put it, 'if "communities" are notoriously hard to find, it is because they are everywhere – not *places* but *practices* of collective identification'.[2]

To write about working-class life, to the exclusion of middle-class existence, as some of the women I look at in this chapter do, is to be susceptible to criticism for narrowness of range, 'special pleading', and lack of development – criticisms that are never voiced in relation to writers who write about middle-class subject matter to the exclusion of all else. As Reva Brown writes of *The Century's Daughter*, 'beneath the story line there is an amount of special pleading for working-class life as uable and interesting because of the necessity to struggle for existence and not despite of it'.[3] In much the same way, to focus as Pat Barker, one of the writers whose work I shall look at closely, does on a particular locality – particularly a place like Thornaby which many of her readers would have difficulty in locating in an atlas – is to risk being pigeonholed as a regional writer, with nothing to say about aspects of human existence which are not associated with any particular *topos*. As Raymond Williams has pointed out, the designation of some places as regional only holds true if certain others are not seen in this way. 'This is in its turn a function of cultural centralisation: a modern form of the 'city–country' discrimination' and 'an expression of centralised cultural dominance'.[4]

What has often been missing from the delineation of working-class lives lived out in the back-to-back terraced streets of Britain's towns and cities is psychological complexity. In Carolyn Steedman's autobiographical account of her own life and her mother's, *Landscape for a Good Woman*, Steedman sets her own experience of growing up in a working-class family apart from the fixed townscapes 'where mothers who don't go out to work order the domestic day, where men are masters, and children, when they grow older, express gratitude for the harsh discipline meted out to them'. Her priority in *Landscape for a Good Woman* is to 'particularise this profoundly a-historical landscape'. Her book tells of a mother who goes out to work and is a single parent and of a father who is not a patriarch. The point for the author 'is *not* to say that all working-class childhoods are the same, nor that experience of them produces unique psychic structures' but 'to find a way of theorizing the result of such difference and particularity'.[5]

In the twenty-year period with which I am concerned, many of the certainties of the left in relation to social class in Britain have been questioned. It is no longer possible to assign to the working-class the status of a privileged historical subject, or to assume that the emancipation of working people will in itself bring an end to all exploitative relationships. Women have always had a more complicated relationship to the class system than men. Because they have traditionally had a different relationship to the means of production, they have been assigned the class identity of their husbands and fathers. But women's sense of their own class identity has also been complicated in recent years by changes in the patterns of marriage, education and employment.

The time with which this book is occupied is one of extraordinarily rapid social change in the social structure of Britain. At the start of the 1960s, class identities were, in the main, still easily recognisable and the factors which determined them, such as place of residence, occupation, education, and social attitudes and expectations appeared relatively stable. The old class loyalties were routinely reflected in well-established voting patterns; in the massive sizes of Labour majorities in the inner cities and of Conservative majorities in the rural heartlands. The belief that ordinary people had 'never had it so good', the slogan which under-pinned Harold Macmillan's election victory in 1959, appeared to be borne out by statistics that showed full (male) employment and general prosper-ity. But the effects of greatly improved standards of living on the attitudes of the traditional working class is by no means clear. While some social commentators like Jeremy Seabrook have lamented the loss of kinship, dignity and neighbourliness as casualties of an economy dominated by the market place,[6] J.H. Goldthorpe's study of '*embourgeoisement*' among affluent workers in the car industry in Luton showed that prosperity did not make them jettison old habits and affiliations.[7]

None of the respondents in Elizabeth Roberts's oral history of working-class family and social life 1940–70 looked back with nostalgia to the houses without bathrooms or other modern facilities. However, few believed that, by moving, they had improved the social climate within which they lived.[8] In 1964 thirteen years of Conservative government came to end with the modernising Labour government under Harold Wilson, narrowly elected with the support of substantial middle-class voters attracted by his pledge to harness the power of science and technol-ogy to the creation of a new Britain. Labour was returned with an increased majority in 1966. As Stuart Laing has put it, 'even if the working class had disappeared, this was of no consequence if Labour could still win elections.'[9]

By the end of the 1970s, a seismic shift had taken place in British society, with two million people unemployed, the largest figure since 1931. The long-term decline of Britain's economic, manufacturing and industrial base also appeared irreversible. Widespread mobility and changes in the patterns of family, education and work made the old class identities and loyalties problematic for many people and produced different voting patterns. The election of Margaret Thatcher's govern-ment in 1979, after the famous 'winter of discontent' in which a series of strikes by public-sector workers had helped to turn public opinion against the Labour government in power, saw the return for the first time of a radical reforming government of the right pledged to destroy the consensus which had dominated British politics for most of the post-war period, to dismantle public ownership, and to undo what many regarded as the most significant advances since the war: full employment and the welfare state. Its objectives pursued via free-market economics and public-expenditure cuts, were to bring about a 'classless society' and to weaken the industrial power of the organised working class. The latter was achieved by the defeat of the miners, who were hitherto thought to be invincible and stood for 'the magic of masculinity, muscle and machinery'[10] in the popular imagination, after a prolonged and painful strike in the coal fields in 1983–84. The government of Edward Heath had adopted a more conciliatory attitude towards earlier miners' strikes in 1971 and 1973.[11]

In 1954 a young, middle-class photographer, Grace Robertson working for *Picture Post* accompanied a party of older working-class women from Battersea in south London on their annual outing to the seaside town of Margate. It was their warmth and exuberance which initially attracted Robertson: They 'were certainly showing a young woman from a different background what stamina and frank, unaffected enjoyment could mean'.[12] Three generations of women lived in the small terraced houses in the streets surrounding the local pub which was the centre of their social life. But even as early as 1954 Robertson was stopped short by the realisation that such women's lives would shortly change for ever: 'Soon the new housing estates and high-rise flats would break into this extended family network, with its unique circle of comradeship and circle of supportive friends. The nuclear family would change all that; grandmothers would be left alone, and there would no longer be nearby aunts to take in a young couple's children for the evening.'[13]

When Nell Dunn went to live in Battersea in 1959 as a young, married woman, the picture of south London street life which Robertson had recorded, was still recognisable, 'back gardens had rabbits and pigeons, dogs wandered the streets and people sat out on doorsteps on hot summer evenings eating fish and chips'.[14] Dunn was a stranger to the urban neighbourhood to which she moved, having been born into a privileged middle-class background – her grandfather was the man who broke the bank at Monte Carlo. But she had her hair bleached and done in a beehive, wore skin-tight white jeans, rode on the back of a motor bike,[15] and soon made friends with the local women who were to provide her with the subject matter of her first two novels and came into her house to use her bathroom, the first in the street, and to try on one another's clothes. Her young son went to nursery school with their children and her new friends took her to work in their factory packing sweets and butter.

Perhaps the most surprising thing about Nell Dunn's fiction in the 1960s, *Up The Junction* (1963) and *Poor Cow* (1967), is its very existence. There is a notable absence of white working-class women within contemporary cultural representation in Britain – the best-selling romances of Catherine Cookson are the obvious exception – and fiction by white working-class women that aspires to express collective attitudes is in far shorter supply than that by women writing about black or lesbian experience. The function of narratives by all disadvantaged groups is to throw the dominant literary narratives of women's experience into relief. The new opportunities for personal fulfilment through equal opportunities in the workplace and easier access to higher education from which many middle-class women have benefited in this time have not, in the main, been open in the same way to working-class women. Here again, the picture is, of course, subject to regional variations and to variations between rural and urban experience.

With notable exceptions, such as the assertiveness demonstrated by women in the coal fields during the miners' strike of the 1980s, the pride and confidence with which lesbians or black women have reclaimed the specificity of their history and questioned the claims of white feminists to speak for all women is missing. Indeed, the most vibrant representations of working-class women in this period are not from Britain but the characters of Toni Morrison and other black authors in the United States. The badge consistently worn by working-class women across the centuries has been poverty. Although economic necessity has sometimes compelled the middle classes to set up home in 'affordable' areas of London and other cities, they have not usually experienced the extremes of poverty and hardship of those neighbourhoods, and this sets them apart from the communities in which they live.

The question to be asked of Dunn, as I shall ask later in this chapter of Pat Barker, is: What bearing does her class position have on her representations of working-class women? Dunn's early fiction bears an identifiable relationship to a recognisable literary tradition, albeit one that has been historically more closely connected to men than women. This is the tradition of 'slumming', of which George Orwell is perhaps the best-known twentieth-century representative. Why, then, has Dunn unusually chosen to embrace a way of life that could not be more removed from that to which she was born? By the time that she moved to south London, the sense of cultural loss, that often went hand-in-hand with material improvements in living conditions, had already been well documented, and was being widely debated in the press and on television. The work of Richard Hoggart, to which l shall return later, was particularly influential in this respect.

Dunn did not simply stumble upon working class-women by accident. The terraced streets of south London provided her with what she already knew was likely to be there. Like Grace Robertson, her fascination as an artist is precisely with difference, with women who embody a set of values which, to the middle-class outsider, appear to be warmer, more supportive and attractive than the values of those with whom she grew up. Such values are all the more remarkable because they appear to be threatened with extinction, even as they are being described. Dunn's interest in working-class experience is highly selective, and her position of privilege is frequently reproduced within the narrative in the guise of common sense. Aspects of working-class experience which do not interest her, for example working-class politics, are simply omitted from the writing.

Dunn first began to write in the 1960s, which we have seen was marked by far-reaching changes in working-class experience. As I have pointed out in my first chapter, the decade was also characterised by a strong, and sometimes prurient, interest in the sex lives of unattached women. Both feature strongly in her first two novels which appeared as fashionable paperbacks.

Dunn began her writing career with a series of closely observed vignettes of working-class life, four of which first appeared in the *New Statesman*, and were later published as a book, *Up the Junction* in 1963, which won the John Llewelyn Rhys Memorial Prize. She followed this with *Poor Cow* (1967), a study of a young mother coping with life when her husband and lover are sent to prison, which was made into a success-ful film by Ken Loach with Carol White in the title role and Terence Stamp. Her first two books were untouched by feminist ideas, and perpetuate some of the attitudes that the women's movement was to question: she appears to celebrate rather than to problematise the experi-ence of motherhood, and to be relatively uncritical of the assumptions which often underpin sexual practice between men and women. In the second part of this chapter I shall concentrate on a novel with very different and far more critical approaches to sexuality, motherhood and gendered experience in working-class communities, Pat Barker's *Union Street*,[16] a book that offers an insider's view of working-class women's experience, and seems unerringly to reflect the concerns of the early days of the women's liberation movement, and more particularly of the socialist-feminist currents within it.

Like her male counterparts, Alan Sillitoe, Sid Chaplin and Stan Barstow, who were also producing fictionalised studies of working-class life, Dunn's early writing depicts the specific moment in the social history of post-war Britain when there was full employment and growing prosperity. In the 1960s municipal authorities all over Britain were embarking upon wholesale programmes of urban renewal and demol-ishing large areas of inner-city terraced housing, and with them the tradi-tional patterns of working-class life. A character in *Union Street* observes that the local council has done more damage in one year than Hitler did in five. The old way of life – or more precisely, one particular variant of it since the pattern of working-class day-to-day existence was always more variegated than most sociological or historical studies usually admit – was memorably documented in Richard Hoggart's influential study, *The Uses of Literacy* (1957).[17]

In *The Uses of Literacy* Hoggart had placed great store on traditional working-class values such as warm-heartedness, neighbourliness and decency, and believed that the continued existence of a homogeneous working-class culture was threatened by affluence and post-war mobility. The old working-class neighbourhood which was on the verge of extinction was to became familiar to millions who had no first-hand experience of it when the television serial, *Coronation Street* began transmission in 1960.

Focused on a small, tightly knit northern community not dissimilar from those in Lancashire where Hoggart had lived and conducted his research, *Coronation Street* was rapidly to become Britain's best-known soap opera. The television series was filmed in Salford, immortalised as 'the dirty old town' of Ewan McColl's song and some years later to become the location of Robert Roberts's scholarly investigations into working people's lives in the first quarter of a century, published as *The Classic Slum* (1971).[18] Some forty years later, *Coronation Street* still continues to draw massive peak-time audiences. In its early days the serial reflected many of Hoggart's preoccupations. The student Ken Barlow, for example, was a character whose university education has distanced him from others in the street and from the values with which he grew up.

With its profusion of 'strong', mature women characters, *Coronation Street* had a strongly feminine inflection from its first episodes. While male critics have often been critical of the series, its importance to women was recognised from the start by feminist film and media critics. Terry Lovell has pointed out that 'its women viewers recognise certain "structures of feeling" which are prevalent in our society, and which are only partially recognised in the normative patriarchal order', for example the desire of women for sexual relationships in later life.[19] The older women characters who were to become household names in Britain included the waspish Hilda Ogden in her familiar uniform of head scarf and rollers. Hilda was a northern stage type – and the series has always used regional and class stereotypes. The gossip on which the narrative hinges invariably took place in locations used by women. Outside shots taken away from 'Wetherfield' were few and far between. Indoor locations included the front rooms of the small terraced houses, the local garment factory, the Mission Hall, the counter of the corner shop, and the pub, the Rover's Return, which was frequented from the very beginning by chisel-featured characters like Ena Sharples and Minnie Caldwell supping their milk stouts. Pat Barker uses some of the motifs made familiar in *Coronation Street*, such as the 'strong', older women, and domestic interiors and interconnecting plots based on the life of one street, in *Union Street*.

Unlike *Coronation Street*, and the novels of Chaplin, Sillitoe, Storey, all of which are based in the Midlands or the north of England, the urban locations in *Up the Junction* and *Poor Cow* are those of south London. Although there are some working-class novels written at this time which focus on women characters, for example Alan Sillitoe's *The Ragman's Daughter* (1963) and David Storey's *Flight into Camden* (1960), Dunn's early fiction is unusual in that it is concerned almost exclusively with women. Her writing is descriptive rather than analytical, and it is interested in the expression of contemporary social reality, rather than experimentation with form. *Up the Junction* and *Poor Cow* engage with the unsalubrious aspects of working-class existence, and follow on from Shelagh Delaney's acclaimed dramatisation of a troubled working-class mother–daughter relationship in the play *A Taste of Honey* (1959) and prefigure the early fiction of Pat Barker with its naturalistic focus on communities of working-class women in *Union Street* (1982) and *Blow your House Down*. (1984)[20] Dunn has a penchant for depicting feisty, independent characters, an interest in the detail of women's sex lives and, having had three sons of her own – she married the writer and documentary film-maker, Jeremy Sandford in 1956 – a strong belief in the importance of motherhood, and particularly of good relationships between mother and son. She seems unable to envisage fulfilment for women who are not mothers and who are not (hetero)sexually active.

In *A Taste of Honey* enjoyment of sex is the prerogative of the older characters; Helen, Jo's blowsy, self-centred mother, and Peter, her unsavoury boyfriend. Despite her teenage pregnancy, Jo retains an aura of naivety and innocence throughout the play. The young women characters in *Up the Junction* have the interest in sex, the anti-authoritarian instincts, and the vitality of Sillitoe's working-class Nottingham heroes, although their responses are free of the violence that characterises the world of Arthur Seaton. Women like Rube and Sylvie are products of the affluent society of the 1960s and conflate collective and individualistic consciousness. They are trapped in so far as their world is circumscribed by the streets in which they live and escape is an impossibility. But they have turned their backs on working-class respectability, and epitomise new models of subjectivity, in which propriety plays no part, and the quest for individual pleasure is seen as potentially liberating. Their search for excitement is itself a statement against the dehumanising aspects of working-class culture. Unattached, and open to possibilities, they are determined to have a good time on a Saturday night. But there is a very heavy price to be paid: Rube's backstreet abortion – a foetus is wrapped in newspaper and flushed down the toilet by a friend as the ambulance takes the mother away to hospital – is depicted from the point of view of the woman who undergoes it rather than, as in *Saturday Night and Sunday Morning*, from the point of view of a sympathetic male observer.

As Adrian Henri wrote in his introduction to the reissue of *Up the Junction* in 1988, part of the 'scandal attendant on the latter's publication (now needing a little historical imagination to conceive) was that the reader is almost eavesdropping on women talking as uninhibitedly about their sex lives as men would in similar circumstances'.[21] Nell Dunn's south London offers a world where women are sexually and economically independent, and where the full employment of the 1960s ensures that working-class women are able to speak their minds freely and to exercise control over their lives by moving from one relationship and job to another.

Poor Cow is a feminine variant on the narrative made familiar by Dunn's male contemporaries: Sillitoe and Storey in *Saturday Night and Sunday Morning* (1958) and *This Sporting Life* (1960); the disaffected young man out for what he can get for himself against the backcloth of the strident new Britain. The dialogue Dunn deploys in her fiction relies on the closely observed use of language and speech rhythms of working-class communities in which the oral mode is primary and, at its best, her use of the oral mode is powerful and arresting. Dunn tries hard not to patronise; nor does she idealise the working-class women whose lives she depicts. In *Up the Junction* women friends and neighbours form a supportive network for one another in times of need. Like the male heroes, Joy, the central character of *Poor Cow* to whom the title of Dunn's second novel refers, is self-reliant. There is no supportive community of women in *Poor Cow*, as there is often an absence of such support for those families in working-class communities which are thought to be not respectable, or deemed to have something to hide, and it is this absence which largely helps to account for the heroine's sense of isolation. Joy dislikes women because they are 'too catty' (*PC*, p. 119), 'a man will help you when a woman won't' (*PC*, p. 21). Her experience. Her husband is a housebreaker whose takings as a petty criminal finance an expensive car and a luxury flat. As a young, single mother who subsists precariously on the edges of a criminal subculture and has little education to equip her for life – the love letters she sends to her boyfriend in prison are awkwardly misspelled – Joy is identifiable as a member of a much-reviled group at this time: the 'sponger' who gives nothing to society and whose philosophy of 'get-rich-quick' is an affront to the work ethic to which others around her subscribe. But Dunn distances herself from any detached sociological perspective whereby Joy would be constructed primarily as a social problem.

Joy takes the material improvements of Britain in the 1960s entirely for granted. The novel has no middle-class reference points: Dunn is determined to avoid the superimposition of middle-class values and morality on Joy by commenting on her taste in furnishing and clothes or her material aspirations. Nor are there references to earlier modes of working-class life where other values compete with material success. Apart from her identity as a mother, Joy is happiest in her identity as a consumer, an identity which many chroniclers of working-class motherhood with their interest in the iconography of poverty, have been reluctant to admit.

In *Landscape for a Good Woman*, Carolyn Steedman suggests that her mother's obsession with consumer goods, and her attempt to define herself in terms of material acquisitions, is a response to deeper, unmet needs. Her mother is a 'working-class Conservative from a traditional Labour background',[22] whose carefully concealed status as an unmarried mother and exile from the north where she was born, make her long for the respectability, security, comfort and status that she knows material things provide: 'Out of a childhood lived in the streets of "the old defensive culture of poverty", my mother brought away a profound sense of insecurity and an incalculable longing for the things she didn't have. She was self-indulgent and selfish in a way that "our mam" is not allowed to be, and she learned selfishness in the very landscape that is meant to have eradicated it in its children. She wanted things.'[23] Steedman notes that, 'The other side of waiting is wanting. The faces of women in the queues are the faces of unfulfilled desire; if we look, there are many women driven mad this way as my mother was. This is a sad and secret story, but it isn't just hers alone.'[24]

Poor Cow was also one of the first novels to provide a view of work in the sex industry from a woman's point-of-view. Joy works as an enthusiastic photographic model, posing in the nude. She clearly enjoys flaunting her body, at one point describing this as her 'vocation'. *Poor Cow* constructs Joy not only as a desiring subject but, more problematically, as an object of desire. Because her body is fetishised and its parts itemised and proudly displayed – ostensibly for the gratification of the men who pay for her services but also for the gratification of the reader – she is reduced to her body as the total of its constituent parts. The novel is restricted to Joy's consciousness and her experiential world – there are no sequences narrated from any one other point of view – and her behaviour is not critiqued but naturalised in relation to gendered expectations.

In the successful but controversial staging of the first production of her play *Steaming* (1981) at the Theatre Royal in Stratford East, which invited the audience to contemplate the bodies of middle-aged women in various states of undress, Dunn attempts to challenge the usual equation of physical beauty with youthfulness. In *Poor Cow* she attempts to break down the inhibition which prevents women deriving pleasure from their own body. But in both the novel and the play the reader or viewer is, albeit uncomfortably, positioned in the role of voyeur, made an involuntary party to the commodification of women. With her male-orientated sexuality, symbolised in her sexy underwear, her enjoyment of sex on male terms, without any questions or complaints, and the absence of the sense of alienation that is frequently reported by women who work in the sex industry, the reader today might well view Joy 'not as a symbol of liberation', but, as Drabble has suggested, 'someone to be liberated'.[25]

Joy's pleasure-seeking promiscuity makes her the antitype of the good heroine faithful to one man. But she is, at a time in the 1960s when the responsibility for juvenile delinquency was often placed at the door of working-class mothers, indisputably a capable and loving mother. Her attitude to sex is instrumental: sex is a marketable commodity. When the boyfriend she loves is in prison a succession of men step in; sometimes money changes hands and sometimes not. The only power she has lies in her youth and sexual attractiveness and she is prepared to exploit these to the full; there is a bungled attempt to seduce her driving instructor, an official in the housing department, and the solicitor whom she sees about her divorce. The acquisition of a driving licence is for her, as for so many working women, a symbol of freedom and independence.

The space which Joy inhabits is very different from the young woman in older working-class fictions whose poverty and beauty makes her a prey to predatory men, as is Sally Hardcastle in *Love on the Dole*, or from the 'angry' narratives in which young women are assigned to the margins of a criminal, rebellious or delinquent male subculture. She is also, as Maggie Humm points out, significantly different from the senti-mentalised picture of the working-class 'mum' Hoggart lauded in *The Uses of Literacy*[26] – Hoggart's own mother died when her children were very small and he had little personal experience of the particular type of family, with the mother at the centre, which he described. While their rebellions may be qualitatively different, Joy is no less a sexual and class rebel than the disaffected characters of Sillitoe and company whose 'anger' in retrospect appears more selective, misogynistic, distasteful and conservative in its targets than it appeared at the time. The image which Joy cultivates is a characteristic image of the 1960s, the 'glamour girl' (a term she uses herself). Her preferred self-image is a challenge to the patriarchal idea that the overt display of sexuality in a woman and being a 'good' mother are incompatible. But when her husband returns from prison, his controlling jealousy and possessiveness put an end to any thought of her being allowed to separate sexual pleasure from reproduction and its responsibilities; of being permitted to be a 'glamour girl' and a mother at the same time.

The narrative resists any attempt to punish Joy for her transgressive sexual behaviour or to restore women to their 'proper place' within the family and normative social relations. Throughout the novel Joy is a free spirit, comfortable with her precocious sexuality, self-possessed rather than man-possessed, preferring the excitement of cohabitation to the boredom of marriage. The novel ends with Joy bridling at the security which she is offered ('being bogged down every blessed moment and all day among women' *PC*, p. 124). Like Jo in *A Taste of Honey*, Joy has an inchoate sense of being hemmed in by her world and a growing awareness of unrealised possibilities. But she stays in an unfulfilled marriage for reasons which are very much of their time: she does not want her son to be the product of a broken home. The only affectionate relationship which is sustained in the novel is that between mother and son.

In *Wigan Pier Revisited*, Beatrix Campbell retraces Orwell's steps across the England of the Great Depression. Her findings counter the pessimism which sees affluence as the enemy of 'authentic' working-class culture, and which dismisses the possibilities of radical change in a class which is no longer poor. 'Just as the middle class have been both proletarianised and radicalised, so have many sectors of the working class itself discarded the 'slough of respectability'.[27] This is especially true of the first university-educated generation which embraced revolutionary change in 1968. For Campbell, the lesson of the 1960s is that socialism thrives on plenty and pleasure and that political radicalism is not dependent on unendurable poverty. Campbell cautions against the attempt to conjure up older working-class solidarities without asking the question, Whose work was it that kept the old neighbourhoods alive?, pointing out the importance of the unpaid labour of women whose economic, social, sexual, cultural and political interests were never represented within the patriarchal organisations of the labour movement. *Wigan Pier Revisited* is at once a refutation of the idea that poverty has been eradicated in working-class areas and a council of hope in new forms of grass-roots community organisation: 'Most importantly, the radicals I met within the working class were women. They were the most reflective and imaginative, it was they who affirmed democratic ways of working, it was they who affirmed egalitarianism.'[28]

Pat Barker is no stranger to the importance of women in working-class communities. She was brought up in Teesside by her grandparents, who ran a fish and chip shop; three generations of women in her family, her mother, sister and grandmother, all worked as cleaners. Barker was encouraged to write by Angela Carter who read an unpublished story about her grandmother on a creative writing course and advised her to write about her past. In *Union Street* Barker acts upon Virginia Woolf's injunction to think back through our mothers. Barker's achievement in *Union Street* is to make visible the 'unsung heroines' of the labour movement; the clerks, cleaners and caterers whose absence in the iconography of the labour movement Campbell decries. Many of the pleasant and enjoyable aspects of working-class women's lives are carefully excised from the novel. As Flora Alexander points out, it is by virtue of this exclusion that she is able to creates 'what is effectively a political statement about the lives of women who have for all practical purposes been silenced'.[29]

Union Street, a modern 'condition of England' novel, which took Barker ten years to get published, is set at the time of the miners' strike in 1973. The name of the novel is a reminder of the nation's present and the past – Union Street was the name historically attached to any street in England where the local workhouse was to be found. Thornaby on Tees where *Union Street* is set is a potent symbol of Britain's industrial decline. Once the largest manufacturer of pig iron in the world, the area was transformed into an area of desolation and high unemployment as the steel industry contracted and thousands of people were made redundant. The male characters in *Union Street* are the walking wounded of a post-industrial Britain in which the old heavy industries which invested their daily lives with purpose have been dismantled and nothing else put in their place. In *Union Street* Barker is writing about the shared experiences of powerlessness of working-class women, and about the relationships of both sexes to the gender and class roles that their environment imposes on them.

A sense of place is integral to Barker's writing. The streets in the novel carry precise connotations. Her characters partake in a semaphore which signals each woman's restricted place in the cosmos she inhabits. The solidarity of the neighbourhood in which everyone is known to everyone else is maintained through the gossip which is an integral part of women's lives and confirms the sense of belonging to a social group with shared traditions, history and expectations of behaviour. The street signifies more than it can ever do in areas without the social cohesion which underwrites the novel, and the subtle gradations of social class, place and respectability produce an exact sense of a woman's place in a man's world. For old Alice Bell, Union Street is a step down the social ladder. Her last house had a bathroom, an indoor lavatory, a patch of green grass and a bay window. But for another character it is a step up: Iris King was born and brought up in Wharfe Street by the river and had fought her way out of it. Before Union Street her neighbours had consisted of men in prison, women spending social security money on bingo, and children left to run wild. Though she is no longer in Wharfe Street, which is the home of the prostitute, Blonde Dinah, Wharfe Street still remains in her. Her former haunts represent the abyss out of which she has risen, and it costs Iris dearly to have to make her way back there in search of a kitchen-table abortionist for her daughter. Union Street is poor but respectable. Iris's house is fanatically clean and she takes pride in her reputation as the cleanest woman on the street. The function of gossip is to maintain standards. The street turns on Mrs Brown, a single parent, because by letting her children roam around in the night she does not live up to their standards. Kelly Brown is accepted by the street in a way her mother is not but when the child is raped she too moves outside the street's understanding.

It is the intimate relationship between hardship and affective experience which *Union Street* brilliantly illuminates. Barker's emphasis in the novel is on the material basis of women's oppression. Women's desires and needs are shown to be inseparable from the harsh social conditions which give rise to them. The extraordinary power of *Union Street* lies in its precise evocation of the dereliction of women's lives and the restrictions imposed on women by a degree of poverty which is incomprehensible to those who have not experienced it. This is very far from the diluted and anodyne version of northern life which, as Stuart Laing points out, was assimilated into the new national (southern and London-based) culture of Britain in the 1960s.[30] Barker refuses to make linguistic concessions to an international readership which may be unfamiliar with the vernacular of her native Teesside. In a (albeit limited) survey Peter Hitchcock was unable to find a single American who could successfully explain the meaning of the following words and phrases selected at random from Barker's fiction: on the hump, nowt, sodding, bairn, skyvying, skint, lost a bob and found a tanner, lugful, poked, clocked, chippy, sneck, and breeching.[31] In the United States where the discourses and meanings of class are very different from in Britain, *Union Street* was divested of its original class and regional referents when it was filmed as *Stanley and Iris*, a Hollywood romance between two bakery workers in Boston, costing millions to make and starring Jane Fonda and Robert de Niro in the title roles.

Though its setting is post-industrial, the milieu of *Union Street* is curiously untouched by signs of consumerism, modernity or recent changes in working-class patterns of life. *Union Street* is situated within the socialist-realist traditions of working-class fiction which it challenges by its focus on a *group* of working-class women rather than the usual male hero or on a single woman protagonist. *Pace* Ian Haywood, the novel has a very specific sense of time.[32] As in Tony Harrison's epic poem 'V', Barker's subtext is a miners' strike. The strike with which Barker is concerned occurred at the time of Edward Heath's Conservative government. The setting of Harrison's poem is the strike of 1984 in which the miners faced a more determined and ruthless opponent in Margaret Thatcher. As in 'V', direct reference to the conflict in *Union Street* is minimal, although the class issues which are at stake are made clear. There is an animated discussion of the rights and wrongs of the forthcoming strike which the women anticipate by stockpiling supplies of coal in their homes. Alice compares her personal situation in the 1930s and the 1970s and concludes that she was better housed and had more money then. But the urban streetscape of the novel is virtually indistinguishable from that of earlier proletarian writing. There is a pub but no disco, night club or other evidence of any youth culture or remnants of the affluence of the 1960s; a supermarket but few references to cars or to any consumer items more sophisticated than a vacuum cleaner. Apart from Bertha in the cake factory there are no black immigrants in the area.

There is an elegiac quality in Barker's depiction of the industrial north-east. The sense of history and cultural loss which sometimes permeates working-class memory is reflected in the older characters. In *The Century's Daughter* (1986) issued in the United States as *Liza's England*, a social worker takes an old woman to where the steel works in the town used to be. Although there is no longer anything there, Liza can feel the ghosts of the dead and sees the furnaces as they had once burnt, at a loss as to why the authorities are trying to rehouse her and take away her sense of place. In *Union Street* the ageing prostitute, Blonde Dinah and her client, George, discuss the demolition of familiar little streets around them with sadness as they recreate a lost community and talk about the past they have shared and the people they have known.

The Marxist critical tradition has historically relegated women to the domestic and reproductive spheres. As a consequence, women are structuring absence in Marxist or socialist theoretical, autobiographical and creative writing because the areas with which they have been primarily associated have been of peripheral concern. The only working-class woman commonly identifiable in cultural representations has been the mother-figure ('Our Mum') whose existence is predicated on sacrifices for her children – the working-class equivalent of the middle-class 'angel in the house'. In *Class Fiction* Pamela Fox has argued that the private sphere is the place where 'we can glimpse the greatest anxieties and longings concerning working-class culture and writing – where we can begin to track the debilitating, as well as empowering effects of both marginality and incorporation'.[33]

In *Union Street* the family and home remain the dominant concerns in women's lives although a woman's place is no longer exclusively in the home. The women are not conscious of gendered inequality in the public domain. They have low-paid and low-status jobs as carers, cleaners, and in the local cake factory. But they do not assert their own rights and no one has a career as distinct from a job or has taken and kept a position with prospects of advancement, responsibility and promotion. The expression of their femininity and their most important concerns are anchored in private life. And as all their reserves of resourcefulness are deployed in survival there is little involvement in anything outside the home. The solidarity which is engendered in the novel is in an important sense feminist – it is one to one and woman to woman – although this is not a term that the women in the street use or recognise. It is predicated on new configurations of gender rather than the older class solidarities and forms of association reliant on institutional forms of education and self-help. There is no wider voluntary association in Union Street; no church, adult education centre, trade union or branch of the Labour Party. Such traditional northern working-class (male) pastimes as leek-growing and pigeon-fancying are also absent. The need to belong, to bond with others, to create families and communities, to protect children, which is common to all human societies, is represented in *Union Street* as a gendered activity at which women are shown to excel.

The continuities in this unremittingly bleak novel are of struggle, resistance, and oppression. What is absent in *Union Street* is the normative family of two parents with a male breadwinner at work and a woman at home. Instead, the community is emblematic of female self-sufficiency. The dominant image in the novel is of a woman struggling valiantly to bring up her children on her own. But *Union Street* is not a community of women by choice but through necessity. As Nina Auerbach reminds us, a 'community of women may suggest less the honor of fellowship than an antisociety, an austere banishment from both social power and biological rewards'.[34] It is women (all powerful figures in the home but powerless once they step outside it) who are working to see that the home and the family stay together. Women as workers are a rarity even in working-class fiction. Like her American counterparts, Agnes Smedley in *Daughter of Earth* and Tillie Olsen in *Yonnondio*, Barker depicts both the tedium of the work expected of

women in the factory or the home and the resilience of those who refuse
to let this destroy their spirit. However needy, hostile or ambivalent their
responses to the fathers of their children may be, the women in *Union
Street* are, in the main, loving mothers trying their best to give their
children a better life even if this invariably means conflict with the men
in their lives. Lisa is abandoned by a husband who departs with a glass jar
of savings put aside specifically for the new baby. Iris is driven to blows
with a feckless husband to protect what belongs by right to her and the
children. The success of such women in bringing up children is a refusal
of the male-defined reality; of the conventional idea of a single woman
living for and through men; attaining status and security through the
approval which men bestow on her. As Nina Baym once put it, the
concerns and subject matter of literature have often been masculinist,
concerned with 'whaling ships rather than the sewing circle as a symbol
of the human community; in favour of satires on domineering mothers,
shrewish wives, or betraying mistresses rather than tyrannical fathers,
abusive husbands; or philandering suitors'.[35] *Union Street* with its
backcloth of domestic interiors and its focus on a street inhabited by
women as a symbol of working-class community belongs to a growing
body of contemporary writing which has helped to swing the pendulum
a little further in the other direction.

There is no one central character with whom the reader is invited to
identify in *Union Street*. The novel spans the seven ages of woman with
characters positioned at various stages of the life-cycle beginning with the
young street urchin Kelly and finishing with Alice who is waiting for the
hearse. The youngest and oldest resident of the street meet on a bench in
the street at the end of the novel and hold hands in a symbolic gesture of
unspoken sympathy. As Alice has been a presence in the story of Kelly's
rape and violent initiation into womanhood, so Kelly is a comforting
presence in the story of Alice's death and represents the promise of continuity and renewal. Only one story, Blonde Dinah's, is registered through
the perspective of a man, and this narrative functions to emphasise the
women's generic humanity rather than their difference, by enabling
George to make unsuspected connections between the naked body of
Dinah and that of his puritanical wife which he has never been permitted
to see unclothed.

Each woman's story is discrete but intersects with the others at
significant moments to produce a kaleidoscopic picture of the cyclical
pattern of any (or every) woman's life. The focus on her potential to give
birth is always a source of hope however inauspicious the circumstances
which surround it. Kelly, playing in the rubble of a partially demolished
street near her home, finds Brenda's aborted foetus buried under a pile

of bricks and rubble. Lisa, weighed down by children and shopping in the supermarket sees in the well-dressed, young and childless Joanne the woman she once used to be. Gladys, who obsessively picks up the used condoms that litter the street, is the wife of George the lavatory attendant who goes to Blonde Dinah and pays her for the sex he does not enjoy in his marriage. Dinah once took care of the motherless Iris who in her turn looks after Alice when she becomes too old to take care of herself. As Raymond Williams notes, 'the isolation of private individuals, whose lives can be closely and intimately explored as if there were no wider social life, is evidently dependent on the social existence of individuals for whom power or money has created the possibility of *practical* distancing or displacement'.[36] In poor communities such as those in Barker's novels association is everything and there can be no such distancing or displacement.

Barker's characters are dominated by their biology and the rites of passage of a woman's life. They are as confined and defined by their bodies as they are by the small streets in which they live and the reader is left no doubt about the correspondence between the two. We are told that the time-honoured method of abortion, gin and a hot bath, is impossible because the houses have no bath. As young courting couples have no domestic privacy, sexual intercourse sometimes takes place under the arches of the bridge. The expression of gender and sexuality is shaped by the experience of class just as the lived expression of class is shaped by gender and sexuality. The desire to be respected for behaving decently, and the need to acquire a good name, or to avoid being tarnished by a bad one, are all important in the street. The traditional silences surround menstruation, contraception, rape and abortion. Moreover, the working-class obsession with respectability is cast in gendered terms and woman's body is the key to feminine virtue and carries the graffiti of her class as well as her gender. It is her body rather than her social situation which is blamed for what goes wrong in her woman's life (often unwanted pregnancy) and her biology rather than anything in society which is perceived to let her down.

Out of the sexed specificity of the woman's body Barker creates a feminist corporeality and politics of the body. Because the emission or transmission of bodily fluids is usually a private, intimate activity this would appear to have everything to do with the body and nothing to do with the social. But what characterises the bodily fluids which leave such a powerful impression on any reader of *Union Street* is their lack of containment, their spillage, their escape from the body, their shocking visibility as they leak into the social domain. Bodily fluids, both male and female – sperm, phlegm, excrement, urine, saliva, etc. – are invested with power and danger because they threaten to pollute the wider community. Fecundity humiliates and oppresses the women in *Union Street* at the same time as it endows their lives with their deepest meanings. Barker intimates how women's bodies incorporate a different form of oppression and signify different forms of resistance from the bodies of men. What is illustrated here is a kind of biological materialism, in which the power to ensure the survival and continuity of others like oneself acquires particular meanings in relation to class and nation precisely because birth takes place in the context of a well-established community whose values and survival are under threat. Although the novel is set at a time of social mobility when it was common to leave home, no woman appears to have middle-class aspirations or to travel far from Union Street. Thus the maternal narrative intersects with the narrative of class survival. In giving birth, women acquire agency and importance which they are denied in the context of a declining industrial nation in which working-class men have been rendered powerless. In impoverished communities the creation of new life is almost always perceived as a symbolic triumph over adversity however much the birth of a new baby may represent a source of anxiety, hardship and financial problems to the hard-pressed mother who is taxed to provide her baby with the emotional and economic support she often lacks herself. The novel resonates with pain and this includes the pain associated with labour. Brenda bleeds uncontrollably after an abortion conducted at a very late stage in her pregnancy – the foetus is fully formed and recognisable as a boy. The imprimatur of birth is the stretch marks that write a women's history on her body – George is surprised to discover that Blonde Dinah, who appears to have no children, has once given birth. Sex in the novel is more often associated with powerlessness, humiliation or unpleasantness than with pleasure. For Joanne the experience of violent sexual intercourse during the course of which it becomes clear to her that her partner is intent on aborting the foetus she is carrying is particularly humiliating.

In a path-breaking essay in *Sea Changes* Cora Kaplan criticised the indebtedness of socialist-feminists to Marxist traditions with their distrust of emotion and the tendency to focus on material factors while ignoring the affective realm.[37] With its emphasis placed equally on the economic and the emotional *Union Street* was a text which was welcomed in radical circles because it was seen to address criticisms of this nature.

I have concentrated so far on those aspects of Barker's writing which commended *Union Street* to many left and feminist groups at the time of writing: her concern with the specificity of women's domestic experience, the importance of working-class subject matter, the empowerment of the poor and dispossessed, the challenge to metropolitan values, the concern with 'communities of women' within English literary traditions, the exploration not only of the material basis of women's oppression but also its relationship to women's desires and needs. The text which is usually taken as a paradigm shift in Pat Barker's work is *Regeneration* (1991) which is situated in the 1914 war and concerned with masculinity and the psychically scarred male victims of war.

If *Union Street* is an example of the importance of thinking back through the mother, *Regeneration* is an example of thinking through the father. The novel was inspired by Barker's childhood memories of her grandfather's injuries sustained in the First World War. But Barker's interest in damaged psyches and with the societies that have damaged them is nothing new. Her concern with damaged men is present in *Union Street* where there is a sympathetic depiction of men like Jos whose growth is retarded or John who is terminally ill or George whose job as a lavatory attendant makes him an object of ridicule. Her later work reflects a greater interest in the discourses of psychoanalysis, although this too is present in *Union Street* and *Blow your House Down*, in both of which she is concerned with exploring the consciousness of men who commit violent crimes against women.

Regeneration with its focus on the male psyche and the male theatre of war, and its setting of Craiglockhart hospital for the officers who have been taught that manliness is synonymous with emotional repression, marks a radical change of direction: from the domestic to the epic. With the *Regeneration* trilogy, *Regeneration* (1991), *The Eye in the Door* (1993) and *The Ghost Road* (1995), Barker moves to a large canvas in preference to the small, to the national rather than the regional, to analyse masculinity and femininity rather than men and women, to depict middle- rather than working-class characters, and to a concern with sexual difference rather than sexual politics. In the incorporation of historical figures and situations into her more recent fiction Barker also reflects contemporary historiographical and postmodern trends. Such changes do not signify a change from an oppositional to a dominant literary practice but a progressive enlargement of discourses of emancipation which are not only discernible in the earlier work but also emblematic of widening feminist concerns in general during this period. As Margaretta Jolly points out, 'her dramatization of differences between women, of masculinities, and the pleasure as well as pain of identity all find their contemporary theoretical and political counterparts: the evolution of identity politics, the new men's movement and feminist and queer theory and psychoanalysis'.[38]

Unlike many postmodern writers, what Barker has not done in her more recent work is to jettison the notion of struggle or to minimise its significance. Her evolving concerns do not signify an abandonment of sexual politics but rather a proliferation and diversification of feminist demands. But neither do her recent writings engage directly with working-class women's experience. The importance of the new agendas with which Barker is now associated should not detract attention from her achievements in exploring working-class women's lives in her early fiction.

NOTES

1 Jeanette Winterson, *Oranges Are Not the Only Fruit* (London: Pandora, 1985), Maureen Duffy, *That's How It Was* (London: Hutchinson, 1962).

2 Francis Mulhern, 'Towards 2000, or News From You-Know-Where', in Terry Eagleton (ed.), *Raymond Williams: Critical Perspectives* (Cambridge: Polity Press, 1989), pp. 67–94, p. 86.

3 Reva Brown, review of *The Century's Daughter*, *British Book News*, December 1986, pp. 709–10.

4 Raymond Williams, 'Region and Class in the Novel', in Douglas Jefferson and Graham Martin (eds), *The Uses of Fiction: Essays on the Novel in Honour of Arnold Kettle* (Milton Keynes: Open University Press, 1982), pp. 59–69, p. 60.

5 Carolyn Steedman, *Landscape for a Good Woman: A Story of Two Lives* (London: Virago, 1986), p. 16.

6 Jeremy Seabrook, *What Went Wrong? Working People and the Ideals of the Labour Movement* (London: Gollancz, 1978).

7 J. H. Goldthorpe *et al.*, *The Affluent Worker*, 3 vols (Cambridge: Cambridge University Press, 1968–69).

8 Elizabeth Roberts, *Women and Families: An Oral History, 1940–1970* (Oxford: Basil Blackwell, 1995), p. 231.

9 Stuart Laing, *Representations of Working-Class Life 1957–1964* (Basingstoke: Macmillan, 1984), p. 219.

10 Beatrix Campbell, *Wigan Pier Revisited: Poverty and Politics in the 80s* (London: Virago, 1984), p. 97.

11 The sense of dislocation as the left was forced to come to terms with the disruption of its certainties is reflected in a set of essays, Martin Jaques and Francis Mulhern (eds), *The Forward March of Labour Halted?* (London: NLB, 1981). This takes its title from an important paper of the same name by Eric Hobsbawm.

12 Grace Robertson, *Grace Robertson: Photojournalist of the 50s* (London: Virago, 1989), p. 22.

13 Ibid., p. 23.

14 Nell Dunn, preface to *Poor Cow* (London: Virago, 1988), p. vii. All quotations are from this edition and enclosed parenthetically (*PC*).

15 Ibid., p. viii.

16 Pat Barker, *Union Street* (London: Virago, 1982).

17 Richard Hoggart, *The Uses of Literacy* (London: Chatto, 1957).

18 Robert Roberts, *The Classic Slum: Salford Life in the First Quarter of the Century* (Manchester: Manchester University Press, 1971).

19 Terry Lovell, 'Ideology and *Coronation Street*', in Richard Dyer (ed.), *Coronation Street* (London: The British Film Institute, 1981), p. 52.

20 Pat Barker, *Blow your House Down* (London: Virago, 1982).

21 Adrian Henri, introduction to *Up the Junction* (London: MacGibbon and Kee, 1963; reprinted London: Virago, 1988), p. xiii.

22 Steedman, *Landscape for a Good Woman*, p. 8.

23 Ibid., pp. 108–9.

24 Ibid., p. 22.

25 Margaret Drabble, introduction to *Poor Cow*, (London: MacGibbon and Kee, 1967; reprinted, with an introduction by Margaret Drabble London: Virago, 1988).

26 Maggie Humm, *Border Traffic: Strategies of Contemporary Women Writers* (Manchester: Manchester University Press, 1991), p. 46

27 *The Road to Wigan Pier*, p. 231

28 Ibid., p. 233.

29 Flora Alexander, *Contemporary Women Novelists* (London: Edward Arnold, 1989), p. 48.

30 Laing, *Representations of Working-Class Life 1957–1964*, pp. 219–20.

31 Peter Hitchcock, *Dialogics of the Oppressed* (Minneapolis: University of Minnesota Press, 1993), p. 197.

32 Ian Haywood, *Working Class Fiction: From Chartism to Trainspotting* (London: Northcote House, 1997), p. 145. In this excellent short study Haywood argues that there is 'no thread of contemporary cultural reference linking the stories' and that the 'general way of life' is almost entirely absent.

33 Pamela Fox, *Class Fictions: Shame and Resistance in the British Working Class Novel 1890–1945* (Durham, NC, and London: Duke University Press, 1994), pp. 200–1.

34 Nina Auerbach, *Communities of Women: An Idea in Fiction* (Cambridge, MA: Harvard University Press, 1978), p. 4.

35 Nina Baym, *Women's Fiction: A Guide to Novels by and about Women in America 1820–1970* (Ithaca: Cornell University Press, 1978), p. 14.

36 Williams, 'Region and Class in the Novel', p. 62.

37 Cora Kaplan, 'Subjectivity, Class and Sexuality in Socialist Feminist Criticism', in *Sea Changes: Culture and Feminism* (London: Verso, 1986), pp. 147–76.

38 Margaretta Jolly, 'After Feminism: Pat Barker, Penelope Lively and the Contemporary Novel', in Alan Sinfield and Alistair Davies (eds), *Post-War British Culture* (London: Routledge, 2000).

4

Continuities and change

I have taken the name of Virginia Woolf in vain, she thought.
Anita Brookner, *Hotel du Lac*

IN 1984 ANITA BROOKNER won Britain's prestigious annual book prize, the Booker, with the elegantly written *Hotel du Lac*. Angela Carter's rumbustious *Nights at the Circus* was not shortlisted. A chorus of voices were immediately raised on Carter's behalf many of them exceedingly critical of Brookner and the winning novel. While an injustice may certainly have been done to Carter by her omission from the prize list, it should be noted that no similar protests had been raised in the previous years in which the Booker Prize had been won by male authors and none of Carter's earlier novels had been selected for the judges' shortlist. In retrospect, the polarisation of literary critics and readers in 1984 probably said less about the respective strengths of the two novels than the critics' own alignment in relation to the different tendencies in women's writing that Brookner and Carter were widely assumed to represent – traditionalism and dissidence respectively.

Isobel Armstrong has argued that Brookner and Carter can be understood as the 'conventional' and 'scandalous' descendants of Virginia Woolf.[1] The two strands that Armstrong identifies them each as inheriting from Woolf are 'the fiction of elegy' and the 'fiction of sport and play'. As Armstrong puts it, 'Brookner takes up that aspect of elegy, that profound sense of separation experienced particularly by women in Woolf's novels, making for a troubled sense of both sexuality and class. On the other hand, Carter takes up that liberated sense of a multiple subject which begins to be discovered at the end of *To the Lighthouse* and leads to an element of fantasy, openness and play.'[2] Armstrong's important and highly illuminating essay pointed out the leylines linking Brookner and Woolf, as nobody else had previously done, although she missed the extent to which Brookner makes explicit reference to Virginia Woolf in her writing, thus indicating a conscious feminist influence on the former writer which has usually been overlooked.

This is most obvious in *Hotel du Lac* in which the heroine, whom we are told bears a strong physical resemblance to Woolf, is unexpectedly overcome by a sense of her own unworthiness: 'I have taken the name of Virginia Woolf in vain, she thought.'[3] But it is also true of *A Start in Life* in which a meal that Ruth Weiss prepares is one which is familiar to every reader of *To the Lighthouse, bœuf en daube.*[4] Armstrong asserts that the novels of Carter and Brookner are respectively progressive and conservative and that the latter is of no interest to feminism: 'One holds to the core of self, and attempts to stabilise the world of middle-class codes, and practices ... The other sports with displaced subjectivities performing themselves in the cultural debris of a multiplicity of histories and spaces, high-kicking with the conventions of class, gender, genre.'[5]

Twentieth-century writers and critics have attached importance, I would argue at times too much importance, to experimentation in literary form. The twenty-year period with which I am concerned has sometimes been distinguished by what Marguerite Alexander has termed as the 'flight from realism',[6] i.e. the desertion of realist modes of writing by novelists and critics who feel such modes of writing to be inadequate to the representation of a deeper reality. But the critical preoccupation with postmodernist writing, which is often seen as the most significant literary development of recent times, is to the detriment of traditional modes of writing, much of this by and about women, which continues to be produced alongside it.

I now want to argue for the importance of a particular type of traditional woman-centred fiction, of which Anita Brookner is an excellent modern exponent. Like its nineteenth-century predecessors, what the early fiction of Brookner does is to ask us to look closely at the moral predicament of a central woman character. Not until her ninth novel, *Lewis Percy*, does she introduce a male hero. Moreover, like other twentieth-century novelists of sensibility – Rosamond Lehmann, Elizabeth Bowen, F.M. Mayor, Daphne Du Maurier, Elizabeth Taylor, Joanna Trollope and E.M. Young come to mind – Brookner's subject matter has ensured that she has been read primarily by women. Indeed, male critics have often exhibited their disdain for the narrowness of Brookner's scope and subject matter, dismissing her as 'the fictional specialist in migraines, flushes and female malaises'.[7] The surprise when she won the Booker was in part because the choice appeared to disprove the widely held conviction that women's intimate experience lies outside the imaginative sympathies of those whose judgements have determined what is good literature.

In the past, woman-centred fiction, of the kind in which Brookner excels, has paraded under various banners: the sentimental novel, the domestic novel, the romantic novel, and the novel of sensibility. Such fiction often deals with women whose private lives are beset with problems and who discover within themselves unsuspected reserves of courage and resilience. It identifies the importance of feeling but usually shows that this must be controlled. The heroines often have as much intelligence and resourcefulness as emotion. Merely to feel is not enough. Indeed, the heroine who lived entirely on her feelings is very little in evidence in much of this fiction; feeling is usually linked to responsibility, rationality and good sense. To represent such aspects of sensibility in fiction other aspects of human experience, particularly the aggressive, brutal and violent, may have to be repressed. The setting of woman-centred fiction is often the home, which is not depicted as a site of entrapment, but of fulfilling social relationships. Woman-centred fiction usually assumes that women as well as men often find contentment in the domestic sphere as the matrix of a set of human relationships defined by supportiveness and love.

Woman-centred fiction of one kind or another has always been the preferred reading of large numbers of women. This may be especially true of women who have not had access to higher education. Such fictions have historically addressed women about issues of primary concern to women. It is therefore important that we do not merely dismiss the woman reader of woman-centred fiction as naive but that we endeavour to understand the variety of reading positions for women inscribed within such fictions. I do not want to lump together radically dissimilar texts or to conflate radically different literary histories. However, as I have argued elsewhere, l believe the importance of woman-centred fiction to be twofold. Firstly, its appeal to women is always illuminating in relation to the specific historical context in which it was written. Secondly, the fact that we know that substantial numbers of women read such fiction attentively, often looking for images of women in which they can recognise aspects of their lives and selves, not only means that such writing may sometimes be instrumental in helping to raise the woman reader's self-esteem but also that it has important uses as the foundation stones of a politics of feminist change.[8] The reader's identification with any fictional characters is never total but always partial. Women readers, like women characters in fiction, are usually all too aware that they have different selves with which they respond to the conflicting and contradictory demands life makes of them. Moreover, in practice, even the most ostensibly recalcitrant of woman-centred texts is capable of producing a reading that is of interest to feminism. Brookner's first novel *A Start in Life* (1981) is a good example of such a text, and I shall compare and contrast this to the title story in Carter's *The Bloody Chamber* (1979). Some reference will also be made to another novel resistant to feminist appropriation, A.S. Byatt's *The Game* (1967).

Of the three writers with whom I am concerned, only Carter has described herself as a feminist. Brookner is uncompromisingly, and at times even belligerently, hostile to feminism: 'You'd have to be crouching in your burrow to see my novels in a feminist way.'[9] Her heroine in *A Start of Life*, an academic who is ironically an authority on women in literature, prefers men in life. Byatt, meanwhile is prepared to accept the importance of feminism as a social and political movement while distancing herself from feminist critiques of the English literary tradition which she holds dear. *The Game* is a meditation on the nature of artistic vision and the female imagination and has much to say about writing as a gendered activity. Indeed, Byatt has described all her novels after *The Shadow of a Sun* as being about 'the problem of female vision, female art and thought' in a world where the visionary female has been associated with men.[10] Like Brookner, Byatt is a successful academic with a greater personal investment in continuity than revolution: 'I like change, not revolution. I like subtle distinctions within a continuing language, not doctrinaire violations.'[11] She has consistently resisted attempts to place her in a feminist pigeonhole: 'It does women a disservice to elevate them as women rather than writers because it prevents their being judged on merit. George Eliot is amazingly good on women but amazingly good on other things as well'.[12] Moreover, her attitudes to literature are stamped with her intellectual formation before the women's liberation movement: 'Literature has always been my way out, my escape from the limits of being female. The writer's profession is one of the few where immense sexual-political battles don't have to be fought.'[13]

By contrast, Carter claims that feminism is at the very core of her literary enterprise ('I'm a feminist in everything and one can't compartmentalise these things in one's life').[14] In an interview with Mary Harron in the *Guardian* she described herself as 'a very old-fashioned kind of feminist' interested in 'abortion law, access to further education, equal rights, the position of black women.'[15] Analysing the momentous changes of the 1960s on her own development ('truly it felt like Year One') she speaks of a 'heightened awareness of the society around me in the summer of 1968, my own questioning of the nature of my reality as a *woman*. How that social fiction of my "femininity" was created, by means outside my control, and palmed off on me as the real thing.'[16]

Carter's language is highly stylised, flamboyant and exuberant where Brookner's is restrained. As critics have often pointed out, there is nothing sacred and nothing natural in Carter's work. Brookner's *forte* is elegant, understated prose which makes much use of intelligent dialogue, and her appeal is to those who prefer the pre-modern to the postmodern and the non-experimental in their choice of literature.

Brookner, unlike Carter, is concerned with the inwardness of private suffering. It is Brookner's feminine subject matter which has largely been responsible for 'an emphatic male hostility towards a certain kind of "woman's novel"',[17] and her dismissal by critics as 'the fictional specialist in migraines, flushes and female malaises'.[18]

Like many of the heroines of Austen and Eliot to which they may be compared, the heroines of both *The Game* and *A Start in Life* are exceedingly intelligent or intellectual. The game which two sisters, Julia and Cassandra Corbett, play in Byatt's novel is based on the Brontë's childhood stories set in the imaginary worlds of Gondal and Angria. Julia and Cassandra stand for two different aspects of the writer's imagination, and for the conflicting claims between women's responsibilities to self and their duty to others. The sisters' secret world nurtures their linguistic skills, fantasies and story-telling abilities. But it is also the locus of the anxieties, competitive impulses and the sibling rivalries which are to haunt their adult relationship. Little in later life approximates to the intensity of the sisters' adolescent imagination and the web which they have woven together as girls entraps them and prevents them attaining autonomy as women and as writers. As Richard Todd has put it, 'the two sisters come to seem, each in her own way, hideously conjoined'.[19]

Byatt illustrates the potentially disastrous effects of literature through the figure of Cassandra, a distinguished professor of medieval literature at Oxford University, through whom Byatt upholds woman's right to be taken seriously in areas in which they have traditionally been derided. As Byatt puts it, 'Female visionaries are poor mad exploited sibyls and pythonesses. Male ones are prophets and poets.'[20] In public Cassandra is a successful academic, a distinguished textual editor, and in private an assiduous compiler of the most personal of all modes of writing, the private diary. But constrained by the rules of academia, she is incapable of writing a work of fiction which gives voice to her imagination, or of using her skills as a writer to express a personal voice, and she seeks refuge from the disappointments of life in the mysticism of her adopted Anglo-Catholic faith.

Julia, the novelist, chooses to write fiction which is effectively about the 'problem without a name', i.e. the situation of the intelligent, highly educated woman who finds herself confined to the home. The relationship between the two sisters is symbiotic. Their dependency on each other is such that imaginative autonomy and freedom are rendered impossible. But the game ceases to be a game and becomes something more sinister when Julia plagiarises her sister's work to launch her own career as a writer. Cassandra's intellectual domain is one in which 'the great images are those of unsatisfied desire, formalized, made into a mode of apprehension'.[21] She never makes the transition from the theorising of passion to its lived experience and eventually has a nervous breakdown and is driven to suicide.

What Carter, Byatt and Brookner all have in common is an interest in how and why desire is central to the literary tradition. In *The Game* Byatt revisits the Arthurian myth of 'The Lady of Shallott' which she uses to symbolise the workings of the female imagination and the potentially disastrous consequences of women's sexual arousal. In Tennyson's poem the woman deserts her weaving and the shadowy world of the tower to look directly out of her window upon Sir Lancelot. As Tennyson's heroine is punished when she forsakes the imaginative for the active life so Julia Corbett is condemned when she chooses love over art and the active rather than the contemplative life.

Brookner's interest in desire leads her to position her work within established traditions of romantic fiction just as Carter's necessitates revisiting and contending the myths of sexual desire perpetuated in the fairy-tale mode. 'The Bloody Chamber', the title story of a collection of the same name, is based on the story of Bluebeard which was set down by Perrault in 1697. His collection, *Histoires et contes du temps passé*, was translated into English by Carter as *The Fairy Tales of Charles Perrault* in 1977. It is written in the Gothic mode which Carter, quoting Leslie Fiedler, describes in an epigraph to *Heroes and Villains* as 'essentially a form of parody, a way of assailing clichés by exaggerating them to the limit of grotesqueness'.[22] Inspired iconoclast and experimenter with language though Carter may be, there are important respects in which her writing is no less dependent on literary traditions than either Brookner or Byatt.

The literary tradition which Carter re-visions in *The Bloody Chamber* is the tradition of the female Gothic, the subversive aspects of which have been usefully discussed in recent studies by Eugenia Delamotte, Kate Ferguson Ellis and others.[23] With its haunted chambers, dark hidden secrets, premonitions of evil, atmosphere of impending doom, and invitation to the reader to identify with a terror-stricken protagonist, the female Gothic has a long lineage in women's writing exemplified in the work of eighteenth- and nineteenth-century women writers including Ann Radcliffe, Jane Austen, Emily Bronte, Mary Braddon and Mrs Henry Wood. It is from this body of work that Carter revives the convention of a protagonist who is at once an active seeker after truth and the hapless victim of mysterious threats to her life and spectral visitations over which she has no control. In *The Bloody Chamber* Carter makes full use of the genre's distinctive features, i.e. its reliance on horror, suspense and entrapment, to explore modern aspects of the erotic and to interrogate the institutions of marriage and heterosexuality in which these have been enshrined.

The grotesquely imbalanced relationship that is dramatised in this story exemplifies Carter's conviction that sex within marriage is always a potential locus of exploitation: 'If one sexual partner is economically dependent on the other, then the question of sexual coercion, of contractual obligation, raises its ugly head in the very abode of love and inevitably colours the nature of the sexual expression of affection.'[24] As Carter has stated, 'a narrative is an argument stated in fictional terms'.[25] What she demonstrates in her reworking of the Bluebeard story is the relationship between domination and desire: '"There is a striking resemblance between the act of love and the ministrations of a torturer", opined my husband's favourite poet'.[26] The narrative centres on the macabre discoveries of the terrified heroine and is narrated in the first person by the nubile young bride who penetrates her husband's secret chamber and discovers that each of the women whom his great riches have enabled him to secure has been tortured, mutilated and put to death.

Even though the Bluebeard figure proudly asserts that in Brittany the aristocracy no longer display the blood on the bridal sheets, a high premium is still placed on the bride's virginity for which he is prepared to pay munificently. 'The Bloody Chamber' makes it clear that the power imbalance between the sexes is largely economic. At its simplest, men have money and want sex. Women want money and to acquire money must sometimes consent to sex with men whom they often do not really want. In the Perrault original, it is Bluebeard's fabulous wealth that persuades the new bride that his beard is not so blue after all. In 'The Bloody Chamber' it is because the bride knows that her suitor is the richest man in France, 'as rich as Croesus' (BC, p. 11), that she consents to an alliance which will remove 'the spectre of poverty from its habitual place at our meagre table' (BC, p. 8). Her youth and innocence makes the bride at seventeen almost a child bride, a *tabula rasa*, but not quite: she asks, 'how could I have failed, even in the world of prim bohemia in which I lived, to have heard hints of *his* world? (BC, p. 17). Patriarchal discourse constructs women not as they want to be but as men want them to be and as the objects of desire rather than desiring subjects. In 'The Bloody Chamber', this is quite literally the case as the Bluebeard-figure dresses his bride to reflect his wealth and status, pre-eminently with the gruesomely symbolic choker of red rubies which he places around her neck.

In *The Sadeian Woman*, Carter argues that because pornography always reveals sexual reality at an unconscious level it is, in theory, possible for it to be deployed in the service of women. She contends that a 'moral pornographer' would 'not be the enemy of women, perhaps because he might begin to penetrate to the heart of the contempt for women that distorts our culture even as he entered the realms of true obscenity as he describes it'.[27] The project on which Carter is engaged in 'The Bloody Chamber' has been described by Merja Makinen as the 'decolonisation of feminine sexuality' and includes the necessity of acknowledging that women may experience a whole range of sexual desires and practices alongside 'normal' sex.[28] In arguing that pornography should be understood as part of a wider regime of representations, and that it is theoretically possible to construct a non-sexist feminist-inspired erotica, Carter controversially prefigured a more general shift in attitude among many feminists and pointed the way to the impassioned and deeply divisive debates on pornography which were to polarise British feminists into opposing groups in the 1980s.[29]

The young bride in 'The Bloody Chamber' is both excited and repelled by the 'rituals from the brothel' in which she partakes on her wedding night: 'I felt both a strange, impersonal arousal at the thought of love and at the same time a repugnance' (BC, pp. 17–18). Carter here uses love as a euphemism for sex and de-romanticises sexual excitement – it is a purely physical sensation divorced from natural feelings of moral revulsion. As Aidan Day puts it, 'the text acknowledges the power and depth of ideological inscriptions which cause a female to respond in certain ways while at the same time exposing and criticising those inscriptions'.[30]

As is often the case in pornography, Carter's reworking of the Bluebeard story makes the body of a nubile young woman freely available to a man who is neither young nor sexually attractive, quite the opposite. The ritual defloration of the virgin bride on the wedding night is inspired by the leather-bound pornographic volumes *(The Initiation, The Key of Mysteries)* secreted in his library. Moreover, the woman derives pleasure from her part in the enactment of male fantasy and her voice is appropriated to enunciate sexual pleasure and pain. But what is absent in pornographic address (directed at a male audience) but disarmingly present in 'The Bloody Chamber' is the woman's criticism of the behaviour, expectations or physical shortcomings of the male. While it is true that the young woman in 'The Bloody Chamber' colludes in the production of herself as the object of the lecher's gaze, this is only up to a point. She intimates both her awareness of the true nature of the exchange – 'And so my purchaser unwrapped his bargain' (BC, p. 15) – and her awareness that her true self is being corrupted – 'I sensed in myself a potentiality for corruption that took my breath away' (BC, p. 12). As Elaine Jordan has put it, understanding the attraction of the pornographic is essential if one wishes to counteract it: 'Where else can you start from, if not where you actually are? ... Where we are may include fascinations from which a rational and ethical self recoils?'[31] In taking on the role of 'moral pornographer' Carter eroticises power imbalances and writes narratives which consistently refer the reader back to the debates about women and sex which were the prerequisite of these narratives' production.

In contrast, *A Start in Life* has virtually nothing to say about sex. This is because the idea of romantic love, at least as Brookner understands it, is essentially redemptive. As Anthony Giddens has pointed out, romantic love 'is incompatible with lust, and with earthly sexuality, not so much because the loved one is idealised – although this is part of the story – but because it presumes a psychic communication, a meeting of souls which is reparative in character'.[32] Anita Brookner intimates the passion that lies beneath the surface of the plain, hard-working and deeply responsible woman: 'Ruth Weiss was scrupulous, passionate, thoughtful, and given to self-analysis, but her colleagues thought her merely scrupulous' (*ASIL*, p. 8). Like Jane Austen to whom she is sometimes compared – such comparisons ignore the strand of intelligent dissent that consistently runs throughout Austen's work – Brookner refuses in her early writing to venture beyond the world of the middle-class women which she knows.

At first it might seem that Brookner and Carter are at different ends of the philosophical spectrum. Carter has generally been taken as a deconstructionist, widely read in modern literary theory, who is sceptical about the fixity of meanings, existing gender roles, and the grand narratives of Western thought. But in his study of her writing, *The Rational Glass*, Aidan Day has argued that 'Carter's wild fables and the pungency of her style may disguise the extent to which her feminism is grounded in the values of reason'. Moreover, in her engagement with the discourses of reason she is at odds with the relativising impulse of an extreme postmodernism 'which threatens to undermine the grounds of a liberal-rationalist, specifically feminist politics'.[33] Anita Brookner has stated that the ideal to which she aspires is Enlightenment rationalism.[34] The heroine of *A Start in Life* attaches great importance to the fact that she is a rational person, and, like another academic, the heroine of *Providence*, prides herself in her ability to interpret the world. She says that 'it is characteristic of the Romantic to reason endlessly in unbearable situations, and yet to remain bound by such situations'.[35] Yet Brookner's reliance on Enlightenment rationalism is in some senses deeply problematic for, as many feminist philosophers have pointed out, Enlightenment philosophers did not include women among those thought capable of emancipating themselves through the appeal to reason. As Jane Flax puts it, the motto of the Enlightenment, '"*Sapere aude* – have courage to use your own reason" rests in part upon a deeply gender-rooted sense of self and self-deception.'[36] Moreover, reliance upon their powers of reason appears to be of little practical help to Brookner's heroines. Because her protagonists are rational, intelligent women, they are fully aware of their status as victims but this awareness does not materially alter their situation. It may be only a short step from interpreting the world to attempting to change it, but it is this one step which her heroines refuse to take.

Brookner is immersed in the Romantic tradition of European litera-ture and art to which her novels make frequent reference. In *Providence*, for example, Kitty Maule's academic specialism is the Romantic tradition 'which still affects us all today, although we may not recognise it'.[37] Brookner has said that 'romantic writers are characterised by absolute longing – perhaps for something that is not there and cannot be there. And they go along with all the hurt and embarrassment of identifying the real thing and wanting it.'[38] Brookner is not, as Angela Carter once famously put it, in 'the demythologising business'.[39] Quite the opposite. Her belief in romantic love remains unassailable and she writes without resort to the pastiche, the carnivalesque, the Gothic, or the parodic which are the hallmarks of Carter's work and make romance acceptable to a sophisticated late twentieth-century readership. But there are, nonethe-less, some important myths and fairy tales which she does wish to decon-struct. There are also significant aspects of the Romantic tradition to which it is clear that she feels deep ambivalence; notably 'that we are deceived into believing that virtue is rewarded, that good will win in the end, and that Cinderella will always get the Prince.'[40] It is these aspects of Romanticism that she interrogates in *A Start in Life*. Ruth Weiss, who thinks that 'the most beautiful words a girl could hear' are 'Cinderella *shall* go to the ball' (*ASIL*, p. 8) is a prime example of romantic self-delusion. *A Start in Life* demonstrates the destructiveness of romantic fantasy at the same time as it argues for its potency. The ball does not materialise and *A Start in Life* begins with the sentence 'Dr Weiss at forty, knew that her life had been ruined by literature.'

Angela Carter's critics have differed in the extent to which they believe that, as Robert Clarke puts it, 'her writings reproduce the consciousness they recognize as unhappy'.[41] This is particularly contentious in narratives such as 'The Bloody Chamber' in which women collude with the representation of themselves as sex objects. Because the position of heroine and victim are synonymous, the reader who wills the heroine/victim to escape may also be positioned in a collusive relation-ship with the masochism of the illicitly desiring female self which can, at least in part, be held responsible for having got her into the predicament in the first place. But, as Paulina Palmer has argued, the representation of femininity in Carter's fiction reflects two contradictory approaches. One is 'femininity as entrapment' and the other 'femininity as self-invention and role mobilisation'. Palmer draws on Irigaray's definition of masquerade as the female enactment of male-orchestrated scripts and roles, which results in women 'submitting to the dominant economy of desire' to argue that this is the position Carter assigns to her female characters in her early writings, but that after *Nights at the Circus* (1984), there is a change of emphasis in her fiction. She shifts from women entrapped in masquerade to the portrayal of women 'subversively playing with mimesis', a strategy, which according to Irigaray 'avoids male scripting',[42] and in which they manage to evade 'the victim's role by the judicious use of their wits'.[43]

Much of Carter's writing illuminates her interest in demystifying the nature of the marriage contract and exposing the illusion that the erotic relationship between a man and a woman can be cast adrift from the other social relationships on which it depends. As Carter puts it in *The Sadeian Woman*, (1979), 'We do not go to bed in simple pairs; even if we choose not to refer to them, we still drag there with us the cultural impediments of our social class, our parents' lives, our bank balances, our sexual and emotional expectations, our whole biographies.'[44]

In the Perrault story a bride is forbidden to enter the one private room which contains the bodies of Bluebeard's previous wives whom he has murdered and dismembered. When the unnamed woman disobeys her husband's instructions she too is doomed but is saved by the arrival of her two brothers. A number of feminist critiques of 'The Bloody Chamber' have argued that it is impossible for any writer to inscribe new meanings into existing fairy tales because these are irredeemably misogynistic. According to Patricia Duncker, 'Carter is rewriting the tales within the strait-jacket of their original structures. The characters she re-creates must to some extent, continue to be abstractions. Identity continues to be confined by role, so that shifting the perspective from the impersonal voice to the inner confessional narrative as she does in several of the tales, merely explains, amplifies, and reproduces, rather than alters, the original, deeply, rigidly sexist psychology of the erotic.'[45] But not all fairy tales admonish women for bad behaviour and their substance, form and meanings are amenable to revision, transformation and change. Elaine Jordan has commented that the distinction which Carter attempted to draw between folktales (produced by people to make their lives more exciting) and myths (designed to make people feel less free) is unlikely to hold, but 'some myths have more power than others, overtly or covertly; the more veiled they are, the more dangerously perhaps they lie coiled in and around the psyche and behaviour. Whether a myth is liberatory or oppressive depends on the existing power relations, the company it keeps, the context of its use.'[46] As Marina Warner points out, their greater purpose may be 'to reveal possibilities, to map out a different way and a new perception of love, marriage, women's skills, thus advocating the means of escaping imposed limits and proscribed destiny'.[47]

The subtext of 'The Bloody Chamber' is curiosity. It is curiosity which compels the bride to enter the forbidden room and thus to defy the right of others to determine what she may or may not know. To do what is forbidden is to exercise power. It is precisely through woman's curiosity that she is able to change herself into a spirited, questing, active subject and not merely a cipher who accepts patriarchal limitations on her knowledge and horizons. In the biblical myth of Adam and Eve and the classical myth of Pandora, women are held responsible for the troubles unleashed on the world. Both myths are misogynistic in that disobedience and curiosity are failings for which women must pay a heavy price.

'The Bloody Chamber', like the Perrault original, fails to punish the errant woman for her curiosity. Indeed, Carter's story ends with the seventeen-year-old widow, her lover and her mother established in an unconventional *ménage-à-trois* on the outskirts of Paris. Following Perrault, and playfully making the meaning of the story tantalisingly difficult to fix, Carter retains the bloody imprint of the key on the woman's forehead to advertise her sexual past as in *The Scarlet Letter*. This utopian ending is in contrast to the Perrault which ends with the central protagonist making a good bourgeois marriage.

The other respect in which Carter reworks the original story is the introduction of two characters who are not present in the Perrault; a young piano tuner who is blind and the bride's mother. The tuner's blindness is not merely the 'symbolic castration' and 'mutilation' which Patricia Duncker has suggested.[48] Lack of sight has never made sex impossible, far from it. Neither need blindness induce emotional or economic dependency: the piano tuner has a job and is indeed defined by this job as he has no name. Nor is his situation analogous to Mr Rochester's in *Jane Eyre* as has sometimes been supposed. Although Mr Rochester's blindness democratises his relationship with Jane, which is put on a more equal footing at the end of the novel, the reader of *Jane Eyre* is left with a strong sense of blindness as punishment or retribution. In contrast, the young man's sight is not removed during the course of the narrative – he is blind from the beginning – and there is no suggestion that his blindness is a punishment or mutilation. On the contrary, what his disability does appear to signify is a heightened sensitivity, to music and to the needs of women. His blindness removes the possibility of voyeurism in the relationship because it is impossible for the woman to be the subject of the male gaze.

Since the piano tuner cannot see his wife there can be no doubt that he wants her for her inner self and not as her first husband did merely for her beauty. Even in her bedchamber there were mirrors placed to enhance the Bluebeard-figure's visual pleasure. Moreover, the fact that the young man cannot see has the plot function of removing any possibility of his taking on the role of St George in relation to the distressed damsel. The bride is rescued from the monster neither by her brothers, as in Perrault, nor by her lover who is powerless to help her, but by her mother who had once 'outfaced a junkful of Chinese pirates, nursed a village through a visitation of the plague, shot a man-eating tiger with her own hand' (BC, p. 7).

Lorna Sage suggests that the model for this most inspired and improbable of avenging angels may be Angela Carter's feisty, northern working-class maternal grandmother.[49] The dazzlingly original eleventh-hour rescue – which is for most readers the most memorable aspect of the story – is prompted by *'maternal telepathy'* which testifies to the strength and indestructibility of the mother–daughter bond: 'I never heard you cry before, she said, by way of explanation' for her unexpected appearance at her daughter's side (BC, p. 40). If Carter has followed Freud so far in designating masochism as one distinguishing mark of women's sexuality, she is in defiance of Freudian theory in showing that the primal link to the mother is not broken by the child's separation. Her use of the fantastic here articulates the importance of the mother–daughter relationship. As Nicole Ward Jouve puts it, 'if such fantasy is subversive, it is only because it dares what the decencies of realism forbid. Yet it upholds the decencies. The unreal guarantees the real.'[50]

It is easy to travesty the narrowness of Anita Brookner's range and her subject matter. As Angela Carter once put it, 'her books are all about preparing elaborate meals for men, of standing looking sadly out of the window as she scrapes the uneaten food out into the tidy bin when they fail to turn up'.[51] In Joan Smith's *A Masculine Ending* a character remarks, 'I can't see any point in her books at all. You might as well watch a documentary about depressed women on Channel 4.'[52]

But what is, in my view, crucial to an understanding of Brookner's work is the fact that the affairs in which so much emotional energy has been invested lead to nothing. For this reason they may, as the authors of a recent collection of essays on romance have noted, be situated in a 'strong and powerful tradition of fictional "anti-romance", all those courtship novels from the time of Jane Austen onwards which undermine the "happy endings" of the main plot with instances of loveless marriage or isolated spinsterhood'.[53] While Brookner's writing can also, to borrow Isobel Armstrong's useful phrase, be seen to exemplify a 'poetics of loss'[54] – in so far as it is predicated on the belief that a loving relationship is for her heroines unrealised rather than unrealisable – the inevitable unhappy endings may also be read as illustrating the folly of the romantic dream. If suffering is the corollary of romantic love, as is the case in Brookner's work – albeit a silent, dignified suffering intended to evoke sympathy and respect for the women who undergo it – investing in the Western cultural heritage that values romantic attraction above all else (*amor vincit omnia*) is a strategy that is clearly disadvantageous to women.

A *Start in Life* is a *Bildungsroman* inspired by Balzac's *Un début dans la vie*. The book is in effect an extended dialogue with Brookner's mentor, Balzac – Ruth Weiss, the plain and bookish heroine of *A Start in Life* writes her doctoral thesis on vice and virtue in Balzac's novels. Ruth decides that she has no wish to live as virtuously as Balzac's Eugénie Grandet: 'She would rather be like the lady who spells death to Eugénie Grandet's hopes, a beauty glimpsed in Paris with feathers in her hair. Better a bad winner than a good loser. Balzac had taught her that too' (*ASIL*, p. 136). Manipulative powers, according to Balzac, distinguish the villains from the virtuous, but Ruth is too disingenuous to have manipulative powers. *A Start in Life* is a series of object lessons. Balzac teaches 'the supreme effectiveness of bad behaviour, a matter which Ruth was beginning to perceive' (*ASIL*, pp. 33–4). The lessons which Ruth learns during the course of a brief love affair with a married academic in Paris before she is summoned to London to care for aged parents are carefully set out:

> She perceived that most tales of moralists were wrong, that even Charles Dickens was wrong, and that the world is not won by virtue. Eternal life, perhaps – but who knows about that? Not the world. If the moral code she had learnt, through literature she was now beginning to reinterpret, were correct, she should surely have flourished in her heavy unbecoming coat, in her laborious solitude, with her notes and the daily bus ride and the healthful lonely walks. (*ASIL*, p. 99)

As Elaine Jordan has pointed out, Angela Carter has rejected the subject position of the virtuous victim throughout her work, but most obviously in the figure of Justine in *The Sadeian Woman* whose preservation of purity and innocence is 'not the continuous exercise of a moral faculty', but 'a sentimental response in a world in which she always hopes her good behaviour will procure her some reward, some respite'.[55] In contrast, the question that pursues Brookner throughout her writing is the question that connects her novels to the concerns of the eighteenth- and nineteeenth-century conduct book, 'the question of what behaviour most becomes a woman'.[56] The ideal woman, according to Brookner in an early interview 'lives according to a set of principles and is somehow very rare and always has been'.[57] A Start in Life is a study in self-control, moral scruple and disappointment. 'Moral fortitude, as Dr Weiss knew, but never told her students, was quite irrelevant to the conduct of one's life; it was better, or in any event, easier, to be engaging. And attractive' (*ASIL*, p. 8). A Start in Life is also an altercation between pragmatic resig- nation and romantic idealism. What is exposed in Ruth Weiss's romantic longing is the tension between social conformity and emotional dissi- dence. But what is missing is any suggestion that the cards which life has unfairly dealt to women might be refused.

As Linden Peach has noted, Angela Carter is interested in the melan- cholic figures for whom, in the words of Julia Kristeva, 'sadness is in reality the only real object'. While pointing out that the melancholic personality may quite properly be understood other than in Kristevan terms, Peach makes the connection between the absence of mother- figures, the preponderance of characters who have lost their mothers, and the melancholic figures and concerns of Carter's early novels.[58] Similar connections can also be made in the fiction of Brookner. Like Carter, Brookner believes that feminine virtue provides no immunity from suffering although she has little interest in drawing attention to the patri- archal arrangements which brings women's suffering about. The order of the day for Brookner's melancholy heroines is acceptance, albeit a quiet, dignified resignation intended to invoke sympathy and respect. But resig- nation and acceptance are, of course, incompatible with a feminist politics of transformation and change. As Isobel Armstrong reminds us, 'lyricized feminine mourning and melancholy is precisely the trap, the fix which women have to get out of at all costs'.[59]

As is *The Game*, the dynamics of which, as Guiliana Giobbi has suggested, are modelled on *Sense and Sensibility* – Cassandra and Julia Corbett taking roles analogous to Elinor and Marianne Dashwood who represent sense and sensibility respectively in Austen's novel[60] – A Start in Life is carefully situated within the moral framework of the nineteenth- century novel. Brookner insists on high levels of ethical awareness from the heroines of her novels, and Ruth Weiss strives hard to live her life according to exacting moral precepts. But there is a differentiation between sexual propriety and personal morality which provides for some of the interesting tensions and contradictions in the novel. Just as I have suggested that it is not only Brookner but also Carter who is heavily dependent upon traditions of women's writing and influenced by the values of reason, so it is is not only Angela Carter's heroines, but rather less obviously Anita Brookner's heroines who in practice behave badly, or at least behave badly in their willingness to transgress respectable sexual codes. At the same time as the punctilious heroine of *A Start in Life* aspires to be as honest and scrupulous as possible in other aspects of her personal life, she is engaged in an illicit love affair with a married man. But Brookner's heroines are neither disingenuous nor naive. The lessons from Balzac are taken to heart, but the irony is that they are learned too late – Ruth Weiss muses that she is 'much too young for Balzac most women are' (*ASIL*, p. 23). She would have preferred the classic literature which she has read to have been right, but her experience tells her the opposite, that the 'selfishness and greed and bad faith and extravagance', to which she had succumbed when in love with Professor Duplessis, 'had made her into this semblance of a confident and attractive woman' (*ASIL*, p. 100).

A *Start in Life* is a poignant and recognisable study of the loneliness of the woman intellectual. It speaks eloquently of endless days spent eating alone, sleeping too much, and reading too long in research libraries. The bitter-sweet quality of Brookner's writings, which appeals to her many women readers, lies in the acuity with which they pinpoint a deep and unsatisfied longing for emotional closeness. As Patricia Waugh suggests, all Brookner's fiction is marked by its acute 'perception of the relational basis of identity and its portrayal of her woman characters' obsessive need for and fear of connection'.[61] Her heroines' personalities are deeply rooted in childhood insecurities and unfulfilled emotional needs. Their unsatiable desire for commitment and stability can be traced back to inadequate parenting. Ruth Weiss is the daughter of a charming but feckless father, who is discreetly unfaithful to his wife and dabbles in the book trade, and a vain, glamorous and ailing mother who has seen better days as a stage actress. The Bohemian disorder of Ruth's childhood is the antithesis of the domestic order and routine for which she secretly longs.

Brookner's novels are studies in not being loved and in which love is ultimately the only thing that matters. The supportive networks of women friends on which unmarried women are often heavily reliant for their emotional and practical support are a structuring absence in Brookner's fiction. The man whom she loves, a leading philologist at the Sorbonne, is Ruth Weiss's only source of real emotion and the heroine's psychic wholeness can only be guaranteed by connection to the object of her desire. What Brookner states in her fiction is what many feminists still find unpalatable, that intellectual achievement does not remove emotional dependency, and that despite a woman's outwardly convincing display of independence, the latter may be neither willed nor wanted: 'The kindest way to treat a scholar and a person of some dignity and courage is to pretend that she is none of these things and to accord her the nurture and protection expected by less independent women' (*ASIL*, p. 135). The world which Brookner melancholically and pessimistically evokes is a world in which intelligent women are successful in their careers but the price they pay is to be bereft of affection, children, domestic happiness and emotional security. Their unhappy lot is not only to be short-changed by men but also to be untouched by feminist ideas. Although the second wave of feminism was predicated on equal opportunity, it often appeared to have little to offer intelligent, successful women of the type which Brookner usually depicts. With many more examples of successful women in the public sphere effectively managing to combine a career and motherhood, this choice between success at work and domestic happiness, and between public achievement and personal fulfilment, is no longer one which confronts many middle-class, articulate and educated women in quite the same way.

NOTES

1　Isobel Armstrong, 'Woolf by the Lake, Woolf at the Circus: Carter and Tradition', in Lorna Sage (ed.), *Flesh and the Mirror: Essays on the Art of Angela Carter* (London: Virago, 1994), pp. 257–79, p. 258.
2　Ibid., p. 264.
3　Anita Brookner, *Hotel du Lac* (London: Jonathan Cape, 1984), p. 88.
4　Anita Brookner, *A Start in Life* (London: Joanathan Cape, 1981). All references are given parenthetically (*ASIL*).
5　Ibid., pp. 257–8.
6　Marguerite Alexander, *Flights from Realism: Themes and Strategies in Postmodernist British and American Fiction* (London: Edward Arnold, 1990).
7　Peter Kemp, quoted in John Skinner, *The Fictions of Anita Brookner: Illusions of Romance* (Basingstoke: Macmillan, 1992), p. 1.
8　Maroula Joannou, *'Ladies, Please Don't Smash These Windows': Women's Writing, Feminist Consciousness and Social Change 1918–1938* (Oxford: Berg, 1995), p. 158.
9　John Haffenden, 'Playing Straight: Interview with Anita Brookner', *Literary Review*, September 1984, pp. 25–31, p. 28.
10　A.S. Byatt, *Shadow of a Sun* (London: Chatto and Windus, 1964) reissued with an introduction by the author as *Shadow of the Sun* (London: Vintage, 1991), p. ix.
11　A.S. Byatt, 'Give Me the Moonlight, Give me the Girl', *New Review*, 11, 1975, p. 67. Quoted in Elaine Showalter, *A Literature of their Own: British Women Writers from Brontë to Lessing* (London: Virago, 1978), p. 316.
12　Quoted by Olga Kenyon, *Women Novelists Today: A Survey of English Writing in the*

    Seventies and Eighties (London: Macmillan, 1988), p. 52.

13 Ibid., p. 53.

14 Angela Carter, 'Notes from the Front Line', in Micheline Wandor (ed.), *On Gender and Writing* (London: Pandora, 1983), p. 69.

15 Angela Carter, Interview with Mary Harron, 'I'm a Socialist, Damn it! How Can You Expect Me to be Interested in Fairies?, *Guardian*, 15 September 1984, p. 10.

16 Carter, 'Notes from the Front Line', p. 70.

17 John Skinner, *The Fictions of Anita Brookner: Illusions of Romance* (Basingstoke: Macmillan, 1992), p. 1.

18 Peter Kemp, 'The Mouse that Whinged', Review of *Lewis Percy, Sunday Times*, 27 August 1989, G6, quoted in Skinner, *The Fictions of Anita Brookner*, p. 128.

19 Richard Todd, *A.S. Byatt* (London: Northcote House, 1997), p. 11.

20 Byatt, *Shadow of the Sun*, p. ix.

21 *The Game* (London: Chatto and Windus, 1967), p. 97.

22 Angela Carter, epigraph to *Heroes and Villains* (London: Heinemann, 1969), p. 27.

23 Eugenia Delamotte, *Perils of the Night: A Feminist Study of Nineteenth-Century Gothic* (Oxford: Oxford University Press, 1990), Kate Ferguson Ellis, *The Contested Castle: Gothic Novels and the Subversion of Domestic Ideology* (Urbana: University of Illinois Press, 1989).

24 Angela Carter, *The Sadeian Woman: An Exercise in Cultural History* (London: Virago, 1979), p. 9.

25 Angela Carter, interview with John Haffenden, *Novelists in Interview* (London: Methuen, 1985), pp. 76–97, p. 79.

26 Angela Carter, *The Bloody Chamber and Other Stories* (London: Victor Gollancz, 1979) p. 33. All quotations are given parenthetically – (BC).

27 *The Sadeian Woman*, p. 20.

28 Merja Makinen, 'Angela Carter's *The Bloody Chamber* and the Decolonization of Feminine Sexuality', *Feminist Review*, 42, Autumn 1992, pp. 2–15.

29 The three principal groupings in Britain were the Campaign against Pornography which was opposed to pornography and argued that this was demeaning to women; the Campaign against Pornography and Censorship which was opposed to pornography but also to censorship by the state which it argued could be abused; and Feminists against Censorship which defended the rights of women to produce and enjoy heterosexual or lesbian erotica.

30 Aidan Day, *Angela Carter: The Rational Glass* (Manchester: Manchester University Press, 1998), p. 162.

31 Elaine Jordan, 'The Dangers of Angela Carter', in Isobel Armstrong (ed.), *New Feminist Discourses: Critical Essays on Theories and Texts* (London: Routledge, 1992), pp. 119–31, pp. 124–5.

32 Anthony Giddens *The Transformation of Intimacy: Sexuality, Love and Eroticism in Modern Societies* (Oxford: Polity/Blackwell, 1992), p. 45.

33 Day, *Angela Carter: The Rational Glass*, p. 12.

34 Shusha Guppy, interview with Anita Brookner, *Paris Review*, Fall 1987, pp. 325–42, p. 336.

35 Anita Brookner, *Providence* (London: Jonathan Cape, 1982), p. 134.

36 Jane Flax, 'Postmodernism and Gender Relations in Feminist Theory', in Linda Nicholson (ed.), *Feminism/Postmodernism* (London: Routledge, 1990), pp. 39–62, p. 43.

37 Brookner, *Providence*, p. 177.

38 Shusha Guppy interview, pp. 335–6.

39 Jenny Uglow (ed.), *Shaking a Leg: Journalism and Writings, The Collected Angela Carter* (London: Chatto and Windus, 1997), p. 38.

40 Shusha Guppy interview, p. 328.

41 Robert Clarke, 'Angela Carter's Desire Machine', *Women's Studies*, 14, 1987, pp. 147–61, p. 159.

42 Paulina Palmer, 'Gender as Performance in the Fiction of Angela Carter and Margaret Atwood', in Joseph Bristow and Trev Lynn Broughton (eds), *The Infernal Desires of Angela Carter: Fiction, Femininity, Feminism* (London: Longman, 1997), pp. 24–43, p. 31.

43 Angela Carter, introduction to *Wayward Girls and Wicked Women* (London: Virago, 1986), p. xii.

44 *The Sadeian Woman*, p. 9.

45 Patricia Duncker, 'Re-Imagining the Fairy Tales: Angela Carter's Bloody Chambers', *Literature and History*, 10(1), 1984, pp. 3–14, p. 6.

46 Elaine Jordan, 'Enthralment: Angela Carter's Speculative Fictions', in Linda Anderson (ed.), *Plotting Change: Contemporary Women's Fiction* (London: Edward Arnold, 1990), pp. 1–40, p. 23.

47 Marina Walker, *From the Beast to the Blonde: On Fairy Tales and Their Tellers* (London: Chatto and Windus, 1994), p. 25.

48 'Re-Imagining the Fairy Tales: Angela Carter's Bloody Chambers', p. 11.

49 Lorna Sage, *Angela Carter* (London: Northcote House, 1994), p. 5.

50 Nicole Ward Jouve, 'Mother Is a Figure of Speech', in Lorna Sage (ed.), *Flesh and the Mirror: Essays on the Art of Angela Carter*, pp. 136–71, p. 151.

51 John Mortimer, 'The Stylish Prime of Miss Carter', *Sunday Times*, 24 January 1982, p. 36.

52 Joan Smith, *A Masculine Ending* (London: Faber and Faber, 1987), p. 125.

53 Lynne Pearce and Gina Wisker (eds), introduction to *Fatal Attractions: Rescripting Romance in Contemporary Literature and Film* (London: Pluto, 1998), pp. 1–20, p. 15.

54 Armstrong, 'Woolf by the Lake, Woolf at the Circus: Carter and Tradition', p. 258.

55 'The Dangers of Angela Carter', p. 120.

56 Brookner, *Hotel Du Lac*, p. 40.

57 Shusha Guppy inteview, p. 336.

58 Linden Peach, *Angela Carter* (London: Macmillan, 1998), p. 17.

59 Armstrong, 'Woolf by the Lake, Woolf at the Circus: Carter and Tradition', p. 257.

60 Guiliana Giobbi, 'Sisters Beware of Sisters: Sisterhood as a Literary Motif in Jane Austen, A.S. Byatt, and I. Bossi Fedrigotti', *Journal of European Studies*, 87, September 1992, pp. 241–6, p. 242.

61 Patricia Waugh, *Feminine Fictions: Revisiting the Postmodern* (London: Routledge, 1989) p. 126.

5

The feminist confessional novel

> Madam, I am a full-blooded, *bona fide* lesbian. As for the way I look, most
> lesbians I know look like any other woman.
> Rita Mae Brown, *Rubyfruit Jungle*

THE SEXUAL CONFESSIONAL moved into literature in the work of
writers like J.D. Salinger's *Catcher in the Rye* and Kingsley Amis's
Lucky Jim in the 1960s, although sexual outspokenness and sexual
bravado have had a long provenance among twentieth-century male
writers, including Jean Genet, Ernest Hemingway, Vladimir Nabokov
and Lawrence Durrell. By the end of the 1970s the sexual confessional
had become closely identified with women writers, with the 'sexual
revolution' of the 1960s, and with a number of texts that were destined to
become classics of the women's movement including Verena Stefan's
Shedding (1980), Lisa Alther's *Kinflicks* (1977), Anja Meulenbelt's *The
Shame Is Over*, and Kate Millett's *Sita* (1977).[1]

In the modern woman's confessional novel, the central character's
understanding or knowledge of herself is often focused on sexual
encounter, love, marriage, or divorce. The woman's confessional, a
contemporary variant of the old-fashioned novel of ideas, is usually traditional in form. What Jane Marcus has termed the relationship between 'art
and anger'[2] is inscribed in the production of these texts in a peculiarly
direct, urgent and provocative manner. The woman's confessional novels
of the 1970s have often been criticised for their lack of an ironic approach
to subjectivity. They are not, in the main, 'literary', that is to say that they
do not signal to the reader that they are fictions of quality through the
lexical surface of their text. There is also a tendency within them to present
male characters in a reductive and one-dimensional light. This sometimes
produces a somewhat different response from the reader to that intended.
Angela Carter once wrote of an unnamed novel, which is clearly *The
Women's Room*, 'I finished the book with every sympathy for the men: they
seemed to have awful lives surrounded by such dreadful women.'[3]

The woman's confessional novels with which I am concerned are
usually perceived to have an intimate connection to the concerns of the
woman's movement. What they therefore raise are important questions

about the nature of the relationship between imaginative writing, cultural analysis and political praxis. Texts such as *Kinflicks, Rubyfruit Jungle* and *The Women's Room*, with their traditional linear narratives, and their emphasis on the importance of woman's subjectivity and agency, are the antithesis of the kind of postmodernist experimental fiction which points to the unstable nature of human identity and the notion that women are discursively constructed in language. Moreover, French feminist critics such as Julia Kristeva, Luce Irigaray and Hélène Cixous have argued that there is a special relationship between feminism and avant-garde modes of writing. As Molly Hite has put it, 'to give the problem its most radical formulation, it would seem that in the contemporary period, fictional experimentation has everything to do with feminism and nothing to do with women – and emphatically nothing to do with women as points of origin, as authors.'[4]

In 1979 Ros Coward raised the distinction between feminist fiction and women's fiction in an article that referred directly to the publishers' claim with which *The Women's Room* was then being marketed, 'This Novel Changes Lives': 'Are Women's Novels Feminist Novels?' Coward pointed out that the feminist best-seller was something of a contradiction at a time when feminists were themselves often unpopular and caricatured in the media: 'Is it that these novels are carrying out subversive politicization, drawing women into structures of consciousness-raising without their knowing it? Or is it that the accounts of women's experiences which they offer in fact correspond more closely to popular sentiment than they do to feminist aspirations?'[5]

To some extent, the extraordinary popularity of the feminist confessional blockbusters, like Erica Jong's *Fear of Flying* (1974), Rita Mae Brown's *Rubyfruit Jungle* (1973) and Marilyn French's *The Women's Room* (1977),[6] rested on the fact that they shared the imperative to 'tell it like it is' with other modes of writing, with which large numbers of women readers were already familiar; popular fiction, family sagas, psychotherapy and personal-growth manuals, biographies of well-known women, and historical novels. Confessional and autobiographical modes of writing are particularly close and the distinction between them is sometimes difficult to sustain. The traditional novel of woman's development also has affinities with the modern woman's confessional novel. In *The Voyage In*, Elizabeth Abel has distinguished between the novel of woman's development, which details a protagonist's formative experiences, and the 'neo-feminist' novel which is largely concerned with an awakening consciousness.[7]

The women's liberation movement was centrally concerned with changing women's lives. This is why the novels that claimed to change lives sold in huge numbers and had the cachet that they did. But what has changed since the publication of these novels is the political context which imbued their content with freshness and urgency. With the demise of the women's liberation movement – and the assimilation of many of its ideas into the political mainstream – the very novels which empowered and helped to politicise a generation of women may appear lacking in subtlety, formally conservative, and sometimes even hectoring in tone. This is especially true for a new generation of readers, who do not remember the days in which these books constituted an important intervention in radical cultural politics, and simply take much of what seemed new and exciting at the time of publication for granted. There are now many feminists within academia who first encountered feminism on their undergraduate degrees as a discursive practice and method of cultural analysis and not as a form of political praxis. As Sally Ledger puts it, 'I myself instinctively associate those years more with my dad's flared trousers and the marvellous arrival of colour telly in our household than with "Women's lib"'.[8]

What the legacies of Thatcherism and Reaganism have erased is the importance that many feminists in the 1970s attached to the notion of agency and to cultural artefacts as key sites of political struggle. Cut adrift from their moorings in the women's liberation movement, such novels read very differently today, and they must to some extent be held responsible for the widespread perception that feminist fiction is often 'bad fiction', that is to say that it is narrow, tedious, prescriptive and formulaic. As Terry Lovell points out, 'polemic writings do not usually last beyond the moment of controversy'.[9] But as Rita Felski argues, 'subjectivity remains an ineradicable element of modern social experience, bringing with it attendant needs – for autonomy, but also for intimacy, which must be addressed in the context of emancipatory politics'.[10] While the notion of the decentred subject may be of great interest within academia it is, as I have argued elsewhere, of very little interest to women outside it, who may be struggling to assert their identity as full human subjects which has often been denied them.[11] In that it is centrally concerned with women's subjectivity, is an accessible mode of fiction with a proven appeal to women readers, addresses questions about subjectivity, class and sexual politics that continue to demand our attention today, and has the potential to link subjective experience to broader currents of historical and social change, I would contend that the confessional mode of writing has not outlived its usefulness but is still of great strategic value to feminists.

There is, of course, nothing intrinsically radical about the idea of the confessional and, as Foucault has argued, the confessional in history has

been constructed in terms of social convention and to promote conformity. Kate Millett has taken exception to the use of the word 'confession'
since it implies 'the acceptance of sin, an unnatural, wrong action for
which the writer wishes atonement'.[12] Confessional writing proceeded
from the subjective experience of problems and contradictions that
women experienced in their lives. The central character derives satisfaction from her accomplishment in overcoming the societal and psychic
obstacles which have impeded her own personal development as a
woman, and she desires to share her new-found understanding with
others. Such writings encourage their readers to believe that more
women would find happiness if they too were prepared to transgress. In
some of these novels there is direct contact with feminist characters and
ideas within the narrative, but in others the encounter with the women's
movement is less explicit.

At the heart of much of this confessional writing, exemplified in
writers as disparate as Erica Jong and Rita Mae Brown, is the belief that
sexual pleasure is itself liberating. In *The Re-Making of Love*, Barbara
Ehrenreich *et al.* have argued that the sexual revolution of the 1960s was
essentially a *women's* sexual revolution and that the changes it has
brought about in women's lives went far deeper than the removal of
sexual taboos and inhibitions. They write that 'if either sex has gone
through a change to sexual attitudes and behaviour that deserves to be
called revolutionary, it is women, and not men at all'.[13] *In Female Desire*,
Ros Coward argues that the significance of sexual experience for men and
women in confessional fiction is different: 'For men sexual encounters
represent access to power in having control over women's bodies. Sexual
experiences in women's novels represents access to knowledge rather
than power. Sexual experience becomes the way in which a woman finds
out about herself.'[14]

The teleology of the confessional narrative is politically inspired and
is analogous to the structure and organisation of the consciousness
group. A woman writer, like a woman participating in a consciousness-
raising group, selects from the possible events in her life those which
appear to illustrate her philosophy and to make her into the woman
whom she now is. Elizabeth Wilson was oppressed by 'the twin poles of
suffering and triumph': she writes that she 'felt strongly that the protag-
onist(s) or author of a feminist work should not have to embody feminist
virtues in the way that western art for centuries has used the female form
to represent uplifting abstract qualities'. Wilson 'wanted to write about
experiences freed from the imperative of affirmation, to explore
ambiguity, complexity and the politically incorrect'. Moreover, 'Since
most women cannot possibly achieve the fame and success of a Maya

Angelou, a Rita Mae Brown, or a Simone de Beauvoir', the force of their examples 'may inhibit or depress rather than inspire'.[15]

It was the 'courage-kindling fires of the Women's Movement, which above all, decreed that women's emotions had as much validity as men's',[16] that persuaded Erica Jong to throw away her experimental novel influenced by Nabokov and to begin her first novel *Fear of Flying*. It was also the women's movement that underpinned the sales of the book. *Fear of Flying* was not considered to be a commercial book when it was first published by Holt, Rinehart and Winston in hardback in 1973. But Harper/Collins, the publishers of the paperback in the United States, believed that it could reach a massive audience and promoted it as a commercial volume. Commenting on its extraordinary success – *Fear of Flying* came tenth on the *New York Times Book Review* list of bestsellers of the 1970s in the United States with five million and seven hundred thousand paperback copies in print[17] – Jong said that she had 'captured the zeitgeist of the decade. Isadora Wing's effort to transcend her fear of being alone and free reflects the lifestyle of many contemporary women.'[18] But as John Sutherland points out, 'the superselling novel with its emancipated themes (*Fear of Flying, Perdido, The Women's Room*) was inevitably suspect as being indirectly exploitative of women (making money for male publishers, fuelling male masturbation fantasies) or indicative of a repressive tolerance which insidiously sapped revolutionary energy and confused protest with entertainment'.[19]

Like Shere Hite's investigation of women's sexual preferences and responses, *Sexual Honesty, by Women for Women* (1974),[20] *Fear of Flying* excited attention because it offered the reader new insights into women's sexuality. With a heroine who was a feminist – explicit and uninhibited descriptions of sex are interspersed with disquisitions on the problems of being both a woman and an artist – *Fear of Flying* received the attention of feminists. Moreover, as a serious work of literature, published by a respectable publisher, and carrying endorsements from Henry Miller and John Updike, it also received the critical attention of the literary world. As Maria Lauret has pointed out, *Fear of Flying* 'was aimed, at one and the same time, at women's feminist curiosity and at male voyeurism – after all these novels promised an insight into "what it is really like for her", and an answer to that age-old conundrum of what a woman wants.'[21]

Both the cover of *Fear of Flying*, and its marketing intimated Jong's willingness to transgress not only the rules of decorum in her uninhibited use of four-letter words and descriptions of the intimate bodily functions, but also many of the unwritten rules of feminism. At a time when many heterosexual feminists were feeling shortchanged by depersonalised sex, the publisher's blurb in the British edition lauded the 'zipless fuck' and proclaimed that what men and women want from sex is satisfaction 'with the minimum of time-wasting preliminaries'. *Fear of Flying* was a problematic book for many feminists, who, while recognising the importance of subjectivity as a central category of feminist politics, disliked the particular type of subjectivity which it depicted. They also often disliked the sexual politics of the novel as a whole which did not 'reveal any serious questioning of the existing basis of male–female relations or any sustained refusal of the values of a male-dominated society'.[22]

John Updike's endorsement of *Fear of Flying* as 'the most uninhibited, delicious, erotic novel a woman ever wrote' appears prominently on the cover. Neither Updike nor Henry Miller, who championed Jong's right as a woman to enter the terrain of sexual fiction, were sympathetic to feminism. Miller, in particular, was suspected of using the literary to exonerate the pornographic in his own writing. On the back of *Fear of Flying* is a photograph of the author (perfect teeth, a dazzling smile, high cheekbones and blonde, dishevelled hair). Like Gloria Steinem, to whom she bears a passing resemblance, Erica Jong is a conventionally beautiful woman. The promotion of the novel through her glamorous, youthful image did little to recommend the book to those who disliked self-advertisement, vanity and feminist 'stars' – a tendency that was always stronger in Britain than in America.

Jong's willingness to be interviewed by the 'girlie' magazine *Playboy*,[23] a feminist *bête noir*, whose stock in trade was the exploitation of women's bodies, was sufficient to damn her in the eyes of many. *Fear of Flying* rapidly accrued a symbolic importance that resonated far beyond the literary. It was eagerly seized upon both by feminists in the anti-pornography lobby and by those who were in favour of sexual permissiveness, all of whom saw it as vindicating their own positions in the heated debates about pornography of the time. My discussion of *Fear of Flying* attempts to provide a more nuanced reading of the novel which retrieves it from the context of pornography and reclaims it for literary history.

Susan Suleiman, one of Jong's few admirers in academia, is, I think, right in insisting that the novel is parodic.[24] What *Fear of Flying* does is to invert the conventions of pornography, in that the beautiful but quiescent woman who is the stock object of the salacious novel, appropriates both the pornographer's vocabulary and his prerogative of contemplating the opposite sex predominantly in terms of its sexual functions, parts and performance. Isadora herself is an expert on the erotic, having published a book of erotic poems which causes strange men to call her up in the middle of the night with 'propositions and prepositions' (*FOF*, p. 234). The adjectives used about this volume are the ones that one suspects Jong would use for her own book, 'brave' and 'bold'. Isadora is a woman who experiences herself as sexual rather than a woman who is depicted as an object of male sexual desire. By the summer of 1965, the twenty-three-year-old heroine and a friend have toured Europe together, breaking class, sexual and racial taboos, sleeping with black musicians, men selling wallets outside the Uffizi, ticket clerks and mail clerks from American Express. The fact that Isadora has both a ravenous sexual appetite and a low opinion of men is one of the central contradictions in the novel: 'Their minds were hopelessly befuddled, but their bodies were so nice. Their ideas were intolerable, but their penises were silky. I had been a feminist all my life ... but the big problem was how to make your feminism jibe with your unappeasable hunger for male bodies. It wasn't easy' (*FOF*, p. 88).

The time in which *Fear of Flying* is set is the mid-1960s and the world in which Isadora moves is the world of the New York radical chic: 'The Diem regime had just fallen and Buddhists kept immolating themselves in a funny little country whose name was growing more and more familiar – Vietnam. Barry Goldwater was running for President on the programme of sawing off the entire Eastern seaboard and floating it out to sea. John F. Kennedy was not one year dead' (*FOF*, p. 190). The Vietnam War has drafted Isadora's first husband into the army and made her into an army wife. She accompanies her second husband on a visit to Vienna for a congress of psychoanalysts of whom she is highly critical: 'Their mildly leftist political views, their signing of peace petitions and decorating their offices with prints of *Guernica* were just camouflage. When it came to the *crucial* issues: the family, the position of women, the flow of cash from patient to doctor: they were reactionaries. As rigidly self-serving as the Social Darwinists of the Victorian Era' (*FOF*, p. 23).

Isadora leaves her second husband for an existentialist with whom she sets out on a tour of Europe. Existentialism, as he explains it to her, entails making no plans for the future, seizing the day and feeling no guilt. In practice, it involves living by his rules, even if in theory there are no rules. The plans which her lover omits to disclose to her include his intention to go back to his wife. Approaching the outskirts of Paris, Isadora comes across some graffiti which relates to her own situation. This reads '*FEMMES! LIBERONS-NOUS*' (*FOF*, p. 238).

'With a name like Isadora Zelda it was clear what I was supposed to choose: everything my mother had been offered and had passed up' (*FOF*, p. 44). The subtext of *Fear of Flying* is the problem of becoming an artist. Isadora wants a particular kind of role model 'the female Chaucer' who is able to combine 'juice and joy and love and talent too' (*FOF*, p. 110). She notes: 'If you are female and talented, life was a trap no matter which way you turned. Either you drowned in domesticity or you longed for domesticity in all your art' (*FOF*, p. 238). Isadora refuses the 'glorious image of the ideal woman, a kind of Jewish Griselda' (*FOF*, pp. 230–1), and has a love–hate relationship with domesticity: 'I suddenly had a passion to be that ordinary girl. To be that good little housewife, that glorified American mother, that mascot from *Mademoiselle*, that Matron from *McCall's*, that cutie from *Cosmo*, that girl with the *Good Housekeeping* Seal tattooed on her ass and advertising jingles programmed in her brain' (*FOF*, p. 230).

Jong is a literate writer, and there are many literary precedents for the bawdy woman in fiction by male writers to which *Fear of Flying* contains oblique references. These include Chaucer's Wife of Bath, Defoe's Moll Flanders and Cleland's Fanny Hill. In his review of the novel in the *New Yorker*, Updike commends Jong for 'having more kind words for the male body than any author since the penning of *Fanny Hill*'[25] – Jong's second novel, *Fanny: Being the True History of the Adventures of Fanny Hackabout-Jones* (1980), is an epistolary novel and a pastiche of the eighteenth-century bawdy of writers like Cleland and Fielding. In *Fear of Flying*, the most important intertextual reference is to Joyce's Molly Bloom with whom Isadora Wing shares a relish for the physical pleasures. *Ulysses* is Isadora's favourite novel. The scene in which Isadora sits contemplatively on a toilet seat is reminiscent of Molly Bloom's defecation in *Ulysses*. But although Jong incorporates Joycean imagery into her narrative, it is without the radical changes to the form of the novel which we associate with Joyce. Instead she revives realism to subvert its assumptions.

Jong has argued that she 'wanted to show Isadora as a survivor – in opposition to all those 19th century heroines who die for the one sexual transgression … and to all those 20th century heroines who suffer madness, breakdown, the deaths of their children, imprisonment in dying marriages, and the like'.[26] While Isadora does survive she has no intention of surviving alone and opts to return to her husband. All her fantasies 'included marriage' (*FOF*, p. 78). The fear of flying which afflicts Isadora is a metaphor for fear of independence and of living on one's own. Jong makes no attempt in the novel to envisage new ways of living: 'Being unmarried in a man's world is such a hassle that *anything* had to be better. Marriage was better. But not much' (*FOF*, p. 78).

What such attitudes appear to confirm is that erotically charged relationships induce dependency in women and disrupt the attainment of an autonomous self. Indeed, *Fear of Flying* can be read as an exploration of the idea that 'everywoman adores a fascist' – the line is taken from Sylvia Plath's poem, 'Daddy', and is used as heading to chapter two. Isadora believes that women are their own worst enemies and that everywoman wants 'to submit to some big brute' (*FOF*, p. 124).

There are two subversive forces in the novel which are used to deflate the male ego: sex, and gossip. Sex, which can in places appear ridiculous, exposes male inadequacy. Isadora's lover, the improbably named Adrian Goodlove, is 'impotent when I wanted him in private, but he became voraciously virile in the most public places' (*FOF*, p. 169). Moreover, 'Men have always detested women's gossip because they suspect the truth: their measurements are being taken and compared. Gossip is the original form of consciousness-raising. Men can mock it, but they can't prevent it. Gossip is the opiate of the oppressed' (*FOF*, p. 97).

In attempting to define women in terms of their sexuality, Jong risks reducing women to their sexuality alone: 'One's body becomes the landscape, the sky, and finally the cosmos' (*FOF*, p. 257). But a preoccupation with sexuality and the human body is not in itself necessarily liberating. As Ros Coward points out, the 'idea that a woman could become her own person just through sexual experience and the discovery of sexual needs and dislikes again establishes sexual relations as separate from social structures. The emphasis on sex as knowledge may well obscure the fact that sex is implicated in society as a whole'.[27] In so far as *Fear of Flying* did little to challenge the predominant ethos in which what mattered about women was their youth and physical attractiveness, it helped to perpetuate it. In *Fear of Fifty* (1994), Jong candidly admitted to having been caught in a self-set trap:

> I am no longer the youngest person in the room, nor the cutest. I will never be Madonna, or Tina Brown, or Julia Roberts. ... For years those were my values – whether I admitted this to myself or not – but I cannot afford such values any more. Every year another crop of beauties assaults me on the streets of New York. With thinner waists and blonder hair, and straighter teeth, with more energy to compete (and less cynicism about the world).[28]

Much of the suspicion of the novel that Charlotte Templin discusses in *Feminism and the Politics of Literary Reputation*[29] centred on Isadora's privileged background. The milieu which she inhabits is that of the monied, cultured metropolitan intelligentsia. It is true that *Fear of Flying* explores the relationship between Jewish suffering and female identity – Isadora's travels takes her to Auschwitz and the book makes pointed references to the Nazi atrocities in Europe. But for many of her readers, Isadora's Jewish identity confirmed membership of a powerful New York elite rather than of a persecuted racial minority. Moreover, the stylish, confident, assertive heterosexuality and liberated individualism of the novel made it an easy target for those who criticised the women's movement for being a white middle-class movement. One suspects that much of the feminist distrust of *Fear of Flying* can be attributed to the fact that the novel appears too male-identified, too 'pro-sex', and too heterosexual even for white, middle-class heterosexual feminists. Indeed, many feminists came to see *Fear of Flying* as the literary epitome of what Adrienne Rich has termed 'life-style liberation, personal solutions to the few – and those few overwhelmingly white.'[30]

Erica Jong's fiction proclaims that women want and need sex as much as men. As an outspoken opponent of sexual puritanism Jong exemplified women's right to participate in the new discourse on sexuality; to 'speak her own body, assume her own subjecthood'.[31] But it is naive to assume that the lifting of restrictions on sex in itself removes male privilege, or that it produces changes in how men relate to women in other kinds of relationships. As Foucault has argued, to see the sexual liberationism of the 1960s as a sufficient end in itself is to miscontrue the nature of power and how it is distributed.[32] I agree with Gayle Greene that *Fear of Flying* 'confuses liberation with sexual liberation and confuses sexual liberation with the freedom to act and talk like a man, but the bold language that so impressed readers, masks a conventionality, a failure to imagine otherwise'.[33] As Anne Mickelson puts it, 'Isadora's flaunted lack of inhibition has not yet successfully embraced the debatable Joycean idea that the indecorous, the vulgar, the commonplace reveal the higher things.'[34]

After many rejections by publishing houses, Rita Mae Brown's semi-autobiographical novel, *Rubyfruit Jungle* was finally published by a small collective which only published books by women, the Daughters Publishing Company, before being taken over by Bantam Books, and coming out worldwide as a Corgi paperback. By its seventh printing it had sold seventy thousand copies in the United States alone, much of its reputation spreading through personal recommendation in the lesbian community where it soon acquired the status of a classic.

The explicit representation of lesbian sexual practice in *Rubyfruit Jungle* needs to be understood in a historical context in which lesbian sexuality had been outlawed. The dominant literary images of the lesbian, until the 1970s, was the guilt-ridden central character in Radclyffe Hall's *The Well of Loneliness* (1928). Lesbian feminism emerged in the late 1960s and the 1970s in the United States where many lesbians found themselves unhappily positioned between the women's liberation movement in which heterosexual women were predominant and the male-dominated gay liberation movement. Like *Fear of Flying, Rubyfruit Jungle*, published in 1978 but set some ten years earlier, equates sex with rebellion. *Rubyfruit Jungle* is a *Künstlerroman*: an account of the formation of woman as an artist. Molly Holt's ambition is to become a film-maker. The traditional mode in which the novel is written is a statement against formalist aesthetic practice in which form is privileged over content. Those with whom Molly finds herself in competition at film school are male avant-garde film-makers, whose stylish, depoliticised experimental form disguises vacuousness and rampant misogyny.

Molly Bolt is orphaned, illegitimate and, like the author, kept in ignorance of the identity of her natural father. She begins life in poverty in the small town of York in Pennysylvania, the clever, mischievous adopted daughter of a straitlaced working-class couple. Like most women who become lesbians Molly is brought up in a traditional family and develops her lesbian identity in tension with and in reaction against the example offered by her parents and other members of her family. Before the family has moved south to Florida, Molly has already had adolescent sexual experiments with members of both sexes, including a love affair with the lovely Leota Bisland, to whom she makes an absurdly humorous proposal of marriage. Breaking decisively with the precedent of *The Well of Loneliness*, Brown carefully avoids providing anything in Molly's psychological make-up, formative experiences, or family history, to suggest that she is in any way different from other women, or to make her sexual orientation anything other than a matter of informed choice. *Rubyfruit Jungle* was written in the context of impassioned debates about the meaning(s) of lesbian identity within the lesbian community, and it reflects deeply held differences about how much importance should be attached to emotional identification with women and how much to sexual practice. To borrow a phrase which became popular after the publication of Jill Johnstone's *Lesbian Nation* in 1973, *Rubyfruit Jungle* set out to 'liberate the lesbian in every woman'.[35]

What lesbianism predominantly signifies for Molly in *Rubyfruit Jungle* is good sex. Unlike Radclyffe Hall, Brown could assume the presence of lesbian readers who were sufficiently liberated to want to read forthright descriptions of sex and did not wish to have their enjoyment diminished by puritanical inhibitions. If heterosexual society has traditionally demanded that sex be treated with secrecy and circumspection then, as Eve Kosofsky Sedgwick has observed, homosexuality is *the* sexual secret which demands even more discretion and concealment.[36] At Fort Lauderdale Molly becomes the most outstanding student in high school and wins a scholarship to the University of Florida. But although her academic work is excellent, she learns that her scholarship cannot be renewed on 'moral grounds' (*RFJ*, p. 131). There follows a chilling description of how Molly is relegated to the realm of the abject; of the homophobia which her presence among women students evokes, and the hostility which the heterosexual community evinces towards the homosexual. The abject, according, to Kristeva, is defined by its potential for social disruption and by the terror of pollution which it produces in the individual and the community.[37] Molly finds herself ostracised by her fellow students, and is expelled, both for admitting to a lesbian relationship in which she feels no shame and for refusing to accept the 'help' which is offered. *Rubyfruit Jungle* is one of the earliest of the post-Stonewall 'coming-out' narratives. It textualises the possibility of sexual defiance through theatrical forms of protest. These contest the homophobic representation of the lesbian as an abject and polluting presence.

Molly prides herself on having 'no mother, no father, no roots, no biological similarities called sisters and brothers' (*RFJ*, p. 88). As Paulina Palmer notes, 'alternative familial forms and social structures furnish the site where the lesbian achieves self-definition and emotional fulfilment'.[38] Finding a lesbian community entails finding a big city: 'There are so many queers in New York that one more wouldn't rock the boat' (*RFJ*, p. 136). Molly works as a waitress in New York and has a number of affairs with women whom she picks up in gay bars at weekends. She also fulfils her ambition to become a radical film-maker: 'Not soppy romances about hapless heterosexuals, not family dramas about sparkling white America' (*RFJ*, p. 174). The film that secures her a graduation *summa cum laude* from the film school is a quietly understated old-fashioned portrait of Carrie, her mother, sitting in her rocking chair talking about herself, her life and the price of food. In 1968, Molly hitch-hikes back to Philadelphia to meet Leota, who at the age of twenty-four is already a wife and mother and has wilfully obliterated all memory of her lesbian past.

The quest for one's 'real' origins, often accompanied by improbable fantasies, is a common motif in lesbian narrative. The mystery of Molly's parentage is eventually disclosed. Her biological father was French and there is some suggestion that it is from him that Molly may have inherited her romantic and Latinate temperament. There follows a somewhat improbable reconciliation with her ageing mother who is dying of cancer, cannot bring herself to accept her daughter's sexual orientation, and stipulates that 'no women are coming to this house while you're in it – not even the Avon lady' (*RFJ*, p. 226). As Patricia Duncker has noted, 'Despite the implausible sentimentality of the leavetaking and the unlikely gush of love which Molly feels for the woman who treated her with nothing but cruel brutality, the political message is absolutely explicit. Carrie's story of unhappiness and betrayal has its counterpart in Molly's history. Women have more in common with each other than they do with any man.'[39]

Like *Fear of Flying*, *Rubyfruit Jungle* is an excellent example of the female sexual picaresque: Molly is a trickster who recounts her adventures in first-person episodic narrative like the Spanish picaro, rogue or scoundrel, revelling in the realistic descriptions of life in New York, where she takes on the role of the flâneuse, and puts as great a distance between herself and bourgeoise respectability as possible: 'And for a future I didn't want a split level home with a station wagon, pastel refrigerator, and a houseful of blonde children evenly spaced throughout the years. I didn't want to walk into the pages of *McCall's* magazine and become the model housewife' (*RFJ*, p. 88).

What distinguishes *Rubyfruit Jungle* from earlier fiction is its defiant, and unapologetic pride in the expression of lesbian sexuality. The cover proclaims that it is 'a novel about being different – and loving it!' *Rubyfruit Jungle* is not only concerned with lesbian erotics, but also with the importance of sexual fantasy to the inner life, and the part played by imagination in all kinds of sexual practice. As Teresa de Lauretis has suggested, in order to contest the existing representations of women the writer must reinscribe the lesbian 'in excess – as excess – in provocative counterimages sufficiently outrageous, passionate, verbally violent and formally complex to destroy the male discourse on love and redesign the universe'.[40] Because Molly has had consensual sex with both men and women – the novel is very much of its time which was before the threat of AIDS made people cautious – she is in a position to make comparisons, and to know that sex with women is altogether more interesting: 'Once you know what women are like, men get kind of boring. I'm not trying to put them down, I mean I like them sometimes as people, but sexually they're dull. I suppose if a woman doesn't know any better, she thinks it's good stuff' (*RFJ*, p. 159).

Rubyfruit Jungle inverts the societal and sexual norms: heterosexual practices are represented as freakish and bizarre and lesbian relationships are celebrated. While all her sexual affairs are described with touches of humour, her sexual relations with men verge on the absurd. As one example, when Molly is almost destitute she agrees to take part in an elaborate charade of throwing grapefruits at a man in exchange for money: this is the kind of parodic performance of oppressive sex roles which Judith Butler suggests has the effect of 'reworking abjection into political agency, recasting it into defiance and legitimacy'.[41]

Women's genitals are like a 'ruby fruit jungle' (*RFJ*, p. 203), and women are 'thick and rich and full of hidden treasures' (*RFJ*, p. 203). The difference between sex with men and with women is that between 'a pair of roller skates and a Ferrari' (*RFJ*, p. 199). Molly is 'a devil-may-care lesbian' (*RFJ*, p. 220), who will never marry a man, but will never marry a woman either. She is also determined to defy the processes of ageing and to be arrested 'for throwing an orgy at ninety-nine' (*RFJ* p. 219).

Rubyfruit Jungle is a lesbian success story which asserts the rights of lesbians to autonomy and self-determination. But, as in *Fear of Flying*, it is made clear that sexual liberation does not necessarily bring happiness. At the end of the novel the heroine is left to face the future on her own, 'to go my own way and maybe find some love here and there. Love, but not the now and forever kind with chains around your vagina and a short circuit in your brain. I'd rather be alone' (*RFJ*, p. 88). *Rubyfruit Jungle* avoids the isolated, misunderstood lesbian made famous in *The Well of Loneliness*. There is no longing for the world of childhood innocence, no sense of a lost Eden, or of lesbianism as exile from the things that matter. But what Molly's experiences have taught her to expect are homophobic attitudes from those around her, and the likelihood of rejection, even from the *soi disant* radicals of her own age.

The conclusions that Molly draws from her experiences closely mirror the author's. Rita Mae Brown had been among the first to raise the issue of lesbianism in the New York chapter of the National Organisation of Women. She had been strongly opposed by Betty Friedan and others who did not wish the organisation to take a public stand on lesbian rights for fear of alienating its respectable heterosexual supporters.[42] In 1970 Brown, resigned her editorship of the NOW-New York newsletter complaining angrily that '"lesbianism" is the one word which gives the NOW Executive Committee a collective heart attack'.[43] *Rubyfruit Jungle* ends on a note of pessimism about the inevitable divergence of feminist and lesbian agendas after the revolutionary stirrings at the end of the 1960s.

> The news, full of stories about people of my own age raging down the streets in protest. But somehow I knew my rage wasn't their rage and they'd have run me out of their movement for being a lesbian anyway. I read somewhere too that women's groups were starting but they'd trash me just the same. What the hell. I wished I could be that frog back at Ep's old pond. I wished I could get up in the morning and look at the day the way I used to when I was a child. I wished I could walk down the streets and not hear those constant, abrasive sounds from the mouths of the opposite sex. Damn, I wished the world would let me be myself. But I knew better on all counts. I wish I could make my films. (*RFJ*, p. 246)

The Women's Room has the most direct relationship of any of the confessionals to the women's liberation movement, and to the consciousness-raising groups that were prevalent in its early days. The back cover of *The Women's Room* carries endorsements by two women associated with the movement in its early days, Betty Friedan, author of *The Feminine Mystique*, and Fay Weldon, whose description of the book as 'the kind of book that changes lives' is transposed on the front of the book into the publishers' claim that 'this novel changes lives'. Although her newly found capacity for sexual pleasure is a landmark in Mira Ward's journey of self-discovery – her first husband is sexually inept and leaves her dissatisfied while her lover enables her to experience a clitoral orgasm – the central character's sexuality is not central to the book.

As a girl growing up in post-war America Mira Ward had received a narrow and restrictive upbringing: 'She looked for books about adolescents, books she could find herself and her problems in. There were none' (*WR*, p. 27). She offends by going to bars and parties on her own, and by appearing to advertise herself as available (*WR*, p. 49). Mira sees her choice 'clearly as being between sex and independence, and she was paralysed by that' (*WR*, p. 41). 'Armed by the title of Mrs., property of some man, she felt stronger in the world' (*WR*, p. 53). After she marries, 'the word *freedom* drops from her vocabulary, the word *maturity* replaces it' (*WR*, p. 55). What changes Mira is a combination of her formative experiences as a child, a near-rape in adolescence, marriage, motherhood, and divorce set in process her disintegration. She takes to drink, attempts suicide, and returns to formal education as a mature student. Before that she has acquired the habit of ransacking literature to make sense of her life.

Central to the process of consciousness-raising is the transformation of personal dissatisfaction into collective feminist political analysis and struggle. As Rochelle Gatlin puts it, consciousness-raising was 'usually a gradual process of unlearning all the internal and external aspects of the culturally prescribed female role. Along with this, there is the emotional and intellectual understanding of the ways they, as women, have been oppressed.' In talking about their childhoods, sexual relationships, education, children, etc. women come to the 'understanding that many of the situations described are not personal at all, and are not based on individual inadequacies, but rather have a root in the social order. Thus the personal becomes political.'[44] The events of Mira's early life are discussed in her consciousness-raising group in 1968 (*WR*, p. 77). Asked by a women friend at Harvard if she had a raised consciousness even as a young woman, Mira replies that she had a 'raised *unconsciousness*', which she explains means that she had 'no words to describe what I felt' (*WR*, p. 150).

The shift between the authoritative third-person narration of Mira's life and the first-person confessional mode of the narrator do not at first indicate a relationship of identity between the central protagonist and the narrator: 'Perhaps you find Mira a little ridiculous. I do myself' (*WR*. p. 10). The effect of the distanciation is to make Mira indistinguishable from other women. It is through Mira's ordinariness, her typicality, that, as Lukács suggests, we can see the force of history at work.[45] The importance of Mira's subjectivity is counterbalanced early in the novel by an element of communal solidarity which prefigures Mira's later politicisation and her rejection of liberal individualism. She writes out a cheque to help an impoverished woman friend, thus incurring the wrath of her husband who sees another woman's problems as having nothing to do with himself and his wife. Mira is set apart from the other mothers in the neighbourhood only by her bookishness. She could just as well be one of any of the other suburban women – Natalie, Martha, Samantha, Adele, Lily, Geraldine, Bliss, whose lives are depicted. But as the novel progresses, the distance between the narrator and the character of Mira is reduced. The character and the narrator merge as Mira's feminist awareness becomes stronger. As the narrator had hitherto possessed a feminist awareness which Mira lacked, there is no longer reason for the distance between the two to be maintained. It might indeed be argued that *The Women's Room* can be read as a confessional novel only with hindsight, since the identity of the narrator is not disclosed until the very last page of the novel. Because Mira has a double function, as commentator and character, she is able to meditate on suburban life, motherhood, loneliness, men, the situation of women in the university, and the situation of women in general.

The high point of the traditional female *Bildungsroman* which the young Mira avidly consumes, is usually the heroine's marriage. As Ellen Morgan has noted, in an essay which makes useful distinctions between the traditional *Bildungsroman* and the modern 'neo-feminist novel' (i.e. the novel influenced by the ideas of the women's movement), the former often follows a recognisable pattern: 'At physical maturity, woman was treated as if she were at the peak of her natural development because her potential for growth, and her potential to be interesting, were construed as physically sexual. When she entered physical adulthood, she was loved. That was her story.'[46] Mira's narrative does not conform to the usual pattern of the woman's *Bildungsroman*. Her marriage is a prelude not to happiness but to disenchantment. Mira embarks on a journey of self-fulfilment by returning to study as a mature student at a point when her marriage is in trouble. This is a well-trodden route in the consciousness-raising novel of the 1970s and Mira's pursuit of happiness through further education is similar to Ella Price's in *Ella Price's Journal*.[47]

The setting of much of the novel is American suburbia: Meyersville or Beau Reve (beautiful dream) in the 1950s. The rejection of the values of middle America, and the discovery of feminism, autonomy and personal liberation are informed by the changes in American society after the certainties of the 1950s, and by the changing place of the United States in the world. For all her wealth and armaments, the United States had not won the wars in Vietnam or Korea, and seemed unable to stem the tide of rebellion among her own minorities and young people. Events in *The Women's Room* are perceived through Mira/the narrator's heightened political awareness, and are mediated by her gradual absorption of the ideas of the women's liberation movement.

The use of two very different women characters, both feminists, in *The Women's Room*, allows French to introduce topical debates about the varieties and forms of feminism open to women. Mira is heterosexual and a liberal feminist. Her friend Val epitomises feminist anger and espouses a radical feminist analysis of power. She is a lesbian separatist, who lives in a women's community, and will work only on projects with other women. Despite her unhappy experiences, Mira is still willing to work politically with men, has a somewhat more nuanced attitude to patriarchy than Val, and comes to realise that her husband 'was not the enemy, only the embodiment of the enemy' (*WR*, p. 259). The strategy French uses in the novel is similar to that of Margaret Atwood in *The Handmaid's Tale* and Marge Piercy in *Braided Lives*.[48] In all three novels a 'reasonable' heroine is used to mediate between the reader and a more extreme woman, whose politics appear unattractive because she refuses to compromise. As in *The Handmaid's Tale*, the lesbian has style and panache which the heterosexual woman lacks, and her personal courage and willingness to expose herself to danger for her beliefs, is represented as admirable.

The Women's Room has been much criticised for its monolithic view of male power. The characters are rigidly divided on gender lines and the representation of the two sexes is schematic. There are no good men in the novel nor are there any male characters who display a capacity to learn and to change. Yet criticisms of the novel on these lines miss the point that what French depicts is not objective reality but reality as it appears through the lens of a wounded feminist. As Anne Tyler put it, in a scrupulously fair review of the novel, 'what victimises Mira is not men, but the chasm that she perceives between men and women – the mistrust, incomprehension, and exploitation. Whether we agree that this chasm exists, it exists for her; it affects her whole life. With a narrator like Mira, a certain bias in the telling is not merely forgivable; it serves a clear purpose.'[49]

French labours the point that playing by men's rules is no guarantee that women will not suffer. Mira's lover Ben is ready to abandon her when she refuses to marry him and to have a new child. In this respect, he is little different from her husband, the aptly named 'Norm', a success-ful medical practitioner, by whom she has two sons, and who divorces her, despite the fact that Mira is a good mother, with exacting standards of housekeeping, who goes out of her way to please him. Rape and murder are the strongest exemplifiers of the misogyny which is rampant in the novel. Val's daughter survives sexual molestation from her mother's lover only to be raped on the streets of Chicago. The courts do not administer justice fairly in a system which is shown to be weighted in favour of men, and the law enforcement agencies singularly fail in their responsibility to protect vulnerable women. Val is shot dead in the streets by the police when demonstrating in support of a black woman who killed an attempted rapist in self-defence. Because she is poor and black this woman's truthful testimony is not believed. Moreover, because she is alone on the streets at night she is deemed to be a prostitute whose profession made it impossible for her to be raped: 'Thus Anita Morrow was found guilty of murder on the grounds of illiteracy' (*WR*, pp. 674–5).

The central focus of the novel is the neighbourhood in which women share the experiences of pregnancy, motherhood, childcare (and often divorce and separation) around the kitchen table, and the student community in which the importance of the nuclear family is minimised. Here the feelings and actions which are generally considered to be the most private are shown to be the most universal. The two settings are brought together when Mira's naive reportage of her experiences as a young wife and mother are discussed in a consciousness-raising group in Cambridge in 1968. For all their education and intelligence, the young university wives are subject to exactly the same pressures to subjugate their own desires to those of their male partners as the women whom Martha has left behind in suburbia.

The Women's Room is a study in disillusionment. The dream that the novel exemplifies is the dream of escape from suburbia and domestic entrapment through the route of academic success. This is counterpoised to both the American Dream of material success, which a changed Mira no longer wants, and to the more alluring dream of the 'humming house' (*WR*, p. 457). This vision of domestic harmony, in which all members of a household are present and purposefully absorbed, continues to haunt Mira even at Harvard, and must also be decisively rejected before she can become a free woman. The revolutionary events of the year 1968 at Harvard University are the pivotal ones for the process of self-transformation. 'That year itself was an open door, but a magical one; once you went through it, you could never return' (*WR*, p. 11).

It is at Harvard that Mira becomes fully politicised by becoming politically aligned with other feminists. It is also at Harvard that she attends mixed political-action groups with the secret hope of finding a new man. But until she meets Ben the men in these groups are 'idealistic, intense, egotistic and asexual' (*WR*, p. 388). After the violent suppression of student dissent at Kent and Jackson State University, fear sweeps around the campus. The radicalism on the campus is counterpoised to the staunchly Republican values of her parents' generation: 'Hard work, frugality, suppression of desire: that was the recipe for success and success was goodness and virtue. And one stayed faithful to one's wife, and one made one's mortgage payments, and one created a semblance of order because if one did not, the world would fall apart' (*WR*, p. 484). But even the 'carefully wrought surface of their social life' (*WR*, p. 474) is broken through by drugs and rumoured abortion. One of the few consciousness-raising novels of the time to insist from the very beginning on the need for change in both the private and public domain by focusing on the experiences of a political activist, *The Women's Room* ends with an impasse.

Mira is left with little except a raised consciousness and a supportive network of friends who have all dispersed. Mira secures a teaching position in a community college in Maine, where she seeks companionship in the brandy bottle, and watches the waves dash themselves against the rocks. This is a bleakly pessimistic concluding metaphor for the predicament in which women frequently find themselves in the confessional works of the period, which often have surprisingly little to say about how long-term change may be brought about.

NOTES

1 Verena Stefan, *Shedding* (London: The Women's Press, 1980); Lisa Alther, *Kinflicks* (Harmondsworth: Penguin, 1977); Anja Meulenbelt, *The Shame Is Over* (London: The Women's Press, 1980), and Kate Millet *Elegy for Sita* (New York: Targ, 1979).
2 Jane Marcus, *Art and Anger: Reading Like a Woman* (Columbus: Ohio State University Press, 1988).
3 Quoted in John Haffenden, *Novelists in Interview* (London: Methuen, 1985), p. 93.
4 Molly Hite, *The Other Side of the Story: Structures and Strategies of Contemporary Feminist Narrative* (Ithaca: Cornell University Press, 1989), p. 17.
5 Rosalind Coward, '"This Novel Changes Lives": Are Women's Novels Feminist Novels? A Response to Rebecca O' Rourke's Article "Summer Reading"', *Feminist Review*, 5, 1980, pp. 53–64, p. 53.
6 Rita Mae Brown, *Rubyfruit Jungle* (London: Corgi, 1978); Marilyn French, *The Women's Room* (London: Sphere Books, 1978); Erica Jong, *Fear of Flying* (London:

Panther, 1974). All quotations are from these editions and given parenthetically in my text.

7 Elzabeth Abel, Marianne Hirsch, and Elizabeth Langland (eds), *The Voyage In: Fictions of Female Development* (London: University Press of New England, 1981), pp. 12–13.

8 Sally Ledger, 'Feminist Criticism in the Nineties: Review Article', *Literature and History*, 2(2), 1993, pp. 76–82, p. 72.

9 Terry Lovell, *Consuming Fiction* (London: Verso, 1997), p. 132.

10 Rita Felski, *Beyond Feminist Aesthetics: Feminist Literature and Social Change* (London: Hutchinson Radius, 1989), p. 68.

11 Maroula Joannou, *'Ladies, Please Don't Smash These Windows': Women's Writing, Feminist Consciousness and Social Change* (Oxford: Berg, 1995), p. 6.

12 Kate Millett, 'The Shame Is Over', *MS*, January 1975, pp. 25–7, p. 27.

13 Barbara Ehrenreich, Elizabeth Hess and Gloria Jacobs *Re-Making Love: The Feminization of Sex* (London: Fontana, 1987), pp. 1–2.

14 Rosalind Coward, *Female Desire: Women's Sexuality Today* (London: Paladin, 1984), p. 184.

15 Elizabeth Wilson, 'Tell it Like it Is': Women and Confessional Writing', in Susannah Radstone (ed.), *Sweet Dreams: Sexuality, Gender and Popular Fiction* (London: Lawrence and Wishart, 1988), pp. 21–45, p. 21, p. 35.

16 Erica Jong, quoted in John Sutherland, *Best Sellers: Popular Fiction of the 1970s* (London: Routledge and Kegan Paul, 1981), p. 83.

17 Ibid., p. 30.

18 Erica Jong interviewed by Wendy Martin in Janet Todd (ed.), *Women Writers Talking* (New York: Holmes and Meier, 1983), pp. 20–32.

19 Sutherland, *Best Sellers: Popular Fiction of the 1970s*, p. 83.

20 Shere Hite, *The Hite Report* (New York and London, Macmillan, 1976).

21 Maria Lauret, *Liberating Literature: Feminist Fiction in America* (London: Routledge, 1994), p. 85.

22 Felski, *Beyond Feminist Aesthetics*, p. 14.

23 Erica Jong interview with Gretchen McNeese, *Playboy*, September 1975, pp. 61–78.

24 Susan Suleiman, *Subversive Intent: Gender, Politics and the Avant-Garde* (Cambridge, MA: Harvard University Press, 1990).

25 John Updike, 'Jong Love', Review of *Fear of Flying*, *New Yorker*, 17 December 1973, pp. 149–51, p. 149.

26 Erica Jong, 'Comments on Joan Reardon's *Fear of Flying*: Developing the Feminist Novel, A Letter to the Author', *International Journal of Women's Studies*, 1(6), November/December 1978, pp. 625–6, p. 625.

27 Coward, *Female Desire: Women's Sexuality Today*, p. 184.

28 Erica Jong, *Fear of Fifty* (London: Chatto and Windus, 1994), p. 17.

29 Charlotte Templin, *Feminism and the Politics of Literary Reputation: The Example of Erica Jong* (Lawrence: University Press of Kansas, 1995).

30 Adrienne Rich, *On Lies, Secrets and Silence: Selected Prose, 1966–1978* (New York: Norton, 1979), p. 309.

31 Susan Suleiman, '(Re)Writing the Female Body: The Politics and Poetics of Female Eroticism', in Susan Rubin Suleiman (ed.), *The Female Body in Western Culture: Contemporary Perspectives* (Cambridge, MA: Harvard University Press, 1985), pp. 7–29, p. 7.

32 Michel Foucault, *Power, Knowledge: Selected Interviews and Writings*, ed. Colin Gordon (Brighton: Harvester, 1980) and *The History of Sexuality*, vol. 1. An Introduction (Harmondsworth: Penguin, 1981), p. 114.

33 Gayle Greene, *Changing the Story: Feminist Fiction and the Tradition* (Blooming-

ton: Indiana University Press, 1991), p. 91.

34 Ann A. Mickelson, *Reaching Out: Sensitivity and Order in Recent American Fiction by Women* (Metuchen, NJ, and London: The Scarecrow Press, 1979), p. 35.

35 Jill Johnstone, *Lesbian Nation: The Feminist Solution* (New York: Simon and Schuster, 1973).

36 Eve Kosofsky Sedgwick, *Epistemology of the Closet* (Hemel Hempstead: Harvester, 1990), pp. 66–7.

37 Julia Kristeva, *Powers of Horror: An Essay on Abjection*, trans. Leon Roudiez (Hemel Hempstead: Harvester/Wheatsheaf, 1991), pp. 3–4.

38 Paulina Palmer, *Lesbian Gothic: Transgressive Fictions* (London: Cassell, 1999), p. 18.

39 Patricia Duncker, *Sisters and Strangers: An Introduction to Contemporary Feminist Fiction* (Oxford: Blackwell, 1992), p. 182.

40 Teresa de Lauretis, 'Sexual Indifference and Lesbian Representation', in Henry Abelove, Michele Aina Barale and David Halperin (eds), *The Lesbian and Gay Studies Reader* (London: Routledge, 1993), p. 150.

41 Judith Butler, *Bodies that Matter: On the Discursive Limits of Sex* (London: Routledge, 1993), p. 21.

42 Sidney Abbott and Barbara Love, *Sappho was a Right-On Woman* (New York: Stein and Day), 1985, pp. 111, 112.

43 Flora Davis, *Moving the Mountain: The Women's Movement in America Since 1960* (New York and London: Simon and Schuster, 1991), p. 263.

44 Rochelle Gatlin, *American Women Since 1945* (Basingstoke: Macmillan, 1990), pp. 129–30.

45 Georg Lukács (1937), *The Historical Novel*, trans. Hannah and Stanley Mitchell (London: Merlin Press, 1962), p. 58.

46 Ellen Morgan, 'Humanbeing: Form and Focus in the Neo-Feminist Novel', in Cheryl L. Brown and Karen Olson (eds), *Feminist Criticism: Essays on Theory, Poetry and Prose* (Metuchen, NJ, and London: The Scarecrow Press, 1978), pp. 272–8, p. 273.

47 Dorothy Bryant, *Ella Price's Journal* (Philadelphia: Lippincote, 1972).

48 Marge Piercy, *Braided Lives* (New York: Summit, 1982).

49 Anne Tyler, 'Starting Out Submissive', Review of *The Women's Room* by Marilyn French, *New York Times Book Review*, 16 October 1977, pp. 7, 38, p. 38.

6

Science fiction and detective fiction

Now, in imagination, she consulted her mother. It was just as she
expected: her mother thought it an entirely suitable job for a woman.

P.D. James, *An Unsuitable Job for a Woman*

A NUMBER of women writers, including Joanna Russ, Ursula Le Guin
and P.D. James, were instrumental in changing two popular genres
of writing, science fiction and detective fiction, in the 1960s and 1970s,
taking advantage of the opportunities for fantasy, revenge and wish-fulfilment which both genres allowed, to make important interventions which
propelled them into more radical and feminist dimensions.

Traditional detective fiction has been a locus of anxieties about
society which often reflect matters of great importance to women such as
sexual violence or street crime. It is usually the function of the (male)
detective to track down offenders and see that they are brought to justice.
The detective novel has sometimes been criticised by feminists on the
grounds that it is about the restoration of the law. But it should be
remembered that the law is something in which women – who are
usually the victims rather than the perpetuators of violent crime – have
always had a strong investment, and that detective fiction usually tells us
as much about transgression and the breaking of rules which always
precede it as it does about the restoration of the status quo. As Sally Munt
has put it, 'within the fictional world of the crime novel all appearances
are ambiguous, the protagonist is the sole repository for our trust, a lone
stable point surrounded by chaos.'[1] By making that protagonist a woman
– the powers of deduction and reasoning have not traditionally been
thought of as feminine attributes – detective writers have destabilised the
conventions of the genre. In so doing they have sometimes moved the
novel to a more thoughtful, social and psychological analysis of crime and
punishment.

The history of detective fiction differs radically from the history of
science fiction in that women writers have had a very strong influence on
the development of the genre from the beginning. The 'golden age of
detective fiction' is usually dated from the first novel of Agatha Christie,
The Mysterious Affair at Styles (1920), in which Hercule Poirot is intro-

duced, to the last of Dorothy L. Sayers, *Busman's Holiday* (1937) in which Harriet Vane marries Lord Peter Wimsey.[2] Both Sayers and Christie made use of independent, single women as detectives: Miss Jane Marple, the ageing spinster with intrepid curiosity and famed powers of deduction, who is a benign, unthreatening figure of authority in the village of St. Mary Mead, and the younger, more stylish Harriet Vane, who supports herself by writing detective fiction, and has often been taken as the prototype of P.D. James's Cordelia Gray. The two detective novels I shall discuss, James's *An Unsuitable Job for a Woman* (1972) and Valerie Miner's *Murder in the English Department* (1982), are influenced by Christie and Sayers respectively, although James and Miner are both affected by feminist ideas, in ways which the earlier writers were not. But before I return to them, I shall look at the relationship between feminism and science fiction.

Science fiction is a literature largely concerned with ideas and not individuals. Until the 1960s, much of what was published under its imprint appeared irretrievably masculinist and inhospitable to women. But feminism and SF have not always been antithetical, as Mary Shelley showed in *Frankenstein* (1817). It is precisely because it is uniquely receptive to exploratory thinking outside the perimeters of established social conventions, that SF has had a long and distinguished provenance in the hands of nineteenth- and early twentieth-century feminists such as Charlotte Perkins Gilman (*Herland*, 1915), Charlotte Haldane (*Man's World*, 1930), Katharine Burdekin (*Swastika Night*, 1937), who have been interested in its potential to express dystopian and utopian visions of the future. Such work, however, has constituted a tiny fraction of the total output produced under the SF subgenre.

Science fiction came into its heyday between the 1930s and the late 1950s when SF as a profitable commercial genre developed alongside a community of dedicated readers. Unlike their counterparts writing detective fiction, who became household names, the best-known practitioners within the SF community, such as Robert A. Heinlein and John W. Campbell were virtually unknown outside it. Although women, such as C.L. Moore, Leigh Brackett and Marion Zimmer Bradley, were published between the wars, it was often with little developed sense of gender consciousness. They tended to use sexually ambiguous names or to write in collaboration with popular male writers of SF. But what constituted a 'golden age' for some was an intellectual backwater for others. With honourable exceptions, such as Naomi Mitchison's *Memoirs of a Spacewoman* (1962),[3] a large proportion of the published work was, as Roz Kaveney put it, 'viciously militaristic, devoted to intensely stratified models of society, often overtly or at least implicitly racist, and deeply misogynistic and patriarchal'.[4] As late as 1970, Joanna Russ was able to conclude that all too often 'speculation about the innate personality differences between men and women, about family structure, about sex, in short about gender roles, does not exist at all'.[5] In 1975 Ursula Le Guin pointed out that only about one in thirty writers of SF were women.[6]

What was to open up the genre to far greater numbers of feminists, and to other radicals, who saw its potential to question many of the 'natural' assumptions prevalent in society, was the questioning of many of the underlying principles of science which got underway in the 1960s. As Anne Cranny-Francis has put it, 'the objectivity of scientific *knowledge*, its status as some kind of non-ideological mode of inquiry and way of knowing, had been exposed as fallacious from within by theorists of relativity and uncertainty ... Then scientific knowledge itself came under scrutiny as an ideological construct: the way scientific knowledge is compiled as well as the way it is used was analysed as a function of bourgeois ideology, with its characteristic class, race and gender discourses articulated within scientific experimentation and theory.'[7] Furthermore, the 'New Wave' of science fiction writers 'introduced a tone of knowingness and literary sophistication, with an almost obligatory commitment to formal experiment' and also 'reflected (and to some extent anticipated) popular disillusionment with scientific advance'.[8]

The SF imprint introduced in Britain by The Women's Press brought science fiction to many new readers for the first time. But as Lucie Armitt noted in her introduction to a collection of critical essays on women writers, *Where No Man Has Gone Before*, women seeking to contest the deep conservatism of the genre faced an uphill struggle, and were likely to encounter a 'peculiarly defensive hostility aimed at any would-be progressive (a relative term in this context) who might wish to challenge the authority of the old guard'.[9] Ursula Le Guin welcomed the new readership: 'Now more women are reading it, and that's good because a lot of women can't do anything much more than dream and propose alternatives, and science fiction is a great way of doing it.'[10] Writing which reflected a desire to politicise the genre – much of it appearing in The Women's Press series – aroused suspicions that it was really polemic masquerading as literature. Moreover, works by women (and radical men), which were textually experimental or focused on non-traditional themes, tended in critical discussion to be relegated to the category of 'soft' science fiction (considered to be well intentioned but less weighty or 'authentic'), as opposed to the 'hard' science fiction produced by established writers in the field. Much of this continued to reflect the traditional concerns and stock ideas of the genre, such as adventures between men in space, technological development and survivalist fantasies.

At the forefront of the attempt to question the male hegemony were Ursula Le Guin and Joanna Russ, both of whom had been writing science fiction for some years. Russ and Le Guin were known in the SF community, but their outlook was changed in the late 1960s by the women's liberation movement, and, in the case of Russ, by her decision to 'come out' as a lesbian. Another established writer who turned her attention to science fiction for the first time was Marge Piercy, whose *Woman on the Edge of Time* (1976)[11] is as memorable for its chilling depiction of the life of a poor Hispanic woman in contemporary America as for the vision of a feminist utopia to which this dystopian present is radically counterpoised. All three women writers used fiction to redesign sexual identity and to ask whether or not it is it possible for men to live in harmony with women in an imagined future. In the 1970s, looking back over her career so far, Le Guin wrote: 'I don't see how you could be a thinking woman and not be a feminist; but I had never taken a step beyond the ground gained for us by Emmeline Pankhurst and Virginia Woolf.'[12] She wrote *The Left Hand of Darkness* (1969) as part of her own need 'to define and understand the meaning of sexuality and the meaning of gender, in my life and in our society'.[13]

Le Guin and Russ are at opposite poles of the feminist spectrum: Roz Kaveney has designated Le Guin 'the soft cop' of American feminist SF as opposed to Joanna Russ, whom she invites us to think of as the 'hard cop'.[14] Le Guin is a liberal feminist whose chief priority has been a respect for the individual and a desire to create a moral universe governed by humanistic values and principles. Her concerns are largely spiritual and ethical. She believes that human beings have a strong moral sense and remain moral creatures only as long as they are responsive to the experience of others. To neglect the need for balance and for moderation in social and personal relationships, says Le Guin, is to nurture egotism and to invite catastrophe. *The Left Hand of Darkness* is strongly influenced by the author's interest in Taoist ideas, reconciling conflict and expressing the unity of supposed opposites, such as light and darkness and night and day. It is also rich in folktales and legends, and the protagonist's story itself becomes a legend which will be transmitted to generations to come.

In *The Left Hand of Darkness*, Le Guin envisaged an imaginary society whose citizens are all androgynous. In thirteen thousand years of recorded history, the planet Gethen has known no war and, although it has made considerable technological advances, environmental exploitation has been carefully avoided. The inhabitants of Gethen/Winter exist in a quiescent state in which there is no such thing as sexual feeling until, for a few days of each month, they involuntarily go into a state of 'kemmer' and develop the sexual attributes of a woman or a man. They have no way of knowing in advance whether they will be male or female during this fertile period, and the mother of several children may be the father of several others. If conception does not take place, the Gethenians revert to an androgynous state and the cycle begins anew.

The society which Le Guin offers the reader is one in which the importance of sexuality has been minimised. Sexual impulses can no longer determine individual or group behaviour, since for most of the time such impulses do not exist. There is no family unit and no sexual violence. Gethen is matriarchal: descent is calculated through the mother. Bringing up children is the collective responsibility of all adults. In sharp contrast to the practices of all known societies, persons are not treated differently according to their sex. For some readers a world without sexual conflict and biological imperatives represented a denial of adult pleasures, but for others, as Sarah LeFanu has noted, this represented a welcome release: 'The book offers a retreat from conflict, a retreat from the symbolic order and the construction of the subject within language, back to the pre-Oedipal imaginary order, or, as Fredric Jameson puts it, the ancient dream of freedom from sex.'[15]

An envoy from the Ekumen, or The League of Known Worlds, is sent to the planet of Gethen in order to persuade its inhabitants to join the League. Genly Ai is at first disorientated by, and then draws close to, Lord Estraven, a statesman who is depicted as a public figure and who indulges in outdoor adventures, but who is never shown in a domestic context or in the company of children. Together they undertake a long, hazardous journey across the ice, from one extremity of the planet to the other, at the end of which Estraven forfeits his life. The two strive to establish communication and find that Genly Ai's preconceptions about gender roles impede this. There are no women as such in the book and there is only one chapter, 'A Question of Sex' in which the voice of a woman is heard. Le Guin later observed that 'Men were inclined to be satisfied with the book, which allowed them a safe trip into androgyny and back, from a conventionally male viewpoint. But many women wanted it to go further, to dare more, to explore androgyny from a woman's point of view as well as a man's.'[16] Criticisms of the novel from its feminist readers were to centre on its lack of linguistic experimentation and its use of the male third-person pronoun, on the fact that the Gethenians were locked into heterosexuality, and they protested that the Gethenians appear more like men than men/women.

Le Guin is a writer of commanding stature within the world of SF. Since *The Left Hand of Darkness* she has 'moved on to become perhaps the most successful and critically admired writer ever to produce a substantial body of work within the genre limits of science fiction. In terms of critical recognition, only Vonnegut and Bradbury come close.'[17] She is, however, much given to self-reflexiveness, and even to self-reproach in exchanges with her interlocutors. She addressed each of the feminist criticisms of *The Left Hand of Darkness* in turn in her essay 'Is Gender Necessary?' which was written in 1976 and revised in 1987. On the omission of relationships between members of the same sex, for instance, she writes that *'in any kemmer-house homosexual practice would, of course, be possible and acceptable and welcomed – but I never thought to explore this option; and the omission, alas, implies that sexuality is heterosexuality. I regret this very much.'*[18]

She attributes her use of the pronoun 'he' to her dislike of *'invented pronouns'* which over the years she had came to dislike less than *'the so-called generic pronoun he/him/his, which does in fact exclude women from discourse; and was an invention of male grammarians, for until the sixteenth century the English generic singular pronoun was they/them/their, as it still is in English and American colloquial speech.'*[19] Finally, she observes that the choice of pronoun wouldn't matter at all if she had been cleverer at showing the female component of the Gethenian characters in action, and regrets that we are shown Estraven 'almost exclusively in roles that we are culturally conditioned to perceive as "male"'.[20] Le Guin admitted that this is 'a real flaw in the book'.[21]

By contrast, Joanna Russ's *The Female Man*[22] is a powerful study of women's alienation. Although completed in 1971, it was unable to find a publisher 'because the feminist polemic and experimental narration put off editors in the male-dominated world of science fiction publishing'.[23] Like Le Guin's work, it is marked by playfulness and lack of conventional characterisation. Yet it differs in that *The Female Man* is unashamedly didactic and concerned with the interaction of four women who are brought together from different periods of history. Since they are in many respects similar, Russ is at pains to show that the differences between them are not just due to temperament but to the different environments they inhabit. As Anne Cranny-Francis puts it, 'the difference between society represented in the text and the reader's own society becomes the site of a political critique'.[24] Taken together, these four women can be taken to represent the divided consciousness of women, and their varying responses to patriarchal oppression, from passive compliance to violent revolt. Alternatively, they can be seen as stages through which women can pass on the way to discovering psychic wholeness.

Russ has chosen to challenge the 'old guard' of SF directly by using science fiction as a vehicle to test anti-sexist ideas: it is largely in fantasy that women are permitted to perform feats of daring on a grand scale. Janet is a visitor to earth from the utopian planet of Whileaway, where the male species has been extinct for many hundreds of years. Women reproduce in pairs, with one parent as the biological mother while the other parent contributes the ovum. Endowed with phenomenal intelligence, women have evolved collective modes of education and child-raising over the years, and they have abolished oppressive institutions such as monogamy, the nuclear family and gender roles in the workplace. The arrival of Janet, who has no understanding of how people on earth are expected to behave – the point is underscored when she is presented with a bouquet of chrysanthemums which she holds 'upside-down like a baseball bat' (*FM*, p. 59) – is designed to make the life on earth appear startlingly unfamiliar.

The conventionally feminine, old-fashioned Jeannine works as a librarian in New York, at the time of the Depression, which has not been brought to an end because the Second World War has never taken place. The most pliant and acquiescent of the four, twenty-nine-year-old Jeannine is subjected to relentless pressure from her family to get married, which she is unable to withstand because society offers no other prospects for a woman. The choice of a partner appears immaterial. '"Well, who shall I marry?" said Jeannine, trying to make it into a joke as they entered the building. He said, with complete seriousness: "Anybody"' (*FM*, p. 116).

Like her biblical namesake, who smote off the head of Sisera while he lay asleep, Jael is a female warrior and represents a dystopian civilisation, where the constant war between Womanland and Manland offers a stark contrast to the vision of harmony in Whileaway. Driven to fury by her treatment as a sexual object, Jael affronts her peaceable companions by murdering a predatory man. The fourth character, Joanna whose name is the same as the author's, is writing a book from the present, which is recognisable as 1960s America. It is Joanna who admits to being a 'female man' because she has been told so often that the terms 'mankind' and 'he' refer to all of us, and if 'we are all Mankind, it follows to my interested and righteous and right now very bright and beady little eyes, that I too am a Man and not at all a woman' (*FM*, p. 140). *The Female Man* contains countless examples of how women and girls are conditioned for traditional sex roles. Inevitably, it is Joanna's present time which closely resembles our own, and provides the greatest scope for feminist polemic and the deconstruction of patriarchal behaviour: 'She said that instead of conquering Everest, I could conquer the conqueror of Everest and while he had to go climb the mountain, I could stay home in lazy comfort listening to the radio and eating chocolates' (*FM*, p. 65).

Although Russ is an academic who has taught literature in a number of American universities – *How to Suppress Women's Writing* (1983) was written for her students at the University of Washington at Seattle – *The Female Man* is emphatically non-literary. Her work is for a readership which accepts that the concerns of the women's movement are worthy subjects of representation. *The Female Man* inevitably attracted detractors not only hostile to feminist ideas but also opposed to the importation of ideological concerns into the genre. As Sarah LeFanu points out, 'it is only the beliefs and aspirations of feminist writers that are labelled as ideological; the "normal" androcentric attitude of traditional SF is effectively invisible.'[25]

Joanna Russ is a postmodern writer who combines feminist ideas with radical experimentation with language. The visual appearance of the words on the page throughout *The Female Man* is striking. Much of the text is made up of staccato sentences, boldly indented maxims, disjointed utterances and disconcertingly long lists. As Nigel Wheale has put it, 'viewed linguistically a list is an undermotivated statement, paratactically adding pure names, and offering the reader minimum help in subordinating one item to another'. Lists therefore, 'accord with postmodern interests through their repetition and formality which challenge our interpretative skill'.[26] The anger and outrage that propel Russ's narrative are unremitting. Her acerbic wit brings to mind the humour of the early days of the women's movement, when slogans such as 'a woman needs a man like a fish needs a bicycle' or 'it begins when you sink in his arms and ends with your arms in his sink', helped to counteract the notion that all feminists were humourless. If statements such as 'Men succeed. Women get married', which would find no place in a more traditional novel, but are allocated a whole chapter in *The Female Man* (*FM*, p. 126), now seem clichéd it is precisely because they have become so deeply assimilated into our consciousness that they no longer appear to need utterance.

As Patrick Parrinder has argued, science fiction can be regarded as 'a mode of counter-culture, propagating visions and conceptions of altered modes of life which would normally be ridiculed or dismissed by the representatives of orthodoxy'.[27] This is particularly true in the 1960s, and of later utopian fantasies of liberation, such as Marge Piercy's *Woman on the Edge of Time*, which differ radically from earlier 'classic' utopian writings. John Griffiths points out that the latter were 'the wishful systems devised, by men of goodwill, for the constraint of the turbulent individual by means of institutions and laws', and were rigidly hierarchical, 'written from the point of view at the top of the ladder'.[28] By contrast, a feminist utopia such as Piercy's shifts the focus to the powerless and places an emphasis on utopia as a site of personal liberation, rather than hierarchy.

The subtext of *Woman on the Edge of Time* is the abuse of power by the medical and psychiatric authorities: the novel was published at a time when feminists were campaigning against the misuse of electric shock therapy. As Francis Bartkowski has noted, Bellevue, the psychiatric institution to which the central protagonist in *Woman on the Edge of Time* has been consigned against her will, 'has a status in the mind of New Yorkers reminiscent of that once accorded to Bethlehem Hospital in London'.[29]

Connie Ramos is a heavily sedated patient in a state mental hospital, to which she has been committed for assaulting a pimp who has been exploiting her pregnant niece. A Hispanic, working-class single mother, Connie is in her mid-thirties but has aged prematurely. Her sex, race and class account for her unhappy position at the bottom of the social hierarchy in modern America. Her personal history speaks of her powerlessness: an illegal abortion, a hysterectomy performed without her consent, a history of depression, barbiturate and alcohol abuse, sexual harassment, and rape. She reflects that it was 'a crime to be born poor as it was a crime to be born brown' and to have 'caused a new woman to grow' (*WET*, p. 62). Forced to give up her daughter Angelina, for adoption by a white suburban family, into whose beautiful exotic daughter she would grow, Connie reproaches herself for not having loved the child better, but reasons that to love another you must first love yourself. The fact that she holds the State of New York responsible for the death of her black boyfriend, from hepatitis while in prison, is taken as confirmation of her madness.

The three names by which she is known express aspects of her divided persona. There is Consuelo, a Mexican woman who does menial work and suffers in silence, Connie who manages to get two years of a college education, decent jobs from time to time, and has fought the welfare for extra money for her daughter, and Conchita, the woman with a drink problem, who chooses bad men as partners, ends in gaol and hurts the daughter she loves. But one thing singles her out as a survivor who can control her destiny: the telepathic power that connects her to her alter-ego, the androgynous Luciente, and transports her to the revolutionary utopian society of Mattapoisett in New England in the twenty-first century. Here oppressive class, gender and race differences no longer exist.

Woman on the Edge of Time reflects interest in co-operative living, communal childcare, environmentally sustainable development, and Schumacher's idea that 'small is beautiful', all of which were fashionable among British and North American radicals in the 1970s. Mattapoisett is a society whose foundations have been painstakingly laid by all those who have worked collectively to change the ways in which people brought food, raised children, and went to school, people who made new unions, withheld rent, and refused to go to war. It is a green, environmentally aware society without skyscrapers, spaceports, and traffic jams: 'We don't have *big* cities – they didn't work' (*WET*, p. 68). Most of its buildings are small, surrounded by plots of vegetables, heated by solar energy, and constructed from old bricks and other reclaimed materials. In many respects, Mattapoisett reminds Connie of peasant society in Mexico. It is, moreover, a community which has experimented with linguistic change, and has recognised the important connection between language and power structures. Luciente tells Connie that 'We've reformed pronouns' (*WET*, p. 42).

Those to whom the utopian society offers unique hope are the dispossessed, from whose lives all hope has been hitherto missing. As a recipient of the appalling treatment meted out by the richest country in the world to its poorest citizens, Connie experiences simultaneously both the dystopian present and the utopian future to which it is contrasted. As Luciente, whose name means light, explains, 'most we've reached are females, and many of those in mental hospitals and prisons' (*WET*, p. 196). When Connie expresses her sense of powerlessness, 'Who could have less power? I'm a prisoner. A patient. I can't even carry a book of matches or keep my own money' a character observes that 'the powerful don't make revolutions' (*WET*, p. 198).

Sarah LeFanu has noted that the social organisation which underpins the utopian society in *Woman on the Edge of Time* was strongly influenced by the ideas of an early classic of the women's movement, Shulamith Firestone's *The Dialectic of Sex: The Case for Feminist Revolution* (1970). This emphasised the importance of collective childcare and held motherhood in a large measure responsible for women's oppression.[30] Firestone's ideas were criticised at the time of publication for not discriminating sufficiently between women's ability to give birth – a biological fact which many feminists were quick to point out was impossible to change – and the institution of motherhood, which patriarchally organised societies exploited to place women at an economic and social disadvantage to men.

In Mattapoisett, Connie is assimilated into Luciente's large, extended family. She discovers a non-violent, co-operatively run society, in which women have chosen to relinquish their role as mothers and their special bonds with their biological children. Childcare is communal. Both sexes are able to lactate, and reproduction is parthogenetic and assisted by modern technology: 'It was part of women's long revolution.

When we were breaking all the old hierarchies. Finally there was that one thing that we had to give up too, the only power we ever had, in return for no more power for anyone. The original production: the power to give birth. Cause as long as we were biologically enchained, we'd never be equal' (*WET*, p. 105).

But Luciente makes Connie aware that the vision of social harmony which Mattapoisett offers is dependent on the actions of those like her. 'We are only one possible future ... Yours is a crux time. Alternative universes coexist' (*WET*, p. 177). Connie, who has been asked to submit to brain surgery as a condition for her release, extracts her revenge by attempting to poison the medical researchers, using herbicide obtained from her brother's greenhouse. Her hope is that this will save other patients from the same fate as herself. As Rachel Blau Duplessis has pointed out, Connie's is, to say the least, a somewhat risky gesture. This is not only because we know that she has no means of escape, and will inevitably be apprehended, but also because there is nothing to indicate that her plan is politically motivated. It is therefore possible to interpret Connie's violent outburst as confirmation of the medical diagnosis that she is mad.[31]

Woman on the Edge of Time ends in a different register, switching to Connie's 'official history', compiled in the institutions which are shown to have made mistakes about her age and ethnic background, 'Puerto Rican' (*WET*, p. 379), diagnosed her wrongly as schizophrenic, dismissed her as a 'socially maladjusted individual' (*WET*, p. 380), and questioned her truthful version of events – 'claims to have 2 years college?' – while accepting without dispute that of her brother, 'a well dressed man' (*WET*, p. 381). The 'objective' evidence of her case notes, a disturbing catalogue of errors and prejudice on the part of the authorities, compounds our concerns about how Connie has been treated. The final section of the novel compels us to question the definitions of madness, and the right of the medical and psychiatric professions to label, disregard and institutionalise women.

Maureen Reddy has argued that the origins of the contemporary feminist crime novel go back to the Gothic novels of Ann Radcliffe, and her sister writers, who, in turn, greatly influenced the sensation writers of the 1860s, such as Mrs Henry Wood. Both the sensation novel and the Gothic novel were genres dominated by women authors.[32] The first detective novel written by a woman is usually thought to be the bestselling, *The Leavensworth Case* published by an American, Anna Katherine Green in 1879, although there is an earlier contender for the title, Seeley Register's *The Dead Letter* (1866), which was published even before Wilkie Collins's landmark novel in crime fiction, *The Moonstone* (1868). In *Crime on her Mind*, Michelle Slung lists thirty-four women detectives who had made an appearance before 1918, of which over half were at work in the nineteenth century.[33] The deployment of women as detectives in fiction in the early part of the twentieth century, when the number of women employed as police officers or detectives was minuscule, is in itself a challenge to traditional gender precepts. If one discounts the two women who were put in charge of women prisoners in 1883, there were no women attached to the Metropolitan Police Force until 1905.[34] As Patricia Craig and Mary Cadogan have noted, the phrase 'a curious career for a woman' is used disapprovingly by the character Lady Sharples in Austin Lee's *Miss Hogg Flies High* (1958), the implication being 'that violence and depravity ought to be repugnant to the feminine temperament.'[35] In *An Unsuitable Job for a Woman* the 'critical phrase is voiced three times like an incantation until the assumption is reversed'.[36]

Following in the footsteps of the two doyennes of detective fiction, Christie and Sayers, P.D. James also inhabits a middle-class world, albeit different from the comfortable, ordered and stratified one in which they moved. Sayers's politics were Conservative, her religion Anglo-Catholic, and her outlook on life conventional. Agatha Christie also lived in the pleasant, secure, hierarchical world of the English privileged classes. As Jessica Mann reminds us, Christie was 'an Anglican, bridge-playing, garden-loving, family woman ... her experience – so wide in geographical terms – was socially restricted and that of a lifelong conformist'.[37]

In *Forever England*, Alison Light has described Agatha Christie's works as 'ultimately defensive fictions, looking for an insider on whom to blame the apparent uncertainty of social life'. She adds that the 'refusal to look beyond the Home Counties and their inhabitants for her psychic swindlers could surely open up Christie's readers to the unsettling implication that "it is the middle classes who are the murdering classes", and their victims are their own selves'.[38] I would argue that much the same can be said for the novels of P.D. James. Christie's novels are set after the First World War, a time when many of Britain's two million 'surplus' women entered the labour force. In contrast, Miss Marple is an unpaid amateur who, as Marion Shaw and Sabine Vannecker have pointed out in *Reflecting on Miss Marple*, is an 'insider', who is dependent on feminine intuitive skills, and represents the ability of the community to police itself.[39]

In 1986, Cora Kaplan pointed to the inherent limitations of detective fiction in a piece entitled 'An Unsuitable Genre for a Feminist?': 'But if feminism has made space for a new breed of female protagonists in a traditional field of popular fiction can it really affect the politics, sexual and otherwise, of the genre itself?'[40] Similar reservations have since been outlined in a number of critical studies, including Glen Irons (ed.), *Feminism in Women's Detective Fiction*, Kathleen Gregory Klein, *The Woman Detective*, and Sally Munt, *Murder by the Book? Feminism and the Crime Novel*,[41] in which feminists have argued that detective fiction is a highly formulaic and predictable genre, the rules of which have changed surprisingly little over many years. It has been rigidly defined, they argue, by masculinist values, has marginalised women, and reinforced conservative social attitudes, and the reasons why it has proved resistant to feminist change are therefore encoded within the genre itself. But, as Kathleen Gregory Klein has put it, 'a reinterpretation of detective fiction is crucial: abandoning the formula as an unprofitable site for women's stories merely leaves the old imperatives in place.'[42]

P.D. (Phyllis Dorothy) James is perhaps the most successful of contemporary British women detective writers. She is also among the most literate, the most concerned to position her work within the 'classic' traditions of detective fiction, and the most preoccupied with her characters' inner states of mind. Cordelia Gray excited many readers as a prototype of a feminist heroine when she first appeared in *An Unsuitable Job for a Woman*[43] in 1972. At twenty-two years of age, Cordelia Gray is far younger than most professional women detectives in fiction, and inherits the small detective agency in which she works when its owner commits suicide. Like P.D. James herself, who was not allowed to go to university because higher education for women did not feature highly among her father's priorities, Cordelia was educated only to the age of sixteen by her father, who is described as 'an itinerant Marxist poet and an amateur revolutionary' (*UJW*, p. 27), and after her mother's death in childbirth, moved from foster mother to foster mother and from school to school. Her unconventional upbringing, rather than leaving her emotionally vulnerable, appears to have equipped her to deal with insecurity especially well:

> Gradually out of a childhood of deprivation she had evolved a philosophy of compensation. In her imagination she had enjoyed a lifetime of love in one hour with no disappointments and no regrets ... This belief in her mother's love was the one fantasy which she could still not entirely risk losing although its indulgence had become less necessary and less real with each passing year. Now, in imagination, she consulted her mother. It was just as she expected: her mother thought it an entirely suitable job for a woman. (*UJW*, p. 19)

Cordelia Gray is intelligent, resourceful, and able to recite the poetry of Blake despite her lack of formal education. She is able to mix inconspicuously with the intellectual friends of the Cambridge undergraduate student Mark Callender, whose apparent suicide she has been hired to investigate. Cordelia discovers that Mark has been murdered by his father, Sir Ronald Callender, a distinguished microbiologist who will forfeit his money for research if the true identity of Mark's mother is revealed. Mark's biological mother, Miss Leaming, overhears Cordelia confronting Sir Ronald with the evidence of his crime, and extracts her revenge by shooting her son's killer dead. Cordelia has previously been asked, 'What shall Cordelia do, love and be silent' (*UJW*, p. 73). When faced with an ethical dilemma the appropriateness of these remarks becomes evident. She did care if Mark's mother went to prison. Her sympathy for the mother makes her tamper with the evidence and vulnerable to accusations of professional misconduct. In an act of gendered solidarity she co-operates with the murderer to fake Sir Ronald's death to look like a suicide, so that Miss Leaming will not be arrested. She justifies her conduct on the grounds that Callender was a ruthless and despicable murderer who himself deserved to die.

Like the classic detective heroines of the interwar years on whom she is modelled, Cordelia Gray is attracted by the creative, intuitive aspects of her job, and by the opportunity that it gives her to express the curiosity that she feels about others. When Mark Callender's tutor suggests that detection is not a suitable job for a woman, she responds in impeccable spoken English: 'Not at all. Entirely suitable I should have thought, requiring, I imagine, infinite curiosity, infinite pains, and a penchant for interfering with other people' (*UJW*, p. 100). Confronted by Sir Ronald, Cordelia expresses her belief in the importance of love: 'But what is the use of making the world more beautiful if the people who live it can't love one another?' (*UJW*, p. 162). In allowing herself to be governed by her heart, rather than her head, she more closely resembles a heroine of popular romantic fiction than a clinical, detached investigator: 'She believed that Mark Callender had been murdered because she wanted to believe it. She had identified with him, with his solitariness, his self-sufficiency, his alienation from his father, his lonely childhood. She had even – most dangerous presumption of all – come to see herself as his avenger' (*UJW*, p. 87).

Cordelia Gray's attitudes to death are symptomatic of attitudes to fictional violence which were to change radically in the post-war period. As Jessica Mann has observed, 'to Christie and her colleagues the corpse was the spur to curiosity. Even when it is quite vividly described the reader is unlikely to feel horror, shock or disgust. The immediate emotion is intellectual stimulation'.[44] In contrast, James's biographer, Norma Siebenheller points out that 'P.D. James feels strongly that death is a serious matter and should be written about seriously, even within the confines of the mystery novel'.[45] Even at such a young age, Cordelia has come across death several times before but her response to it is no different from any other sensitive person's. Her knowledge of love and sex – the pornographic material with which Mark is discovered does not disconcert her – makes her an up-to-date heroine, remote from her predecessors in the golden age. Dorothy Sayers, for example, was always dismissive of love interest in the detective novel and regarded affairs of the heart as much less interesting than puzzle-solving. Moreover, as Cora Kaplan has noted, a sexually experienced heroine is used 'to reject the notion that it is women's transgressive sexuality that is "the problem" – the trigger of social disturbance and violence'.[46]

P.D. James is the inheritor of the mantle of the 'genteel' classic interwar writers. She finds violence distasteful, and her biographer, Norma Siebenheller has rightly noted that 'her strength is in her civility'.[47] The escapades of Cordelia Gray, trapped down an abandoned well in *An Unsuitable Job for a Woman*, are more akin to those of the nineteenth-century Gothic heroine, at once victim and sleuth, than the 'hard-boiled', gun-toting women detectives in the mean streets of American cities. The setting of the novel, with its timeless descriptions of the beauty of Cambridge – 57 Norwich Street is still a cite of pilgrimage for P.D. James's admirers – is a world away from the late twentieth-century urban pavements where feminist detective heroines of the eighties are at home. *An Unsuitable Job for a Woman* (1972) was published before the Sexual Discrimination Act of 1975, which made all forms of discrimination against women in the workplace illegal, and at a time in which women still had to struggle to establish their right to enter jobs which were dominated by men – Cordelia was originally trained as a typist and not a private detective.

Nicola Nixon has described Cordelia Gray as 'a touchstone of early seventies feminism'.[48] Discussing whether or not James would ever write another Cordelia Gray story, Nixon suggests that 'the question of her potential reappearance was therefore perhaps less an expression of nostalgic fondness for a particular character than an anticipation of what she might have become in the context of specific feminist achievements'.[49] When it did come, the sequel, *The Skull beneath the Skin* (1982), was a disappointment. This was because 'James's clever and independent heroine of the seventies simply did not translate well into the sociopolitical climate of the eighties'.[50] The Cordelia of *The Skull beneath the Skin* is 'refashioned in a manner rather inconsistent with what readers might have anticipated, given her proto-feminist promise in her first incarnation'.[51]

In the character of Cordelia Gray, James grafted elements of the home-grown 'vicarage garden' detective novel with elements of the 'hard-boiled' thriller, in which North American writers often specialised. But innovation went only so far.[52] In the United States, Sue Grafton's Kinsey Millhone, Marcia Muller's Sharon McCone, Sarah Paretsky's V.I. Warshawski, and Susan Steiner's Alex Winter, all revealed that the women's movement could produce tougher, more resilient and more self-sufficient women than the soft-spoken Cordelia Gray. A succession of lesbian investigators, including M.F. Beal's Kat Guerrera, Barbara Wilson's Pam Nilson, and Mary Wings's Emma Victor,[53] foregrounded issues of gender and sexuality, helping to make detective fiction the 'most popular lesbian adventure genre since the earliest publications in 1977, replacing the science fiction or utopian novel as the quintessential lesbian genre'.[54]

The heyday of the new type of feminist detective novel was to be the 1980s, when the successful Pandora Women Crime Writers imprint, and The Women's Press, both made detective fiction widely available to readers in Britain. As Sally Munt has put it, 'in the mid-1980s a smattering of feminist crime novels appeared, and began to proliferate into *the* feminist book to be reading.' Arguing that the great interest in detective fiction during the Thatcher and Reagan years was 'a manifestation of political defeat', Munt attributes the popularity of the genre to the fact that 'political activism had seemingly transmogrified into oppositional cultural production' and that 'feminists of the 1980s spent more time reading than marching'.[55]

For women readers, the pleasures in the text may often lie in the fact that it is permissible for the tyrannical father to be disposed of by proxy or for the misogynist in the English Department to perish at his victim's hands. But Morag Shiach has suggested that feminist detective fiction often disappoints its critics by 'relying on liberal versions of individual agency; by portraying female detectives as amateur, taking on cases only for family and friends rather than seeing themselves fully as players in the public world of crime; by failing to sustain the (fantasy of) autonomy for its female protagonists'.[56]

Valerie Miner was born in New York and attended the universities of London, and Edinburgh. While living in Britain she became involved in feminist writing groups and was part of a circle consisting of Zoe Fairbairns, Sara Maitland, Michèle Roberts and Micheline Wandor which produced and published a collection of short stories, *Tales I Tell my Mother* in 1978, and a sequel, *More Tales I Tell my Mother* in 1988. *Murder in the English Department*[57] makes use of detective fiction to explore the issue of sexual harassment in academia. The novel may be usefully contrasted to Malcolm Bradbury's *The History Man* (1972) in which there is widespread collusion with the sexual exploitation of women students by a teacher in one of the new universities. The protagonist in *Murder in the English Department* is Nan Weaver, a university teacher. Miner chooses to work within a feminist tradition of crime fiction set in academia which goes back to Dorothy Sayers's *Gaudy Night* (1936), a novel which is concerned with the emotional and rational life of the woman intellectual. Amanda Cross's Kate Fansler, who features in *In the Last Analysis* (1964) and *The James Joyce Murders* (1967), is probably the best-known academic sleuth – Amanda Cross is the pseudonym of the feminist literary critic Carolyn Heilbrun. Like Miner herself, Nan is a Lecturer in English at the University of California, Berkeley, a campus that acquired an international reputation as a hotbed of student radicalism in the 1960s and 1970s. A working-class woman from a small town in California, Nan is a childless divorcee who has worked as a school teacher for ten years, and returns to university as a mature student in the 1960s to begin work on a PhD.

> She thought she had come back to the same campus, but the atmosphere had been changed indelibly by Civil Rights, Free Speech, Black Power, Ethnic Studies and the Anti-War Movement. Nan helped to occupy several buildings, got arrested, then acquitted. They were creating – she was helping to create – a counter-culture, a freedom of the highest order. Academic freedom. Political freedom. Sexual freedom. (*MED*, p. 22)

Nan is forced to change the subject of her dissertation from Lawrence to Woolf after her dissertation adviser makes crude sexual advances. Although she has a prestigious job, and her research has been published widely, she is still beset by low self-esteem: She says she 'still didn't feel like a scholar. She felt like a fraud' (*MED*, p. 28). At forty-eight she is still unsettled and her warmest personal relationship is with her young protégée and niece, Lisa. Her lack of self-confidence contrasts with that of her graduate student, Marjorie Adams, who 'looked as if she had been born in a silk blouse and a velvet skirt' (*MED*, p. 4). From the beginning Nan's relationship with Marjory is fraught, because of the younger woman's patrician manner, and antipathy to feminism. Marjorie suggests, with an irony that is not apparent at the time, that the victims of sexual harassment may be partially responsible for what happens to them. She writes about Iris Murdoch, the subject of her thesis, 'as one mind reading another, not as a woman sympathising with another woman' (*MED*, p. 29).

Like many feminists in academia, Nan feels herself torn in different directions: 'The English Department is embarrassed by my conscience.

My friends think I work for a boring, stuffy academy. And my family sees me as some kind of hippy' (*MED*, p. 6). The extent of her political differences with her colleagues become apparent when, to her utmost dismay, the most sexist professor in the department, Murchie, a Milton specialist, visits the class in which Nan discusses Milton's exploitation of his three wives and his daughters. When Murchie is stabbed to death she is arrested as the prime suspect.

Murder in the English Department breaks one important convention of modern detective fiction: Valerie Miner does not provide a detective, thus responding to feminist objections that the detective in fiction is a representative of patriarchal law, whose function in the narrative is always to restore the status quo. As Rosalind Coward and Linda Semple have noted, 'since feminism sees the law as often defending the interests of men and controlling the behaviour of women, there is no comfortable way in which the law can exist in the background as an embodiment of a shared morality'.[58] The novel breaches a second major convention of the genre in that there is no trail of clues to follow and very little suspense because the identity of the murderer is already known. There may, however, be a question mark about Marjorie's guilt in the reader's mind because we know that Nan heard but did not see the fatal act.

Nan knows who committed the crime because she was the only member of staff present in the building on the night of the crime, and overheard Marjorie leaving Murchie's room after a violent disagreement. Like Cordelia Gray, Nan feels an instinctive feminist urge to protect another woman with whom she ostensibly has little in common: 'It didn't make sense to defend Marjorie, yet Nan knew that she was right' (*MED*, p. 128), and she removes Marjorie's incriminating scarf and her fingerprints from the murder weapon. She is saved by a last-minute confession from Marjorie, who admits that she killed Murchie to prevent him raping her. Twenty-two women make depositions alleging they too had received unwanted sexual advances from him. Nan becomes a feminist hero when Judge Marie Wong rules that 'rape is an act of such physical violence that it warrants substantial use of force in self-defence' (MED, p. 166). *Murder in the English Department* ends with Nan driving into the sunset with a woman friend in search of another teaching post. Other teaching jobs 'won't have as much prestige as Berkeley. Chances are they won't have as much sexism' (*MED*, p. 167).

There is nothing inherently radical about particular modes of writing. Much will depend on what discourses are displaced and what discourses are put in their place and to what effect. The substitution of violent, gun-toting male detectives by equally violent, gun-toting, female ones, for example, may create as many problems for feminism as it removes. While both science fiction and detective fiction have had a long history of relegating women and their concerns to the margins, writers like Le Guin, Russ, Piercy, James and Miner, who worked subversively within established conventions during the 1960s and 1970s have proved the usefulness of both genres to those who wish to challenge traditional notions about gender and to express radical and feminist ideas.

NOTES

1 Sally Munt, 'The Investigators: Lesbian Crime Fiction', in Susannah Radstone (ed.), *Sweet Dreams: Sexuality, Gender and Popular Fiction* (London: Lawrence and Wishart, 1988), pp. 91–118, p. 100.

2 For many years the works of Agatha Christie sold more copies than any book except the Bible and Shakespeare.

3 Naomi Mitchison, *Memoirs of a Spacewoman* (London: Victor Gollancz, 1962).

4 Roz Kaveney, 'The Science Fictiveness of Women's Science Fiction', in Helen Carr (ed.), *From My Guy to Sci-Fi* (London; Pandora, 1989), pp. 78–97, p. 78.

5 Quoted Sarah LeFanu, *In the Chinks of the World Machine: Feminism and Science Fiction* (London: The Women's Press, 1988), p. 13.

6 Quoted in Joe de Bolt, 'A Le Guin Biography', in Joe de Bolt (ed.), *Ursula K. Le Guin: Voyager to Inner Lands and to Outer Space* (Port Washington, NY, and London: Kennikat Press, 1979), pp. 13–28, p. 25.

7 Anne Cranny-Francis, *Feminist Fiction: Feminist Uses of Generic Fiction* (Cambridge: Polity Press, 1990), p. 45.

8 Patrick Parrinder, *Science Fiction: Its Criticism and Teaching* (London: Methuen, 1980), p. 17, p. 18.

9 Lucie Armitt (ed.), *Where No Man Has Gone Before: Women and Science Fiction* (London: Routledge, 1991), pp. 2–3.

10 de Bolt, 'A Le Guin Bibliography', p. 25.

11 Marge Piercy, *Woman on the Edge of Time* (New York: Knopf, 1976, and London: The Women's Press, 1979). All quotations are from the latter and are given parenthetically – (*WET*).

12 Ursula K. Le Guin, 'Is Gender Necessary? Redux' (1976/1987), in *Dancing on the Edge of the World: Thoughts on Words, Women, Places* (London: Victor Gollancz, 1989), pp. 7–20, p. 16.

13 Ibid.

14 Kaveney, 'The Science Fictiveness of Women's Science Fiction', p. 88.

15 LeFanu, *In the Chinks of the World Machine*, p. 140.

16 Le Guin, 'Is Gender Necessary? Redux', p. 16.

17 Barry N. Malzberg, 'Circumstance as Policy: The Decade of Ursula K. Le Guin', in *Ursula K. Le Guin: Voyager to Inner Lands and to Outer Space* pp. 5–9, p. 5.

18 'Is Gender Necessary? Redux', p. 14. I have retained the italics as used in the original text.

19 Ibid., p. 15.

20 Ibid.

21 Ibid.

22 Joanna Russ, *The Female Man* (New York: Bantam Books, 1975, and The Women's Press, London, 1985). All references are from The Women's Press edition and are given in the main body of my text.

23 Quoted in Tom Moylan, *Demand the Impossible: Science Fiction and the Utopian*

Imagination (London: Methuen, 1986), p. 57.

24 Cranny-Francis, *Feminist Fiction*, p. 61.

25 Sarah LeFanu, 'Sex, Sub-Atomic Particles and Sociology', in Lucie Armitt (ed.), *Where No Man Has Gone Before: Women and Science Fiction* (London: Routledge, 1991), pp. 178–85, p. 180.

26 Nigel Wheale, *The Postmodern Arts: An Introductory Reader* (London: Routledge, 1995), p. 47.

27 Parrinder, *Science Fiction: Its Criticism and Teaching*, p. 36.

28 John Griffiths, *Three Tomorrows: American, British and Soviet Science Fiction* (London: Macmillan, 1980), p. 98.

29 Frances Bartkowski, *Feminist Utopias* (Lincoln and London: University of Nebraska Press, 1989), p. 62.

30 LeFanu, *In the Chinks of the World Machine*, p. 57.

31 Rachel Blau Duplessis, 'The Feminist Apologues of Lessing, Piercy and Russ', *Frontiers*, 4, Spring 1979, pp. 1–8, p. 4.

32 Maureen Reddy, *Sisters in Crime: Feminism and the Crime Novel* (New York: Frederick Ungar, 1988), p. 7.

33 Michelle Slung, *Crime on her Mind* (New York: Random House/Parthenon Books, 1975).

34 Patricia Craig and Mary Cadogan, *The Lady Investigates: Women Detectives and Spies in Fiction* (London: Victor Gollancz, 1981), pp. 92–3.

35 Ibid., p 223.

36 Ibid., p. 241.

37 Jessica Mann, *Deadlier than the Male: An Investigation into Feminine Crime Writing* (Newton Abbott and London: David and Charles, 1981), pp. 150, 151.

38 Alison Light, *Forever England: Femininity, Literature and Conservatism Between the Wars* (London: Routledge, 1986), p. 97.

39 Marion Shaw and Sabine Vannecker, *Reflecting on Miss Marple* (London: Routledge,1991).

40 Cora Kaplan, 'An Unsuitable Genre for a Feminist?', *Women's Review*, 8, June 1986, pp. 18–19, p. 18

41 Glen Irons (ed.), *Feminism in Women's Detective Fiction* (Toronto: University of Toronto Press, 1995), Kathleen Gregory Klein, *The Woman Detective: Gender and Genre* (Urbana and Chicago: University of Illinois Press), and Sally Munt, *Murder by the Book? Feminism and the Crime Novel* (London: Routledge, 1994).

42 Klein, *The Woman Detective: Gender and Genre*, p. 229.

43 P.D. James, *An Unsuitable Job for a Woman* (London: Faber and Faber, 1972). All references are given parenthetically – (*UJW*).

44 Mann, *Deadlier than the Male*, p. 237.

45 Norma Siebenheller, *P.D. James* (New York: Frederick Ungar, 1981), p. 3.

46 Cora Kaplan, 'An Unsuitable Genre for a Feminist?', pp. 18–19, p. 19.

47 Siebenheller, *P.D. James*, p. 5.

48 Nicola Nixon, 'Gray Areas: P.D. James's Unsuiting of Cordelia', in *Feminism in Women's Detective Fiction*, pp. 29–45. p. 30.

49 Ibid., p. 32.

50 Ibid.

51 Ibid., p. 33.

52 James objected strongly to Cordelia going to bed with Ronald Callender in the television drama based on the book. See Helen Birch, 'P.D. James's Stylish Crime', *Women's Review*, 10, 1986, pp. 6–7, p. 7.

53 See Sue Grafton, *'A' is for Alibi* (New York: Signet, 1984); Marcia Muller, *Games to Keep the Dark Away* (New York: St. Martin's Press, 1984); Sarah Paretsky, *Killing Orders* (New York: William Morrow, 1985); Susan Steiner, *Murder on her*

Mind (New York: Fawcett, 1985); F. M. Beal, *Angel Dance* (New York: Daughters, 1977); Barbara Wilson, *Murder in the Collective* (London: The Women's Press, 1984); Mary Wings, *She Came in a Flash* (London: The Women's Press, 1988).

54 Kathleen Gregory Klein, 'Habeas Corpus: Feminism and Detective Fiction', in *Feminism in Women's Detective Fiction*, pp. 171–89, p. 176.

55 Munt, *Murder by the Book?* p. 27.

56 Morag Shiach, 'Domesticating the Detective', in Maya Slater (ed.), *Women, Voice Men: Gender in European Culture* (Oxford: Intellect Books), 1997, pp. 97–102, p. 97.

57 Valerie Miner, *Murder in the English Department* (London: The Women's Press, 1982). All quotations are given parenthetically – (*MED*).

58 Rosalind Coward and Linda Simple, 'Tracking Down the Past: Women and Detective Fiction', in *From My Guy to Sci-Fi*, pp. 39–57, p. 52.

7

The Commonwealth

I am the pure product of an advanced, industrialised, post-imperialist country in decline.

Angela Carter, 'Notes from the Front Line'[1]

THE POST-WAR PERIOD marked the end of the British Empire and the certainties about Britain's place in the world which had accompanied the Empire from its inception. Two important colonies, Jamaica and India, had received their independence in 1944 and 1947 respectively but the process of decolonisation accelerated rapidly in the late 1950s and the 1960s as many nations, including Cyprus, Ghana, Kenya, Malawi, Nigeria, Uganda and Zambia, acquired their freedom. With Harold Macmillan's 'winds of change' speech in 1957, even the Conservative government of the day bowed to the inevitability of the loss of the colonies. In this chapter I am concerned with three novels by women from the British Commonwealth which deal with the crisis signified by the end of empire: one by an author originally from the Caribbean living in Britain, Jean Rhys's *Wide Sargasso Sea* (1966), one by a Nigerian immigrant, Buchi Emecheta's *Second-Class Citizen* (1974) and one by an English woman living in India, Ruth Prawer Jhabvala's *Heat and Dust* (1976). While each of these texts help to dislodge some of the literary myths of empire, little or no attempt is made within them to envisage different community relationships or alternative forms of societal organisation that might take its place.

In *Second-Class Citizen*, Emecheta, like many of the black British writers who were to follow her, is primarily involved in resistance to British racism which she experienced at first-hand. Both Jhabvala and Rhys were white women with an ambivalent relationship to colonial history, and thus were unable to partake wholeheartedly in any project of post-colonial reconstruction; both were regarded as 'outsiders' within their adoptive communities. Their situation may be understood with reference to what Susan Stanford Friedman has termed 'cultural narratives of relational positionality', i.e. narratives whereby situational identities and entities shift with a changing context dependent always on a point of reference so that 'power and powerlessness, privilege and oppression, move fluidly through the axes of race, ethnicity, gender, class and national origin' and can be understood differently according to the vantage point of their formation and function.[2] In rewriting the place of women in the coloniser's history and interrogating the notion of Englishness, I shall argue that their work opens up a space in which it becomes possible for a more developed post-colonial feminist critique to evolve.

What these three texts reveal is a close relationship between women, dispossession, struggle and resistance to patriarchal authority, which cannot be understood only in relation to gender, race and class – the heroines of *Wide Sargasso Sea* and *Heat and Dust* are white, middle class and privileged – but which places the experiences of women within a context of social injustice and exclusion in Britain, and a history of exploitation of the poor by the rich across the world. The experience of exile and the importance of place and displacement is ubiquitous in *Wide Sargasso Sea, Second-Class Citizen* and *Heat and Dust*. Rhys, Emecheta and Jhabvala devise different strategies to deal with their characters' experiences of dispossession, power and powerlessness. The subjectivities of migrant and marginalised women in each of these three novels are gendered and racialised in relation to ideologies of dominance.

The historical context for Jean Rhys's *Wide Sargasso Sea*, originally to have been called *The Revenant*, which was written over a long period but published in 1966, is the arrival in Britain of the first major influx of immigrants from the Caribbean in the 1950s. Jean Rhys was rediscovered in Britain at about the same time as the race riots in Nottingham and Notting Hill in London. For much of the thirty-year gap between the publication of *Good Morning, Midnight* (1939) and *Wide Sargasso Sea* (1966), Rhys had disappeared from public view. She had only resurfaced when the actress Selma Vaz Dias sought permission to perform her dramatic adaption of *Good Morning, Midnight* on the BBC Third Programme, and wrote an article 'In Search of a Missing Author' in the *Radio Times* on 3 May 1957, to which Rhys had responded. Francis Wyndham, Rhys's critic and admirer, persuaded Diana Athill at André Deutsch to purchase an option on the novel in 1957.

Jean Rhys had left the Caribbean in 1907 as a young woman with many unresolved conflicts of identity. In her unfinished autobiography, *Smile Please*, she remembers the pain of rejection on account of her whiteness ('this was hatred – impersonal, implacable hatred'), and her envy of black people, who appeared to her to have greater freedom than whites.[3] Much of the fiction which she published in the 1920s and 1930s, had been concerned with women as victims; with the lives of insecure, emotionally frail and sexually vulnerable characters. The heroines of the earlier fictions, Julia Martin in *After Leaving Mr McKenzie* (1930), Anna Morgan in *Voyage in the Dark* (1934) and Sasha Jenkins in *Good Morning, Midnight* (1939), work on the margins of respectable society as part-time prostitutes, artists' models and chorus girls. These emotionally damaged, loveless and isolated women eke out a precarious living by trading on their physical attractiveness and are relentlessly exploited by the men who dominate their lives. While some feminist critics have been alienated by the helplessness and passivity of Rhys's heroines, her importance to others has lain in her insights into the difficulties faced by the *femme seule* in a male-dominated society. As Rosalind Miles puts it, 'it is her recurrent, almost obsessive theme, that women are permanent and perpetual victims of masculine society. Not only will they be oppressed by individual male bullies; they are everywhere confronted by institution-alised masculine hostility in the shape of the law, the professions, the police and the bureaucrats of every country'.[4]

Wide Sargasso Sea, a haunting study of sexual marginality and exile, is the only novel which Rhys sets in the West Indies, and in which she draws fully upon her memories and understanding of the Caribbean. As a long-established white immigrant in Britain at the time that her final novel was published, Rhys had experienced some suspicion, rejection and hostility in her adopted country. But she had not known the extremes of racial hatred with which the black newcomers from the Caribbean in the 1950s and 1960s were confronted. Her earlier writings often focused upon the alienation felt by the 'foreign' woman in Europe. *Wide Sargasso Sea* deals with the distorted picture of the Caribbean commonly held in England and with the position of the Creole woman who cannot be accommodated comfortably in either British or Caribbean society. *Wide Sargasso Sea* expresses Rhys's preoccupation with the damage that may be inflicted upon a woman's psyche by a man who is in control of her, as well as the discursive and historical formation of the racialised woman's subjectivity. As Judith Kegan Gardiner observes, in *Wide Sargasso Sea* Rhys replaces 'exoticism with reflection on the exotic'.[5]

The subject matter of *Wide Sargasso Sea*, and the thematics of enslavement and resistance, can be read as a response to the changing racial composition of post-war Britain, brought about by what the Jamaican poet Louise Bennett has described as 'colonisation in reverse'. In 1958 serious racial disturbances had broken out in Nottingham in the Midlands, and in the Notting Hill district of London. In the 1964 General Election, a hitherto unknown Conservative candidate, Peter Griffiths, had won the constituency of Smethwick by campaigning on the slogan, 'if you want a nigger for a neighbour vote Labour'. The Commonwealth Immigrants Act had imposed stringent entry controls on black immigrants to Britain in 1962, and tightened them further in 1966, the year Rhys's book was published.[6]

Although she had not read their work at the time,[7] she knew of the impact on English cultural life of the group of newly arrived Caribbean authors based in London including George Lamming and Samuel Selvon. Like her, they were preoccupied with deracination, exile, loss and alienation, the practical difficulties of combating the racism they found in Britain, and adapting themselves to a different way of life. In the Caribbean this was a period of great social turbulence as Black Power, Rastafarianism and movements for colonial freedom gathered momentum. As her biographer, Carol Angier, has noted, Rhys stayed abreast of developments in Dominica where she was born by means of her friendship with the novelist and politician Phyllis Shand Alfrey. The latter kept her informed of the struggle for independence in Dominica,[8] and sent copies of the *Dominica Star* which Alfrey edited. Dominica remained a British colony until 1967 when it became a self-governing associated state. Full independence with republican status within the British Commonwealth followed in 1978. While Rhys was never actively involved in party politics such political sympathies as she had appear to have been on the left.

As Mary-Lou Emery points out, West Indian writers have discovered that 'identity depends on place even as it questions the identity of the place'.[9] Like the Caribbean migrants who journeyed in hope to the 'motherland' in the 1950s, Antoinette Cosway in *Wide Sargasso Sea* finds the prospect of living in England an antidote for her unhappiness: 'I will be a different person when I live in England and different things will happen to me'[10] (*WSS*, p. 92). Instead, she experiences the reality of disillusionment, hostility and rejection. But Rhys's wronged colonial woman does not suffer passively; Antoinette extracts her revenge by burning down the oppressor's house: 'Now at last I know why I was brought here and what I have to do' (*WSS*, pp. 155–6).

The intertext of *Wide Sargasso Sea* is Charlotte Brontë's *Jane Eyre*. Moreover, *Wide Sargasso Sea* is that rarity in English letters: a work which rewrites an earlier novel but is also a major literary achievement in its own right. In order to understand the full significance of Rhys's re-visioning in *Wide Sargasso Sea*, it is necessary to understand the privileged place which *Jane Eyre* has been accorded by Western feminist literary critics; its unique importance as a text which has inspired generations of women readers through its moving evocation of a young orphan's struggle to find fulfilment in work, love and kinship. But from a post-colonial perspective, the novel can be read somewhat differently. Gayatri Spivak takes *Jane Eyre* as 'an allegory of the general epistemic violence of imperialism, the construction of a self-immolating colonial subject for the glorification of the social mission of the colonizer'. As Spivak has put it, 'In this fictive England, [Bertha/Antoinette] must play out her role, act out the transformation of her "self" into that fictive Other, set fire to the house and kill herself, so that Jane Eyre can become the feminist individualist heroine of British fiction.'[II]

Rhys's linking of Antoinette Cosway in *Wide Sargasso Sea* to Bertha Mason in *Jane Eyre* pinpoints the nineteenth-century novel's narrow and exclusionary notion of Englishness. The characterisation of Charlotte Bronte's novel, in which Edward Rochester is depicted as the hapless victim of a mad wife and a scheming brother-in-law, is reversed. The primary responsibility for the breakdown of the arranged marriage is attributed to the European man, who is the product, and even in his turn the victim, of his own society, rather than to the colonial woman. Thus Rhys provides a powerful challenge to the mainstream English literary tradition and questions the distortions and omissions of race in literary accounts of English national and cultural identity.

In their influential reading of *Jane Eyre* in *The Madwoman in the Attic*, Sandra Gilbert and Susan Gubar have taken the 'bad' character of Bertha Mason to be symptomatic of the 'good' character Jane's repressed anger.[12] In *Wide Sargasso Sea*, Rhys overturns the distinction between the good woman and the bad – with its long history of deployment in the service of patriarchy – by making the hidden plot of the earlier novel central to the later one. *Wide Sargasso Sea* is an impassioned vindication of the mad woman in the attic. Rhys's aim in rewriting the Victorian script is to give Antoinette a voice with which to challenge the dominant discourses of gender, empire and sexuality and to question a patriarchal and historically specific set of ideas about women, marriage and property. Both Bertha Mason and Antoinette Cosway's predicaments have their origins in the literal historical experience of gendered property relations. Once the material reasons for the marriage are made transparent, Antoinette can be perceived as a victim of social and economic exploitation. Her husband is the younger son of a respectable English family, who is forced to marry for a munificent thirty thousand pound dowry in order to avoid the humiliation of being financially beholden to his father. It is he who insists on Antoinette's inferiority, finding her 'a stranger who did not think or feel as I did' (*WSS*, p. 59). In the absence of any legislation safeguarding married women's property he is also able to appropriate all that she owns.

The marriage is disastrous precisely because it is the kind of transaction it is. Yet the novel makes it clear that the unnamed husband is not a bad man, but simply a man whose unhappy fate it is to be caught up in a dehumanised and brutalising system of exchange, in which women and black people are routinely sold and bartered. In such a world it is unwise to hope for love, commitment, or trust because such things depend for their existence on at least a partial innocence of the nature of that world. As Elizabeth Bowen once put it, 'it is not only our fate but our business to lose innocence, and once we have lost that it is futile to attempt a picnic in eden'.[13]

Just as slave-owners routinely renamed the slaves they had purchased, so Antoinette is given the stolidly English name of Bertha ('Bertha is not my name. You are trying to make me into someone else, calling me by another name' *WSS*, p. 121). At the same time as her 'master' voices the pieties of the outsider, who has not sullied his hands with slavery (this is 'not a matter of liking or disliking' but a 'question of justice', *WSS*, p. 121), he continues the sexual exploitation associated with slave-owners, by seducing, and shortly afterwards dispensing with, the services of the young black maid, Amelie. As Antoinette tells him, 'You abused the planters and made up stories about them, but you do the same thing. You send the girl away quicker, and with no money or less money, and that's all the difference' (*WSS*, p. 121). Ironically, what Antoinette resents most is not the pain and humiliation of dependency but her inability to become the dependent woman who captures her husband's heart.

In *The Wretched of the Earth*, Franz Fanon argues that 'in the colonies the economic substructure is also the superstructure. The cause is the consequence; you are rich because you are white, you are white because you are rich.'[14] *Wide Sargasso Sea* begins with the Emancipation Act of 1834. This brings bankruptcy to the white slave-owning population whose loss of income has reduced them to objects of ridicule as 'white niggers' ('Old time white people nothing but white niggers now, and black nigger better than white nigger' (*WSS*, p. 21). The marriage of Antoinette's mother to the entrepreneur, Mr Mason, saves her daughter from the disgrace of destitution. But Mason represents continuity as much as change, and intends to run the estate by exploiting black labour, even after slavery has officially come to an end: 'These new ones have Letter of the Law. Same thing. They got magistrate. They got fine. They got jail house and chain gang. They got tread machine to mash up people's feet. New ones worse than old ones – more cunning, that's all' (*WSS*, pp. 22–3).

Like the black slaves, who were removed from their homes in Africa to work on the plantations in the Caribbean, Antoinette is transported across the Sargasso Sea and separated from her family and all that is familiar to her. Her relationship to the man to whom she is in thrall is analogous to that of slave and master; the difference being that hers is also a psychic enslavement which is a product of her emotional neglect and correspondingly low sense of self-esteem. In *Jane Eyre* Rochester charges his wife with sexual excess, with being both mad and lascivious, in contrast to the temperate, virginal Jane. Madness, lust and evil are constructed as demonic and foreign importation to English soil. Madness, far from being a symptom of his wife's situation, is represented as its cause. In *Wide Sargasso Sea* Antoinette's sexual proclivities are depicted more sympathetically, as signifiers of emotional desperation and of her unrequited search for love.

In *Jane Eyre*, Bertha Mason has no language, and is knowable only through Rochester's description of her. As Rhys puts it, she is 'a lay-figure – repulsive, which does not matter, and not once alive, which does. She's necessary to the plot, but always she shrieks, howls, laughs, horribly, attacks all and sundry – *off stage*'.[15] In *Wide Sargasso Sea*, this marginal and mobile figure is transported from the peripheries of the empire, where she has her own voice, to the metropolitan centre, where she is silenced and becomes an object of shame to be hidden away in the attic. As a white outsider, whose history differed radically from the majority in either her native or adoptive countries, Rhys was singularly well situated to provide an imaginative critique of imperial history and literature. The figure of Antoinette enables her to explore the complex interconnections between the treatment of black people in the former British slave colonies and the oppression and silencing of women in nineteenth-century England. The exploitation of women by men parallels the exploitation of black by white and poor by rich. The conflict of interest between coloniser and colonised is displaced on to the conflict of interest between man and wife.

Once Antoinette's home is in England the separation of the metropolis and the peripheries, on which the foundations of empire and slavery depend, appears problematic. What the burning of her master's house effectively signifies is the refusal of the marginalised woman to be confined as the 'difference' within the hegemonic. Antoinette burns down the mansion in England in which her husband has deprived her of her liberty, just as her black playmate, Tia, has earlier been implicated in the burning of the colonial house in which her family has been exploited by her white masters.

As Nancy R. Harrison has put it, 'Rhys's writings are only "marginal" in the sense of constituting a powerful evocation of their heroine's, or the writer's, marginality'.[16] Like many of Rhys's heroines, Antoinette is narcissistic, masochistic and insecure. Her Martinique-born mother has been hurt by the women in Jamaica who would not accept her. Antoinette herself has been emotionally damaged by the absence of her mother's love. Moreover, her feelings of inferiority and powerlessness are compounded by her contact with both her English husband ('Long, sad, dark alien eyes. Creole of pure English descent she may be, but they are not English or European either', *WSS*, p. 56) and the white residents of the island: 'They say when trouble comes close ranks, and so the white people did. But we were not in their ranks' (*WSS*, p. 15). According to Antonio Gramsci, 'each individual is the synthesis not only of existing relations but of the history of these relations. He [sic] is the precis of the past.'[17] Antoinette's sense of self-identity is fragile and her subjectivity is as confused and troubled as the legacy of her slave-owning past: 'So between you I often wonder who I am and where is my country and where do I belong and why was I ever born at all' (*WSS*, p. 85).

In an excellent recent study of Jean Rhys, Helen Carr has argued that Rhys's primary loyalty was not to her sex 'but to the group with which she identifies, in her case the disempowered and dispossessed, which are neither so homogeneous nor so easily identified as a group held together by race, nationality, or even class.'[18] In *Smile Please*, Rhys recollects longing for the lack of restrictions that black people enjoyed, and that she 'prayed so ardently to be black, and would run to the looking-glass in the morning to see if the miracle had happened'.[19] In *Wide Sargasso Sea* the black servant, Christophine, epitomises the freedom which Antoinette lacks. Her three children were fathered by three different men and she has never been constrained by marriage, nor ever given her money to 'no worthless man' (*WSS*, p. 91). As Antoinette runs from a burning planta-tion house, she runs towards Tia: 'We had eaten the same food, slept side by side, bathed in the same river. As I ran, I thought, I will live with Tia and I will be like her' (*WSS*, p. 38). But it is Tia who robs the ingenuous Antoinette of her pennies and her good dress, and who, in a final act of betrayal, throws the stone that injures her former friend. What Tia's actions demonstrate is how loyalties of race override those of gender. In Benita Parry's words, the black woman here returns 'the look of surveil-lance as the displacing gaze of the disciplined' in order to 'menace the colonial authority'.[20]

As Veronica Marie Gregg points out, 'when Rhys invokes her West Indian identity, she assumes the function of historiographer' and she 'challenges History (as European discourse) and posits history as that which is secreted within her experience, memory and imagination', resisting 'the cannibalizing of West Indian history by the dominant European narratives, while producing the Creole's version of that history'.[21] The memory of slavery casts a long shadow throughout this novel. It is not Antoinette's present but her ancestry which make her an object of hatred to the black people who surround her. Try as she might, Antoinette cannot escape the historical determinants of otherness and she is haunted by the dark figure of Daniel Cosway claiming to be her illegitimate half-brother. Cosway embodies the fury of the dispossessed, while the marble tablets in church proclaim that the white masters were 'All benevolent. All slave-owners. All resting in peace' (*WSS*, p. 64). It is only because Antoinette is the daughter of slave-owners that she is separated from Tia, to whom she would otherwise have been close, by the history of racial exploitation in which she, as a white Caribbean Creole woman, like it or not, is heavily implicated.

The subjectivities in *Wide Sargasso Sea* are not only gendered but racialised through the historical and discursive processes, whereby the white self in the Caribbean is constituted in relation to the black 'other', represented in the novel by Tia, Daniel and Christophine. While she is able to discern and resist the ideological character of colonialist discourse, Rhys's history and experience as a white woman imposed limitations on what she was able to write and her participation in any post-colonial project. Because 'she was a colonial in terms of her history ... she was ill placed to join in one major endeavour of postcolonial literature, the creation of a counter-history, a counter-identity, an alternative "imagined community", to free the colonized from a mimicked colonial identity and from their cribbed confinement within the colonizers' history.'[22]

A rather different perspective was provided in the mid-1960s by the critic and novelist Sylvia Wynter whose somewhat clumsily entitled article, 'We Must Learn to Sit Down Together and Talk about a Little Culture: Reflections on West Indian Writing and Criticism', was first published in the *Jamaica Journal* in 1968. Wynter took issue with male critics who had a vested interest in the 'brilliant myth of Europe as the super culture which embraces all other cultures, and obliterates all it absorbs'.[23] This was followed by 'Creole Criticism: A Critique' (1973) in which she argued that it is only by 'drawing from, by feeding from [the peasant culture] that a truly national literature could begin'.[24] *Wide Sargasso Sea*, with its focus on the privileged strata of society and disdain for practices such as obeah (a form of voodoo) may be usefully contrasted to Wynter's only novel, *The Hills of Hebron* (1966).[25] This is steeped in West Indian folk culture and references to the idioms of black people and the spirit world. The working-class women in it, far from being victimised, are the mainstay of the community, providing sustenance and support for each other and their men.

Buchi Emecheta's *Second-Class Citizen* provides a chilling account of the experiences of the first generation of Commonwealth immigrants to

Britain. This forms a sharp contrast to the fictional accounts of immigration to London in novels by black writers such as Sam Selvon's *The Lonely Londoners* (1953), from which women's perspectives are largely absent. Emecheta's first book, *In the Ditch* (1972),[26] had depicted Adah Obi's struggle to survive as a single mother on state benefits. *Second-Class Citizen* (1974), an immediate bestseller, was published by the small firm of Allison and Busby which was looking for new authors, after seven other publishers in London had turned it down.[27]

Emecheta immigrated to London in 1962 to fulfil her childhood ambition of living in the 'mother country'. Like 'many Nigerians, who came into contact with missionaries or British officials, she thought on the basis of that experience, that all whites were pure of heart and pleasant in character'.[28] But she was soon to be disappointed. Wole Soyinka's poem 'The Telephone Conversation' expressed the shock of one unsuspecting black person encountering the racial discrimination in the housing market which was widespread at the time and which Emecheta was to discover when looking for accommodation herself. In her semi-autobiographical novel, Adah Obi leaves a good job in Lagos to join her feckless husband in Britain, and is quickly stripped of her illusions about British society. Francis Obi explains that racism is endemic to British society: in Lagos 'you may be earning a million pounds a day; you may have hundreds of servants; you may be living like an elite; but the day you land in England, you are a second-class citizen' (*SCC*, pp. 42–3).

Second-Class Citizen is a novel of social protest bereft of the touches of humour that make Selvon's accounts of black immigrants in London palatable to a British readership. Adah has to contend with poor job opportunities, bad housing, unwanted pregnancies and blatant racial prejudice. Like Bessie Head, Emecheta is an outspoken critic of African patriarchy and, like Dikeledi, the heroine of the title story in *The Collector of Treasures* (1977), Adah is a resourceful single parent whose patience is stretched to breaking point by the sexist and misogynistic attitudes of her husband. As a naive young wife, 'she still yearned to be loved, to feel really married, to be cared for' (*SCC*, p. 61) but her husband, an eternal student, sits idly at home while Adah takes on the responsibilities of breadwinner for their five children.

Second-Class Citizen recounts Adah's determination to survive by refusing second-class status and earning her own living as a librarian and a writer. Adah leaves Francis when he sets fire to her first novel because he believes African women to be incapable of writing good fiction. Both Christianity and traditional African culture appear to Adah to conspire to set limitations on women's creative aspirations – in Lagos she had been warned by a teacher at her Methodist school against the sin of hubris in wanting to become an author.

Alice Walker ascribes Buchi Emecheta's literary achievement to the experience of maternity, she is a writer 'because of and not in spite of' her children.[29] *Second-Class Citizen* is a study of militant motherhood. The novel is set apart from many other slum novels set in London by its feminist inflection, by the race of its central character, which differentiates Adah from the women of the white working-class, and by her combative perspective on her own situation as an unsupported mother. To provide security for herself and her children as she is resolved to do, Adah must overcome gender, race and class-based oppression. To borrow Zora Neal Hurston's well-known phrase, the black woman carries a hugely disproportionate share of women's burdens: she is the 'mule of the world'. Although the idealised figure of the mother has featured largely in the rhetoric of African nationalist struggles, the double oppression of women, by the colonial power and by the men in their own societies, has seldom been recognised. As Elleke Boehmer puts it, 'Mother Africa may have been declared free, but the mothers of Africa remained manifestly oppressed.'[30]

Adah Obi's aspirations in *Second-Class Citizen* are largely confined to improving her own situation. She voices few objections to domesticity *per se*, but only to the conditions that prevent the fulfilment of maternal responsibilities from being pleasurable and rewarding for women. Moreover, Adah's method of overcoming her problems (reliance on her inner resources) diverts the reader's attention away from the structural problems of inequality. Notwithstanding the extraordinary reserves of courage, tenacity and determination that Emecheta's central character possesses, institutionalised sexism and racism cannot be overcome by individual enterprise alone: 'It seems Emecheta wants to dismantle patriarchy only to make room for her model female rather than to expose its self-privileging arrangements.'[31]

In *Second-Class Citizen*, Emecheta is not overly concerned with either the struggle for women's liberation, which was occupying many white middle-class women in London at the time the book was published, or with the important role that women had to play in the creation of the new African societies which Chinua Achebe was to explore sensitively many years later in *Anthills of the Savannah* (1994). In *The Bride Price* (1976), Emecheta does turn to African myths and traditions as part of an attempt to deconstruct essentialist notions of womanhood in African communities. Despite Emecheta's sociological interests – she was later to study for a degree at the University of London and to obtain work as a sociologist – the novel makes no attempt to be a study of the experiences of the wider

Nigerian community in London. There is, for example, no mention of the Commmonwealth Relations Act of 1962, which became law in the same year as the events depicted in the novel.

Second-Class Citizen resonates with trenchant and uncompromising anger about the traditions which have made African men incapable of regarding women as their equals and their failure to respond to women's emotional needs: 'To him a woman was a second-class-human, to be slept with at any time, even during the day, and, if she refused, to have sense beaten into her until she gave in; to be ordered out of bed after he had done with her; to make sure she washed his clothes and got his meals ready at the right time' (*SCC*, p. 181). There is particularly strong resentment of the fact that Francis regards the birth of a baby daughter as insignificant compared to the birth of a son, and of his neglect of Adah in hospital.

Most of the Nigerian women of Emecheta's acquaintance in London worked in menial jobs and had only received an elementary education. But the heroine in *Second-Class Citizen* is determined to fight her way out of poverty and to acquire middle-class status and all the comforts that go with it. Tuzyline Allan pinpoints the central contradiction of the book, 'if it has been textually predetermined that Adah should both beat and join the system, one wonders why Emecheta should rail against that system, except perhaps to underscore her heroine's preternatural strength of will?'[32] Lloyd Brown also regards Emecheta's aspirations to better herself as symptomatic of her deracination and her unquestioning acceptance of Western individualistic values, as opposed to the collective values prevalent in her own Ibo culture. However, he concedes that by 'linking the disadvantages of women with the handicaps of poverty, Emecheta places the experiences of her women within a broad context of social injustices in Great Britain, the West as a whole and the Third World.'[33]

Ruth Prawer Jhabvala shares the archetypal modern condition of deracination, hybridity, exile, marginality, homelessness and deracination with Jean Rhys and Buchi Emecheta. She was born as Ruth Prawer in Cologne in 1927 and fled as a child with her family to England in 1938 to escape Hitler's persecution of the Jews. Like Rhys, she watched the anti-Semitism that swept through continental Europe and the struggle against fascism in the Second World War from the refuge of her adoptive country, becoming a naturalised British citizen in 1948, and marrying the Indian architect, Cyril Jhabvala, with whom she moved to India from London in 1951.

The British Empire in India appears in several novels written in the 1970s which are concerned with history and national identity. *The Raj Quartet* (1966–75) and *The Seige of Krishnapur* (1973) followed earlier fiction about the British in India such as *Black Narcissus* (1939) and *Bowhani Junction* (1954), all of which were concerned with the British rather than the Indian experience of the Raj. White women characters frequently represent the liberal conscience, expressing qualms about how Indians are treated, while stopping short of any searching criticisms of the British presence. Such Anglo-Indian novels often appear as critiques of the shortcomings of the imperial enterprise rather than its justification. Women who break ranks by having sexual relationships with Indian men are held to be partially responsible for the breakdown of the imperial project.

Jhabvala had been writing fiction with Indian or Anglo-Indian characters to the fore long before *Heat and Dust*. *Heat and Dust* offers a fictional perspective on the rediscovery of India in the 1960s, by a new generation of Europeans, who were dissatisfied with the materialistic values of the West and flocked to India in their thousands. They were often influenced by the 'counter-culture' of Europe and the United States, which had borrowed its fashionable flowing robes, sitars, incense, Afghan jackets, ashrams and communal living from the East. As in *Esmond in India* (1958), this is symptomatic of economic imperialism. The export of Indian arts and crafts to the West was a highly lucrative business at the time. In *Heat and Dust* a couple of young English designers are in India to manufacture clothes for a London boutique. Their partner, the heir to the Nawab, plots with them to get the family art treasures out of the country. *Heat and Dust* illustrates that the reality behind the spiritual pilgrimages to India of the 1960s and 1970s was very different from the illusion. As Richard Cronin has pointed out, 'Young Westerners came to India in flight from the burden of individuality, of self-consciousness, that the West imposes on its citizens as the condition of the industrial society that secures their prosperity. They came out of nostalgia for a life "without personal characteristics", but they did not come to a country where such a life existed.'[34]

Heat and Dust speaks eloquently of the isolation of the European woman, whose flouting of class and racial barriers separates her from other women of her class, culture and background. Jhabvala's novel is carefully situated within Anglo-Indian traditions of writing, staying within the consciousness of white European characters. Both the year in which the narrative takes place, 1923, and the social milieu of the novel, which is the expatriate British community, are the same as in E.M. Forster's *A Passage to India*. *Heat and Dust* is concerned with sexual encounters which break racial taboos, a topic of little interest to Indian writers such as Raja Rao or R.K. Narayan.

In Heat and Dust, the narratives of two English women intersect. In the first, Olivia, the wife of an officer in the Indian Civil Service, abandons her husband for a Nawab by whom she has become pregnant. After an abortion she decides to live alone in a remote village in the Himalayas. Like many of the European and American women who cohabited with Indian rulers early in the century, Olivia is the object of hostility from the Nawab's family, and from the British who despise her, and she is abused by her lover who uses her unscrupulously in power games against the Raj. But as one character is made to comment, 'to have done what she did – and then to have stuck to it all her life – she couldn't have remained the same person she had been'.[35] If the British authority in India in the 1920s has been undermined by Olivia's wilfulness, the novel suggests that this is no bad thing.

Heat and Dust explores the possibility of friendship between different races, but differs from *A Passage to India* in having two women as its central characters. It articulates the connections between the oppression of the Indian peoples under imperialism and the oppression of women within Anglo-Indian society. When she wrote *Heat and Dust* the time that Jhabvala had spent in India was the equivalent of the time she had spent in Germany and England combined. Like each of her two central characters, Jhabvala's own ambivalent relationship to India is mediated through the key man in her life. In *Heat and Dust*, she places European values into narrative tension with the values of the Indians whom the Europeans encounter. She is more concerned with the states of mind of her European characters than with the representation of a country which she has come to believe to be unrepresentable. In 1975, shortly after writing the novel, she left India and took up residence in New York.[36]

Olivia's husband had married a second time and in the modern narrative his grandaughter by that marriage has come to India to recon-struct her great aunt's story of her experiences in India. Intimations of this story are contained in a set of letters which she has inherited. Like her early twentieth-century predecessor, the grandaughter is resolutely independent, a *femme errante*, whose determination to explore India on her own is in sharp contrast to the timid attitudes of the traditional Indian women who are confined to the home. Her choice of sexual partner is anathema within both the Anglo-Indian and Indian communities. When she discovers that she is pregnant, by the poor, married Indian govern-ment official in whose house she has lodged, she retreats to the Himalayas to have her baby. Like Olivia, the unnamed narrator decides to stay on in India.

This modern young woman differs from both the English chorus girl, who has no connections at all to India, and the English missionary,

whose Christian faith reconciles her to dying in exile, in that her reasons
for staying in India are neither mercenary nor idealistic. She stays
because she wishes to make a commitment to the country and cannot do
so by living exclusively with Europeans, or by travelling across the country
as a 'spiritual tourist'. To put down roots, she has to live with Indians, and
it is her baby, whose father is Indian, who will give her a lasting stake in
Indian society. As Laurie Sucher puts it, her exploration of the politics of
passion 'confirms and illustrates the premise of feminism, the societal
derogation of women. It even confirms feminism's imperative: that
women resist that social and psychological derogation'.[37]

Jhabvala is best known for her long association with the 'heritage'
cinema of Merchant–Ivory and her adaption of the work of Forster and
James for the screen. Although she has often been criticised for her
Eurocentrism, for writing which appeals most to the nostalgia of an
English readership ('proper liberal principle jostles uneasily against a
damp-eyed nostalgia for departed glory'),[38] she has no personal investment in empire. Quite the opposite. Her father-in law was a trade
unionist who had been imprisoned by the British. Her Jewish history also
sets her apart.

Like Rhys, her history as an outsider disqualifies her from full participation in any post-colonial literary enterprise: 'I write differently from
Indian writers, because my birth, background, ancestry, and traditions
are different.'[39] In an essay entitled 'Myself in India' she explains that she
was 'not attracted – or used not to be attracted – to the things that usually
bring people to India'. She chose to live there only because her 'strongest
human ties' (her husband and her three daughters) are Indian.[40] Hence,
the knowing irony with which she depicts European characters like
Chidananda in *Heat and Dust*, who apes Indian ways of seeing, dressing
and behaving – the transformation is short-lived, and his reversion to
European dress is accompanied by a vehement dislike of all things
Indian.

Jhabvala, who belongs to an extended Indian family and speaks
Hindi, also appears to be unsympathetic to Hinduism, and to other
Eastern philosophies. She retains a Western, ameliorative belief in
progress, the perfectibility of human beings, and, unlike many Indians
who have become habituated to them, sees the eradication of ignorance
and disease as a matter of the utmost urgency. She writes that the 'most
salient thing about India is that it is very poor and very backward',[41] and
cautions those like herself who 'may praise Indian democracy, go into
raptures over Indian music, admire Indian intellectuals' not to 'lose sight
of the fact that a very great number of Indians never get enough to eat.
Literally that: from birth to death they never for one day cease to suffer

from hunger.'[42] The relationship between the modern narrator and her Indian lover in *Heat and Dust* is circumscribed by awareness of economic disparities; his poverty and her wealth.

Sharp division of opinion marked the reception of *Heat and Dust* in England, where it won the prestigious Booker Prize in 1975, and India, where the novel was seen as anti-Indian. Jhabvala was criticised for catering to the prejudice about India (epitomised in her title) and for her preoccupation with the country as dirty, dusty and disease-ridden. The critic Vasant Shahane objects to her 'constant sneering at the expense of India, as depicted in the attitudes, postures and gestures of the characters in *Heat and Dust*'.[43] Like Rhys, Jhabvala was brought up in a middle-class family whose codes of good behaviour she transgressed. As a Jewish woman married to a non-Jew, and as a white woman married to an Indian, she was doubly marginalised, exciting the suspicion that an informed insider always arouses. As Salman Rushdie has put it, 'looked at from the point of view that literature must be nationally connected and even committed, it becomes simply impossible to understand the cast of mind and vision of a rootless intellect like Jhabvala's. In Europe, of course, there are enough instances of uprooted, wandering writers and even peoples to make Jhabvala's work readily comprehensible; but by the rules of the Commonwealth ghetto, she was beyond the pale.'[44]

Jhabvala focuses on the phenomenon of the woman traveller. The connection she makes is 'between travelling or wandering, on the one hand, and the Gothic sense of sensuality as dark, intense, even hysterical', on the other.[45] Her marginalised, itinerant women are exiled from their homes and cast adrift from the men who could bestow on them sexual respectability and economic security. This is a fate which they share with the exiled and suffering heroines of both Emecheta and Rhys. But Emecheta and Jhabvala depict strong, late twentieth-century women whereas Rhys shows a nineteenth-century woman without their options.

NOTES

1 Angela Carter, 'Notes From the Front Line', in Micheline Wandor (ed.), *Gender and Writing* (London: Pandora, 1985), pp. 69–77, p. 73.
2 Susan Stanford Friedman, 'Beyond White and Other: Relationality and Narratives of Race in Feminist Discourse', *Signs: Journal of Women in Culture and Society*, 2(1), 1995, pp. 1–49, p. 16, p. 19.
3 Jean Rhys, *Smile Please: An Unfinished Autobiography* (London: André Deutsch, 1979), p. 49, p. 51.
4 Rosalind Miles, *The Female Form: Women Writers and the Conquest of the Novel* (London: Routledge and Kegan Paul, 1987), pp. 134–5.
5 Judith Kegan Gardiner, *Rhys, Stead, Lessing and the Politics of Empathy* (Bloomington: Indiana University Press, 1989), p. 36.

6   This legislation was not designed to restrict immigration as such but only black immigration. The Irish, who were the largest immigrant group entering Britain, at about 60,000–70,000 a year, were exempt from controls and there was no upper restriction placed on the number of aliens allowed into the country.

7   Francis Wyndham and Diana Melly (eds), *The Letters of Jean Rhys* (London: André Deutsch, 1984), p. 197.

8   Carol Angier, *Jean Rhys: Life and Work* (London: André Deutsch, 1990), p. 369.

9   Mary-Lou Emery, *Jean Rhys at 'World's End': Novels of Colonial and Sexual Exile* (Austin: University of Texas Press, 1990), p. 14.

10 Jean Rhys, *Wide Sargasso Sea* (London: André Deutsch, 1966). All quotations are from the Penguin edition, 1968 and given parenthetically – (*WSS*).

11 Gayatri Spivak, 'Three Women's Texts and a Critique of Imperialism', *Critical Inquiry*, 12 (Autumn 1985), p. 244.

12 Susan Gilbert and Sandra Gubar, *The Madwoman in the Attic: The Woman Writer and the Nineteenth-Century Literary Imagination* (New Haven: Yale University Press, 1979), pp. 311–66.

13 Elizabeth Bowen, *Collected Impressions* (London: Longmans Green, 1950), p. 265.

14 Franz Fanon, *The Wretched of the Earth* (Harmondsworth: Penguin, 1961), p. 40.

15 *The Letters*, letter to Selma Vaz Dias, 9 April 1958, p. 156.

16 Nancy R. Harrison, *Jean Rhys and the Novel as Women's Text* (Chapel Hill: University of North Carolina Press, 1988), p. 57.

17 Cited in Jonathan Rutherford (ed.), *Identity, Community, Culture, Difference* (London: Lawrence and Wishart, 1990), p. 20.

18 Helen Carr, *Jean Rhys* (London: Northcote House, 1996), p. 18.

19 Rhys, *Smile Please*, p. 42.

20 Benita Parry, 'Problems in Current Theories of Colonial Discourse', *Oxford Literary Review*, 9, 1988, pp. 27–58, p. 41.

21 Veronica Marie Gregg, *Jean Rhys's Historical Imagination: Reading and Writing the Creole* (Chapel Hill: University of North Carolina Press, 1995), p. 73, p. 72.

22 Carr, *Jean Rhys*, p. 18.

23 Sylvia Wynter, 'We Must Learn to Sit Down Together and Talk about a Little Culture: Reflections on West Indian Writing and Criticism', Part 1 *Jamaica Journal* 2, December 1968, pp. 23–32; Part 2, *Jamaica Journal* 3, March 1969; pp. 27–42, Part 2, p. 31.

24 Sylvia Wynter, 'Creole Criticism: A Critique', *New World Quarterly*, 5, 1973, pp. 12–136, p. 20.

25 Sylvia Wynter, *The Hills of Hebron* (London: Jonathan Cape, 1972).

26 Buchi Emecheta, *In the Ditch* (London: Barrie and Jenkins, 1972) and *Second-Class Citizen* (London: Allison and Busby, 1974). All references are to this edition and are given parenthetically – (*SCC*).

27 Emecheta's country of birth, Nigeria, became an independent member of the British Commonwealth in 1962. The number of Nigerians admitted to the United Kingdom between 1962 and 1967 was relatively small. The total of entry certificates issued was 3,573 of which the largest number 1,727 were, like Emecheta's husband, admitted as students and 990 who, like Emecheta herself, were admitted as dependants. See Sheila Patterson, *Immigration and Race Relations in Britain 1960–67* (London and Oxford: Oxford University Press, 1969).

28 Buchi Emecheta, 'It's Me Who's Changed', *Connexion: An International Women's Quarterly*, 4 (Spring, 1982), pp. 4–5.

29 Alice Walker, 'A Writer Because of Not in Spite of, Her Children', *In Search of Our Mothers' Gardens: Womanist Prose* (New York: Harcourt Brace Jovanovich, 1983), pp. 66–70.

30 Elleke Boehmer, 'Stories of Women and Mothers: Gender and Nationalism in the

Early Fiction of Flora Napwa', in Susheila Nasta (ed.), *Motherlands: Black Women's Writing from Africa, The Caribbean and South Africa* (London: The Women's Press, 1991), p. 7.

31 Tuzyline Jita Allan, *Womanist and Feminist Aesthetics: A Comparative Review* (Athens: Ohio University Press, 1995), p. 99.

32 Ibid., p. 100.

33 Lloyd Brown, *Women Writers in Black Africa* (London: Greenwood Press, 1981), p. 39.

34 Richard Cronin, *Imagining India* (Basingstoke: Macmillan, 1989), p. 96.

35 Ruth Prawer Jhabvala, *Heat and Dust* (London: John Murray, 1975), p. 197.

36 Ruth Prawer Jhabvala, 'Myself in India', in *An Experience of India* (London: John Murray, 1971), p. 2.

37 Laurie Sucher, *The Fiction of Ruth Prawer Jhabvala: The Politics of Passion* (Basingstoke: Macmillan, 1989), p. 9.

38 Cronin, *Imagining India*, p. 37.

39 Ramlal Agarwal, 'An Interview with Ruth Prawer Jhabvala', *Quest*, 91, 1974, p. 36.

40 'Myself in India', p. 2.

41 Ibid.

42 Ibid.

43 Vasant A. Shahane, 'Jhabvala's *Heat and Dust*: A Cross-Cultural Encounter', in M.K. Naik (ed.), *Aspects of Indian Writing in English* (Madras: Macmillan, 1969), p. 230.

44 Salman Rushdie, *Imaginary Homelands* (London: Granta Books, 1991), p. 68.

45 Sucher, *The Fiction of Ruth Prawer Jhabvala*, p. 12.

8

To *The Color Purple*

I'm pore, I'm black, I may be ugly and can't cook, a voice say to everything listening. But I'm here.
Amen, say Shug. Amen, amen.

Alice Walker, The Color Purple

I NOW WANT to discuss Toni Morrison's *The Bluest Eye* (1970) and
Alice Walker's *The Color Purple* (1982) in relation to the changes in
American society brought about by the civil rights movement and its
aftermath. In 1966 a young Alice Walker left her job as a caseworker with
the Welfare Department of New York City and went to offer her services
to the Mississippi voter registration programme. It was here that she met
her first husband, Melvyn Leventhal, a Jewish civil rights lawyer with
whom she had her daughter, Rebecca. Walker's novels are deeply
embedded in the 'historically oppressed (racially), economically poor,
rural black Southern community'.[1] In the state of Georgia in which she
grew up, it was illegal for a black person to enter a public restaurant,
library or swimming pool. Her marriage to a white man was also illegal
in the state of Mississippi, where she lived from 1967–74, and in which
her husband worked to desegregate Mississippi's schools. Walker herself
was employed in a variety of desegregationist projects such as registering
voters to teaching in two local black colleges and writing history texts for
the head start program.[2] *Meridian* (1976), which is set at the time of the
civil rights movement, has been discussed by Maria Lauret. Lauret points
out that in Meridian's story, Walker 'charts the historical conditions
(political, social and cultural) that made her own discursive practice as a
Black woman possible. In other words, the story of Meridian, who saves
herself from suicide by becoming politically involved, entails the story of
how Civil Rights engendered Black self-affirmation and later the
Women's Movement'[3] Walker's fiction has been instrumental in helping
to shift the attention of students of the history of the civil rights
movement away from its male leaders such as Martin Luther King,
Junior, to the part played by its female activists including Flo Kennedy,
Fanny Lou Hamer and Rosa Parkes. *Meridian* is a historicised and explic-
itly political text, but here I want to concern myself with a text whose
politics and relationship to history are rather more elusive; Walker's

international best-seller, *The Color Purple.*

Toni Morrison's relationship to the civil rights movement was somewhat different, although its influence on her writing was also profound. Although student sit-ins by civil rights activists swept through college campuses across the South where she was teaching, Morrison did not participate directly, and she expressed some reservations at the time about the devaluation, or possible complete loss of, the existing black education colleges that might result from integration. During her time as an academic at Howard University (1957–64), Morrison had taught Stokely Carmichael, who was to become a leading figure in the Black Power movement. She later came into contact with the ideas of the leading African theorist of decolonisation, Chinweizu, whose writing she had edited in her post as an editor at Random House in New York, which she took up in 1964.

By the time that *The Bluest Eye*[4] came to be published in 1970, two major pieces of legislation, the Civil Rights Act of 1964 and the Voter Rights Acts of 1965, had been added to the Civil Rights Acts of 1957 and 1960 which had given black Americans the right to vote. Although the civil rights movement could claim credit for desegregation in schools, housing and public transportation, the fault-lines that divided America along the lines of colour were still rigidly in place. After the assassination of Martin Luther King in 1968, the civil rights movement appeared weakened, directionless and schism-riven. There was also an important change in mood among many African-Americans. The bus boycotts of the 1950s in the South, and the huge non-violent demonstrations of the Martin Luther King era, had been superseded by the stridency and the assertiveness of the black power and black-is-beautiful movements. These were especially strong in the northern cities where they spoke to the aspirations of the disaffected young.

The relationship of women to the male-dominated movement was problematic from the beginning. Sexual equality did not feature on the agenda in the early days of Black Power – anger had erupted when Stokely Carmichael had famously remarked that the place of women was on their backs. Toni Morrison later told Anne Koenen that 'I was not impressed with much of the rhetoric of Black men about Black women in the Sixties ... But I never made any observations about any of them in print or otherwise, because it was too frail a movement to swish down certain kinds of criticism on.'[5] Black-is-beautiful did much to promote the confidence and self-esteem of African-Americans. As Morrison was to observe, 'of course, young people loved it – beauty, physical beauty, was important to them (like being "popular" in school). After all, they had grown up with *Marilyn, Miss America* and *Mademoiselle*. Older people liked it too, for it seemed to liberate them from the fretful problems of hair and Nadinola.'[6] But it also appeared to many black people who had supported the civil rights movement to belie the complexities that had characterised the thinking behind the earlier campaigns. In 1974 Morrison wrote that 'when Civil Rights became Black Power, we frequently chose exoticism over reality.'[7] Later she told Gloria Naylor that 'nobody was going to tell me that it had been that easy. That all I needed was a slogan: "Black is beautiful"'.[8]

At its simplest, *The Bluest Eye* tells of a little black girl, Pecola Breedlove, who longs for blue eyes (which she associates primarily with Shirley Temple), is raped and impregnated by her father, and subsequently goes mad. *The Bluest Eye* is perhaps the first novel of substance to be centrally concerned with the experiences of a black girl who had hitherto been a marginal character in American literature. Morrison's achievement in *The Bluest Eye* is to illuminate the destructiveness of whiteness as a desideratum by telling Pecola's story. As Richard Dyer points out, 'the invisibility of whiteness as a racial position in white (which is to say dominant) discourse is of a piece with its ubiquity'.[9] In alerting the reader to the dangers of whiteness as a social category, and making visible that which is invisible – white privilege reproduces itself because it is not recognised by others as white but as normal – Morrison lends support to the civil rights movement. At the same time, she distances herself from the black aesthetic movement and carefully avoids what had by then come to be seen as the cliché of black-is-beautiful. Morrison's response to the black aesthetic movement in *The Bluest Eye* is to deconstruct the notions of blackness and of beauty.

The Bluest Eye is set in 1940–41 at the end of the Great Depression. This was a period of major economic restructuring and mass internal migration in the United States. In much the same way as Pauline and Cholly Breedlove in *The Bluest Eye*, thousands of people left their homes to search for employment and economic security in the industrial towns of the north, establishing new communities, identities and families in distant places. This was also a time of important civil rights agitations which prefigured the civil rights activism of the 1960s. The huge march on Washington to complain against racial discrimination in the armament industry started in 1940. The experience of black people in the 1930s and 1940s was of particular interest to Morrison who was old enough to remember some of this history. For her this seemed to have little relation to 'the new Black history being propounded in the streets, in the classrooms, and in the gatherings of Black people in this country' in which 'it is strongly hinted that aside from Marcus Garvey and W.E.B Dubois, we were illiterate worshippers of white people'.[10] Her contribution to debates about the history of black people in the United States was the compilation of *The Black Book* (1973), a pictorial history of African-American society without editorial comment of any kind which was intended to depict the diversity of ways in which life had been lived by black Americans.[11]

In *The Bluest Eye* Morrison sets out to question hegemonic notions of beauty and to show how blackness, ugliness and powerlessness have come to be linked. What matters is not that the ironically named Breedloves, the poor black family whose fortunes the story chronicles, are physically unprepossessing, but the processes whereby they have come to internalise the notion of their own ugliness and inferiority: 'It was as if some mysterious all-knowing master had given them a cloak of ugliness to wear, and they had accepted it without question. The master had said, "you are ugly people". They had looked about themselves and saw nothing to contradict the statement; saw, in fact, support for it leaning at them from every billboard, every movie, every glance' (*BE*, pp. 38–9). In a society in which beauty has been substituted for virtue those who are not endowed with beauty will be made to believe that they are inferior to those who are. In *The Bluest Eye*, a light-skinned character says to Pecola, 'I *am* cute! And you ugly! black and ugly black e mos' (*BE*, p. 69). When Pecola is born even her mother exclaims, '*Lord she was ugly*' (*BE*, p. 116), and because she finds her daughter unattractive she withholds the maternal love that is essential to the development of the growing young woman's sense of self-esteem.

As Morrison puts it, 'when the strength of a people rests on its beauty, when the focus is on how one looks rather than what one is, we are in trouble'.[12] White feminists in both Britain and the United States had, of course, expressed similar concerns – when organising the protests against the Miss World beauty contests which they accused of reducing women to sex objects – but Morrison analyses the specific effects of the pursuit of beauty on the psyche of African-American adults and children. In an article in *Black World*, Morrison wrote 'the point about concentrating on whether we are beautiful is that it is a concentration on a way of measuring self-worth that is wholly trivial and totally white'.[13] Moreover, 'the concept of physical beauty as a virtue is one of the dumbest, most pernicious and destructive ideas of the Western world and we should have nothing to do with it'.[14]

In *Playing in the Dark: Whiteness and the Literary Imagination*, Morrison has argued that black representations have been essential to the fabrication of white racial imagery and suggests that 'it may be possible to discover, through a close look at literary "blackness", the nature – even the cause – of literary "whiteness." What is it for? What parts do the invention and development of whiteness play in the construction of what is loosely described as American?'.¹⁵ *The Bluest Eye* is about the experiences of black people in a white-dominated United States. As Morrison has put it, 'American means white, and Africanist people struggle to make the term applicable to themselves with ethnicity and hyphen after hyphen after hyphen.'¹⁶ Although Lorain, the Ohio steel town in which the Breedlove family lives, and in which Morrison herself grew up, is racially mixed, white characters are a structuring absence in the novel. As Cynthia Davis points out, this is because 'the brutality here is less a single act than the systematic denial of the reality of black lives'.¹⁷ There is, however, one shockingly brutal act perpetuated by a gang of white men who stumble on Cholly Breedlove about to have intercourse in the woods and mock and humiliate the semi-naked man in a way which is to to haunt him for life and to destroy his ability to have loving relationships with women.

The white characters in the book are Mr Yacobowski, a storekeeper who can barely bring himself to touch the hand of the black child to whom he sells candy, and Rosemary Villanucci, the next-door neighbour whom the black children torment. Instead, Morrison's characters exist in a world which is circumscribed by its blackness living in close proximity to white people like the Villanuccis, but defensively opting to distance themselves from a white community whose values and beliefs are different. As Karla Holloway and Stephanie Demetrakopoulos have put it, 'our response to the indignities of racism has been to draw boundaries around our cultural identity that dare anyone's crossing'.¹⁸ It is only Geraldine, who has virtually disavowed her racial identity, who encourages her son to associate with white children, although Louis Junior secretly longs to play with black boys and to share their sense of freedom which he lacks.

But the absence of white characters is offset by the presence of white representations in the novel. White representations reduce the black subject to a mere cipher permitting neither the recognition of similarities nor the acceptance of difference, except as a signifier of inadequacy. The conversation between black characters in *The Bluest Eye* contains references not only to the ubiquitous Shirley Temple but also to other Hollywood actresses whose names have become household words for glamour and beauty: Hedy Lamarr, Claudette Colbert, Greta Garbo and Ginger Rogers. If the coveted blue eyes of Shirley Temple can only be attained by prayers to God (or with recent advances in consumer products and modern technology by wearing blue contact lenses!), the hairstyle of Hedy Lamarr appears to be within easier reach. One little girl tells a humorous anecdote about a black woman who asks her hairdresser to style her hair like Hedy Lamarr's and is told to return when she has managed to grow it like Hedy Lamarr. The point here is that the damage done to the black psyche (and particularly to young children like Pecola) is not always perpetuated by contact with individual white people. More subtly and insidiously, it is perpetuated by a regime of representations which present whiteness as the normative (and therefore desirable) state of existence. As Richard Dyer has put it 'for those in power in the West as long as whiteness is felt to be the human condition, then it alone both defines normality and fully inhabits it'.[19]

Morrison is deeply critical of the standards whereby happiness is judged in terms of material success and of the deleterious effects which the American dream (the acquisition of success, fame, status, riches and happiness) has had on generations of African-Americans. This is not only because the American dream is precisely that – a chimera which eludes the vast majority of the American population which it supposedly encompasses – but also because aspiring to white standards of beauty (blue eyes, light skin), material success (immaculate houses, beautiful kitchens), or behaviour (restrained, individualistic) usually results in African-Americans abandoning their own values, behaviour and traditions. As an example, *The Bluest Eye* provides three contrasting examples of interior, domestic spaces which may be read as synecdoches. The first is the Fisher family's beautiful kitchen with its sparkling surfaces and gleaming utensils over which Pauline Breedlove (patronisingly renamed Polly) presides as a trusted servant. The kitchen gives the black woman all the power and luxury for which she longs, but it is from this kitchen that her own daughter is summarily expelled so that she can tend to a distressed white girl who monopolises her attention. By contrast, the MacTeer's kitchen is a place of communal security and warmth where the whole family gathers. Claudia's dream is to sit on a stool in the kitchen clutching a bunch of lilacs and listening to Big Papa playing his violin. The Breedlove living room is simply a squalid poorly furnished room in which there are no memories to be cherished; no furniture to which anyone is attached; no songs are ever sung around the piano, and no visitors ever call. All that we are told about the Breedlove's kitchen is that it is a room at the back of their shack. It is not a space in which the laughter, gossip, celebrations and rituals which bind families together have ever found expression.

In *The Bluest Eye* Morrison suggests that the socialisation of children in their formative years is largely responsible for their unrealistic expectations of material success and happiness. In reality, there can be very few houses like that in which Jane and Dick live happily with their mother and father which is depicted in the school primer reproduced in the opening lines of the *The Bluest Eye*. But the image of this house was instilled into a generation of American children who went to school in the 1940s, with the first words they were taught to read. *The Bluest Eye* makes use of each familiar item in the primer in an ironic way. Pecola's father is not 'big and strong'. Her mother is not 'very nice'. The ramshackle house in which the family live, an abandoned store which nobody else wants, is not 'very pretty'. Morrison explains that 'the primer with white children was the way life was presented to black people'. She adds that 'as the novel proceeded, I wanted that primer version broken up and confused, which explains the typographical running together of the words'.[20] Geraldine's neat little green and white house into which the hapless Pecola is lured, approximates to the house in the primer. The house is Geraldine's 'inviolable world', from which even her husband is banished to the porch to smoke, as she stands on guard 'over its every plant, weed and doily' (*BE*, p. 78). This is a cold and loveless house in which even the cat is tormented by Geraldine's little sadist of a son but Pecola thinks it beautiful. As Barbara Christian has put it, 'The more confusing, different, poverty-ridden or depressed a child's life is, the more she will yearn for the norm the dominant society says provides beauty and happiness.'[21]

Angela Burton has argued that 'Toni Morrison's status as a recognised commentator on black America seems to rest uneasily with the centrality she gives to black disempowerment in her fiction.'[22] She is right to suggest that the abjection of Morrison's black character should be understood as a response to white dominance. But the characters in *The Bluest Eye* are not only black. They are also poor, and, in the case of the Breedloves, almost destitute: 'Although their poverty was traditional and stultifying, it was not unique' (*BE*, p. 38). Morrison shows how economic deprivation and social class both play a crucial role in determining the expectations and behaviour of individuals and groups. The black community is not romanticised in *The Bluest Eye*. To present it in an entirely positive light would be to deny its heterogeneity, and to erase the problems which must be found in any small and economically disadvantaged community, whether it is black, or mixed, or white. But neither is it demonised. Claudia talks about 'Love, thick and dark as Alaga syrup' (*BE*, p. 15) seeping through her house. It is the presence of love which helps to make Claudia into the person that she is and its absence which propels Pecola over the precipice of insanity. In *The Bluest Eye*, childhood is represented as a time of danger rather than safety; of furtively acquired sexual knowledge rather than innocence. To be a girl is to be especially vulnerable to abuse. Like Alice Walker, Morrison is interested in sexual violence primarily as a domestic phenomenon. In *The Color Purple* a character, Sofia, declaims that 'A girl child ain't safe in a family of men.'[23] In *The Bluest Eye*, Pecola and Frieda are sexually abused by a member of the family and by a friend of the household respectively.

Morrison writes in what she describes as a 'tragic mode in which there is some catharsis and revelation'.[24] There are no magical reunions, transformations, or happy outcomes in this novel as there are in *The Color Purple*. The landscape, like the central character of the novel, is desolate. As the narrator, Claudia sorrowfully observes, 'this soil is bad for certain kinds of flowers. Certain seeds it will not nurture, certain fruit it will not bear' (*BE*, p. 190). The novel is divided into the four seasons of the year and begins not as one might expect with spring, the season of birth and hope, but with autumn.

The Bluest Eye is set at a historical moment when cinema attendances in the United States were at their highest. It was at this time that the child star Shirley Temple became familiar to millions. There is, somewhat ironically, an attractive mulatto girl called Pecola in the movie, *Imitation of Life*, to which *The Bluest Eye* makes reference. In *The Bluest Eye*, Pecola's mother spends many happy afternoons at the movies, transfixed by the image of the bottle-blonde Jean Harlow whose hair-style she unsuccessfully tries to imitate: 'Along with the idea of romantic love, she is introduced to another – physical beauty. Probably the most destructive ideas in the history of human thought. Both originated in envy, thrived in insecurity, and ended in disillusion' (*BE*, p. 113). It is at the cinema that Pauline is able to escape from the drudgery of her day-to-day existence, but it is at the cinema that she learns to be dissatisfied with her own husband and her children: '*Them pictures gave me a lot of pleasure, but it made coming home hard, and looking at Cholly hard*' (*BE*, p. 114).

The cult of Shirley Temple, to which the children in *The Bluest Eye* succumb, also originates in the movies: 'It was a small step to Shirley Temple. I learned much later to worship her, just as I learned to delight in cleanliness, knowing, even as I learned, that the change was adjustment without improvement' (*BE*, p. 25). Shirley Temple becomes a particularly destructive ego-ideal for Pecola, who drinks large quantities of milk just to handle a mug with Shirley Temple's face on it. The child is prepared to go to any lengths to acquire the film star's blue eyes, which she innocently equates with the happiness, beauty and love that are missing in her own life. Pecola also enjoys eating sugar candies with blonde, blue-eyed, petulant but smiling Mary Jane on the wrapper: 'To eat the candy is somehow to eat the eyes, eat Mary Jane. Love Mary Jane. Be Mary Jane' (*BE*, p. 49).

The Shirley Temple mug demonstrates how racial tropes have shaped cultural products that might appear to have nothing to do with race. As bel hooks puts it, 'This contradictory longing to possess the reality of the (white) Other, even though that reality wounds and negates, is expressive of the desire to understand the mystery, to know immediately through imitation, as though such knowing was like an amulet, as mask, will ward away the evil, the terror.'[25]

As Melissa Walker has pointed out, the year in which *The Bluest Eye* is set was the year in which the famous Clark and Phipps doll test was administered to children in segregated schools. The low self-esteem of black children was confirmed when they were asked to choose between a black and a white doll. Most said that they preferred the white doll but recognised the black doll as being the most like themselves.[26] In *The Bluest Eye* Claudia is given a big, blue-eyed baby doll as a Christmas present: 'Adults, older girls, shops, magazines, newspapers, window signs – all the world had agreed that a blue-eyed, yellow-haired, pink-skinned doll was what every girl treasured' (*BE*, p. 23). But hope lies in the fact that not all black little girls are susceptible to such pressures. The strong-willed Claudia, who embodies a different, more compassionate, and more critical, set of values than many of the adults around her, refuses to love the alien doll which she surreptitiously dismembers, carefully examining its parts out of curiosity to discover what it is that all the world finds lovable (*BE*, p. 23).

In contrast to Pecola, Maureen Peal is beautiful, light-skinned, long-haired, rich, spoilt and widely adored. The girl induces feelings of inferiority, hatred, envy and incomprehension in other black children, who are at a loss to understand the secret of her popularity: 'Dolls we could destroy, but we could not destroy the honey voices of parents and aunts, the obedience in the eyes of our peers, the slippery light in the eyes of our teachers when they encountered the Maureen Peals of the world. What was the secret? What did we lack?'(*BE*, pp. 70–1). Embodying the values of the dominant culture as she does, Maureen might simply function as a hate-object. But the young narrator realises that it is not Maureen who is the problem: 'And all the time we knew that Maureen Peal was not the Enemy and not worthy of such intense hatred. The *Thing* to fear was the *Thing* that made *her* beautiful and not us' (*BE*, pp 70–1).

The variability of black as a skin colour has sometimes been used to make distinctions within it even among those whose racial identity is not in dispute. Although the behaviour of the three light-skinned characters in the novel, Maureen, Geraldine, Soaphead, is often despicable, Morrison avoids any suggestion of racial essentialism. She is too astute a commentator on matters of race to represent black skin as superior to white skin, i.e. to endorse racism in reverse. She avoids 'the traditional useful constructs of blackness', i.e. the use of black or colored people or the symbolic configurations of blackness as 'markers for the benevolent and the wicked'.[27] Morrison has expressed regret for her superficial depiction of Maureen ('if I were doing that book now, I would write her section or talk about her that way plus from inside').[28] The tendency to present dark-skinned characters as more attractive than light-skinned in *The Bluest Eye* is moderated in Morrison's later fiction. At the start of her most recent novel, *Paradise* (1998), for example, Morrison does not disclose which character is black and which white.

As Kate Davy has pointed out, 'the meanings of "middle classness" may be virtually the same as the meanings that constitute an institutionalized whiteness'. Middle-classsness, according to Davy, denotes 'a kind of hard-earned as opposed to birthright, "gentility" in the form of civility … that encompasses a plethora of values, morals and mores that determine sexual propriety, as well as the tenets of respectability in general'.[29] In *The Bluest Eye* the self-mutilating behaviour that comes from the pursuance of middle-class respectability is best illustrated in the character of Geraldine. Women of Geraldine's type have moved far from the small southern towns like Aiken, Meridian and Baton Rouge where they were born. They have forgotten their working-class and African-American roots and transformed themselves into bland American women obsessed with 'thrift, patience, high morals and good manners' (*BE*, p. 77). These women 'do not drink, smoke or swear' and guard against 'the dreadful funkiness of passion, the funkiness of nature, the funkiness of the wide range of human emotions'. Geraldine explains the difference between 'colored people' and 'niggers': 'Colored people were neat and quiet; niggers were dirty and loud' (*BE*, p. 81). The 'line between colored and nigger was not always clear; subtle and telltale signs threatened to erode it, and the watch had to be constant' (*BE*, p. 81). In the dirty, helpless and unkempt Pecola, Geraldine sees the other self she has so long fought, the black self she fears to be, and turns in fury upon the child she curses as a 'nasty little black bitch' (*BE*, p. 86).

In answer to the Geraldines who have forgotten their origins, Morrison posits two life-enhancing forces: the community and the ancestor. In an essay entitled 'Rootedness: The Ancestor as Foundation', Morrison explains that ancestors are 'timeless people whose relationships to the characters are benevolent, instructive and protective, and they provide a certain kind of wisdom'. She adds that 'When you kill the ancestor you kill yourself.'[30] As Trudier Harris has argued, Cholly's Aunt Jimmy with her asafetida bag, and head-rags embodies the old Southern black culture and reflects the customs of her ancestors.[31] The resilience of the old black women in the South (Cholly's ancestors) who are not individuated but described in a prose that takes on a poetic quality is a contrast to the petulant self-centredness of Geraldine. But such women belong not to the present but to the disappearing past.

> The hands that felled trees also cut umbilical cords; the hands that wrung the necks of chickens and butchered hogs also nudged African violets into bloom; the arms that loaded sheaves, bales, and sacks rocked babies into sleep. They patted biscuits into flaky ovals of innocence – and shrouded the dead. They plowed all day and came home to nestle like plums under the limbs of their men. The legs that straddled a mule's back were the same ones that straddled their men's hips. And the difference was all the difference there was. (*BE*, p. 128)

As Jan Furman has noted, 'Morrison often calculates the psychological distance her characters have traveled by estimating their proximity to the community. The closer they are, the better.'[32] Both Cholly and Pauline Breedlove are deracinated Southerners who have migrated to the North and have failed to transplant the values of the communities in which they grew up: 'The main characters spring from cultures that are in many respects whole and vital, but because of their orphanhood and their rootlessness, they are unable to use these cultures as sustaining forces in their lives.'[33] If the community in *The Bluest Eye* has its share of charlatans, sadists, child molestors and rapists (Soaphead who purports to interpret dreams; Louis Junior, who derives enjoyment from tormenting animals and children; Mr Henry who abuses Frieda; and Cholly who rapes and impregnates his own daughter), it also functions to ensure continuities; to uphold the importance of kinship and the continuance of African-American traditions.

If it rejects the damaged and unlovable Pecola, it also demonstrates its ability to police itself, and to provide its members with a safety blanket in times of trouble, thus obviating the need for outside interference from welfare agencies. The best representatives of the importance of community in *The Bluest Eye* are the MacTeer family, who retain a sense of the black community as an extended family and despite their own financial problems manage to give Pecola a home when her father is in prison. Claudia is the one loyal friend who struggles to attach dignity and meaning to Pecola's life. If the community's ideas about propriety are outraged by the three prostitutes, China, Poland and Miss Marie, its members also rally around to support Aunt Jimmy in her dying illness and to help young Cholly after his aunt and guardian dies.

Morrison has described herself as writing 'village literature, fiction that is really for the village, for the tribe. Peasant literature for *my* people, which is necessary and legitimate but which also allows me to get in touch with all sorts of people.'[34] In that her concerns are largely rural rather than urban and with a peasant history – an unusual term in the context of the United States although one Morrison has used herself – Morrison has something in common with the other great twentieth-century novelists of peasant communities, George Lamming, Lewis Grassic Gibbon, Chinua Achebe as well, of course, with the other black American writers of the South, and especially with Alice Walker.

Alice Walker conceived of *The Color Purple* as a 'womanist' challenge to patriarchal history. The novel starts not with the 'taking of lands, or the births, battles, and deaths of Great Men' but with an anecdote about a triangular relationship told to Walker by her sister, 'one day the Wife asked the other Woman for a pair of her drawers.'³⁵ The events take place in Georgia early in the twentieth century, but the novel contains no dates, and only a handful of verifiable historical facts. This makes it impossible for it to be repositioned accurately in history. The conundrum expressed by its central character, Celie, who remarks 'what the world got to do with anything, I think?' (*CP*, p. 9) also faces the reader.

But as I have argued in my discussion of science fiction, historically precise narratives are not the only narratives that women who wish to counter oppression have at their disposal. If, as is so often the case, history is the history of the defeated, it is necessary to resort, as Walker does, to allegorical form, myth, fantasy and fairy tale in order to redress injustice, and to envision the triumph of democratic and egalitarian principles. Celie is based on Walker's grandmother who was raped at the age of twelve by her slave-owner, Walker's grandfather. Walker writes, 'I liberated her from her own history. I wanted her to be happy.'³⁶ Walker takes liberties with the notion of historical truth, and subordinates this to myth, because, at its best, history is inspirational myth and, at its worst, it is either irrelevant or damaging to black people: 'White people busy celebrating they independence from England July 4th, say Harpo, so most black folks don't have to work. Us can spend the day celebrating each other' (*CP*, p. 243).

Like Morrison, Walker locates her narrative wholly within the black community and is not directly concerned with white society except to show how racism impinges on blacks – Celie's biological father, a small storekeeper, is lynched by white people, and her daughter-in-law Sofia's insubordinate behaviour ends in a shockingly punitive gaol sentence which bears no relation to the severity of her offence. The one white character who is given any substantial dialogue, Miss Eleanor Jane, is a petulant time-waster who attempts in vain to solicit maternal sentiments about her own son from the honest Sofia: 'I got my own troubles, say

Sofia, and when Reynolds Stanley grow up, he's gon to be one of them' (*CP*, p. 225).

The incidence of rape and sexual violence in Walker's own community of Eatonton, Georgia, was high: 'Ever since I was a child, I had been aware of the high rate of domestic violence in our town, among our people; wives shot or stabbed to death, children sometimes abused and beaten.'[37] The novel begins with the rape of fourteen-year-old Celie by a man whom she believes to be her father, and who also has designs on her younger sister. As in *The Bluest Eye*, the household is depicted as a potentially violent and threatening place for women and children. While the misogynistic attitudes of black male writers like Richard Wright and Ralph Ellison to black women have usually gone unnoticed, Walker has often been accused of vilifying black men. But not all the abusive men in her fiction are black: Mary Agnes is sexually assaulted by a white man to whom she is distantly related, and who is clearly disconcerted by the family resemblance ('He saw the Hodges in me, she say. And he didn't like it one bit' (*CP*, p. 83).

Both *The Color Purple* and *The Bluest Eye* detail the stories of young black women searching for self-esteem. But the question that Pecola asks, 'how do you get somebody to love you?' (*BE*, p. 33) is never answered. In contrast to Pecola, Celie tells the story of the sexual violence which has been inflicted on her in her own language – her letters are barely literate and full of incorrect spelling and syntax – giving her own point of view. What resonates throughout the text is the importance or orality of the individual woman's speaking or singing voice which serves as her instrument of freedom, in marked contrast to the Western literary tradition, in which literacy is the way in which that aspiration to freedom has usually been expressed. The epistolary mode which Walker uses for a large part of the novel was ironically the preserve of privileged, middle-class young ladies in the eighteenth century. Walker engages inventively with the Western literary tradition but in so doing also reminds us of its limitations and cultural specificity. The reader is made critically aware of the dangers of universalising white women's experience and of the distance which separates Celie's use of the vernacular from the elegant sentiments which characterised the earlier letter writers. In many respects, Celie's experiences are analogous to those of a slave woman: she is raped, made to bear children who are taken away from her, separated from the sister she loves, haggled over by two men who both regard her as a marketable commodity, and made to marry a man who abuses her sexually and who uses her as an unpaid servant. Because the context of slavery is invoked through the particulars of Celie's situation, her experiences bring to mind collective rather than individual memories and histories, thus rendering problematic any identification that white feminists might make with Celie as a recipient of sexual abuse, since the context in which the abuse takes place involves race as well as gender.

The Color Purple is an emancipatory narrative in ways which *The Bluest Eye* is not. But to read the novel as the record of one woman's journey from abjection to self-esteem is to misconstrue that journey as an individual narrative of triumph over adversity in the manner of the Western *Bildungsroman*. Its essence is, in fact, collective, and its inspiration is derived from a cultural tradition which is black and very different. Each stage of Celie's transformation and progress on her journey towards happiness and self-esteem is inspired by three 'strong' women, Nettie, Sofia and Shug, who epitomise respectively the importance of three key elements of black culture and history, kinship, defiance and music, in underwriting her resistance and providing her with support. The sex/race analogy, whereby white women spoke of their own exploitation by men as analogous to the exploitation of slaves, was very commonly evoked in the early days of the women's movement. Such an analogy refers to slavery in a symbolic sense recognising its significance as a powerful literary and cultural trope. But in so doing it denies the specificity of the historical experience of black women and underplays the magnitude of their suffering. It is for this reason that any identification of the white woman reader with Celie should be avoided.

Celie comes to value herself as a person through the love of her long-lost sister, Nettie, with whom she is eventually reunited after her husband has hidden her letters away from her for many years. Nettie's influence affirms the importance of the relationship that many women experience as the most sustaining and permanent in their life, that with one's sister. Although sharing Celie's inauspicious start in life, Nettie shows that it is possible to educate oneself and become a teacher. Her range of experience widens Celie's horizons and connects her to black women across the world. Celie is also changed by her respect for the defiant spirit demonstrated by Sofia, who resists the sexism of her husband and goes to prison for her defiance of racism, as many black women were to do in the course of the civil rights movement. Finally, Celie's transformation is brought about by her love affair with the blues singer Shug Avery who makes Celie appreciate her own body, giving her the experience of sexual pleasure for the first time. Shug shares Sofia's irrepressible spirit. Albert describes her as 'upright, honest. Speak her mind and the devil take the hindmost, he say. You know Shug will fight, he say. Just like Sofia. She bound to live her life and be herself no matter what' (*CP*, p. 228).

In *In Search of our Mothers' Gardens* Walker asks how the 'creativity of the black woman was kept alive, year after year and century after century, when for most of the years black people have been in America it was a punishable crime for a black person to read or write'. She suggests that the voices of the great black blues singers may provide an answer. It is this inspirational tradition of women's music and independence which Shug Avery represents in the novel. In *The Color Purple*, Shug represents the liberated spirit of women singers such as Bessie Smith, Billie Holiday, Nina Simone, Aretha Franklin and Roberta Flack whom Walker admired and who have served as role models for so many black women.[38]

Shug is an unrepentant rule-breaker, who refuses to play any of the roles conventionally expected of a woman (attentive mother, faithful wife, the loyal mistress of only one man). She has rejected a patriarchal version of God as an old white man in the sky, and it is largely because of her influence that Celie loses her faith in this conventional God and is converted to a pantheism that takes delight in all things natural, like the fields of purple that give the novel its name. Moreover, Shug is rich, glamorous, successful, and not beholden to anyone either economically or sexually. She embodies the 'funkiness' that, as we have seen in Toni Morrison's fiction, those black women who have learned to ape white behaviour have destroyed in themselves. Although the word 'lesbian' is not used in the novel Shug's relationship with Celie has a physical dimension. Shug demonstrates the pleasure that can be obtained from the clitoris to Celie. The joy of the relationship between Shug and Celie is that it evokes no criticism, surprise or excitement, and is depicted as no less 'natural' than any of the heterosexual relationships in the novel. Lesbian defensiveness does not enter the novel but neither does homophobia: Walker, who is bisexual, 'wanted to give my family and friends an opportunity to see woman-loving women – lesbian, heterosexual, bisexual, "two spirited" – womanist women in a recognisable context. I wanted them, I suppose, to see me.'[39]

Walker shares Morrison's interest in the leylines which connect black women to their ancestors. In *In Search of our Mother's Gardens* Walker suggests that 'black Southern writers owe their clarity of vision to parents who refused to diminish themselves as human beings by succumbing to racism'.[40] Nettie is reconnected to her African ancestry by going to Africa as a missionary to work with the Olinka peoples. But Walker not only criticises the Western developers who desecrate the Olinka's traditional homelands but also the romantic, idealistic view of Africa to which African-Americans sometimes subscribe. The Olinka are a patriarchal community who do not permit their girls to be educated and sanction the brutal practices of clitoredectomy and scarification.

The naming of the characters in *The Color Purple* is matrilineal and reflects Walker's literary and familial debts. As I have mentioned before, Celie is modelled on the author's grandmother. Walker discovered a character called Shug in the work of Zora Neale Hurston, while Shug was also the name of her grandfather's lover as well as the nickname of an aunt after whom Walker herself was called.[41] Nettie is the name of Walker's maternal grandmother.[42] Sofia is the Goddess of Wisdom. Olivia is taken from a line 'Chloe loved Olivia' in Virginia Woolf's feminist classic, *A Room of One's Own*, 'a book that made me happy to be a writer and bolstered and brightened my consciousness about the role other women, often silenced or even long dead, can have in changing the world'.[43]

The Color Purple caused a sensation among feminists, the black community,[44] the reading public and the critical intelligentsia when it was published in 1982. It won the American Book Award and the coveted Pulitzer Prize for fiction in 1983, after which sales of the novel soared to more than two million copies. In 1985 it was turned into a film directed by Stephen Spielberg who made a number of controversial changes to the book – Walker has always defended Spielberg and the film.[45] Jacqueline Bobo's research has shown an overwhelmingly positive response to the film among a selected group of black women viewers whom she interviewed.[46]

In Alison Light's words, *The Color Purple* offers the reader 'passionate hopefulness'.[47] Combining as it did the author's resolutely anti-sexist perspectives, with narration from a black woman's perspective, and a heroine who triumphantly refused the status of a victim, the novel became required reading in radical circles in both Britain and the United States. The impact of *The Color Purple* in progressive academic circles was unprecedented.[48] The novel set into train complex debates about the reception of the text, the dangers of appropriating other women's experience, and the ethical problems raised by facile cross-cultural identifications which still resonate today. These debates focused attention on reader response and cultural context and prompted many to question what happened when, as was often the case, a white middle-class reader identified with experiences of joy and abjection that could not be more far removed from her own.

For many readers, then, *The Color Purple* was quintessentially *the* flagship text of difference, the literary embodiment of the new 'identity politics' *par excellence*. But for others, it merely confirmed the abandonment of collective struggles, the capitulation to commercial pressures, and the pessimistic retreat into private sensibility that was the hallmark of the Reagan and Thatcher years ('a novel for Yuppie and Buppie America, an America that was a bit tired, a bit bewildered, driven to cut losses, consolidate gains, and cultivate its own private, profitable gardens').[49]

Its readers were sharply polarised. Some loved the novel's exuberance, welcoming its depiction of lesbian sexuality, of women's spirituality and communities of women and applauded the way in which it affirmed the resilience of the black woman's spirit. Others disliked its utopianism, deploring its representations of black men, its lack of historical grounding and its counter-cultural spiritual religiosity. *The Color Purple*'s imputed endorsement of capitalist ethics, as well as its happy ending were also criticised.

While many lesbians welcomed the significance Walker attached to the lesbian subtext, others were unhappy because the novel did not appear to reflect the assertive lesbian politics of the 1970s. bel hooks, for example, objected to lesbian sex being shown as compatible with Celie's marriage, and never becoming a controversial issue, or undermining heterosexual and patriarchal institutions, because of 'Walker's refusal to acknowledge it as threatening – dangerous'.[50] Among Walker's most virulent black critics is Trudier Harris, who took exception to Celie's passivity, 'even slave women who found themselves abused frequently found ways of responding to that – by running away', and made the objection that the book 'reinforces racial stereotypes' including the suspicion that 'black people have no morality when it comes to sexuality, that black family structure is weak if existent at all'.[51] The magical transformation of Albert, the sudden return of Nettie, the fairy-tale-like restitution of Celie's lost children, the fortuitous discovery that Alphonso was not Celie's father, and the unexpected legacy from her mother, all provided ammunition for those who saw *The Color Purple* as symptomatic of Walker's decline into wish-fulfilment and sentimentality; as her abandonment of the historicised and socially engaged novels influenced by her history as a civil rights activist and the substitution of a depoliticised fantasy in their place.

In 1983 Cora Kaplan, an American feminist then resident in Britain, and in general sympathetic to the book, noted the importance of the dialogue which *The Color Purple* entered not only with black women writers, like Zora Neale Hurston and Nella Last, but also with a number of 'prior constructions of southern Black social relations' that represent women as either powerless or repressive in the work of black male writers such as Ralph Ellison and Richard Wright, who often depict black women as imperilling the masculinity of the black male.[52] Kaplan also voiced concerns that were to become widespread in relation to the novel's rapturous reception, and the ease with which it appeared that a potentially subversive text could be recuperated into the literary mainstream, co-opted for liberalism, or drained by the critics of its subversive qualities. She warned of the dangers of *The Color Purple* being 'bleached into a pallid progressive homily, an uncontentious, sentimental, harmless piece of international libertarianism'. Kaplan suggested that the 'marketing of the book in the United States has made the most of this anodyne popular appeal' to the 'tradition of the sentimental novel, à la *Uncle Tom's Cabin*, the reconstituted rural family (*The Waltons*) or a vaguely defined and potentially reactionary "spirituality".'[53].

At the root of much of the feminist distrust of the novel is Celie's entrepreneurial success – by the end of the novel she has established an income from her colourful, customised trousers which are merchandised under the designer label 'folksplants unlimited'. But Susan Willis has argued against the dismissal of commodity capitalism *per se*, citing transformation as the site where the desire for black cultural autonomy coincides with fetishisation of commodity capitalism. Willis suggests that 'black culture has at its disposal and can manipulate all the signs and artifacts produced by the larger culture. The fact that these are already inscribed with meanings inherited through centuries of domination does not inhibit the production of viable culture statements, even though it influences the way such statements are read.'[54]

Celie's story, then, is not 'yet another journey into bourgeois bliss'.[55] On the contrary, customised trousers are a co-operatively produced alternative to mass-produced garments, created, as Walker makes clear, in a non-alienated way, as a labour of love. At a symbolic level the trousers are used to break a number of taboos ('Men and women not suppose to wear the same thing, he said. Men spose to wear the pants', *CP*, p. 230). The idiom 'to wear the trousers' means to be the dominant partner. Celie's cottage industry affirms both the importance of women's devising ways to avoid being financially dependent on men, and the continuance of the African-American woman's traditional skills of sewing and needlework, albeit in an updated form.

Walker prefaces her collection of essays, *In Search of our Mother's Gardens* with an explanation of why she has chosen to identify herself as a womanist rather than a feminist. A womanist 'appreciates and prefers women's culture ... Committed to survival and wholeness of entire people, male *and* female'.[56] One significant area in which womanists and feminists often differed at the time was in analysis of the family, which denoted different things to white feminists and to black. In *The Anti-Social Family*, which was published in the same year as *The Color Purple*, Michèle Barrett and Mary McIntosh concluded that the family did not serve the interests of women: 'What is needed is not to build up an alternative to the family – new forms of household that would fulfil all the needs that families are supposed to fulfil today – but to make the family less necessary, by building up all sorts of other ways of meeting people's needs, ways less volatile and inadequate than those based on the assumption that "blood is thicker than water".'⁵⁷

For many white Western feminists like Barrett and McIntosh,⁵⁸ the family was little more than an institution that oppressed women. But to African-American women, whose ancestors had often been separated from their loved ones by the experience of slavery, and whose sons, fathers, lovers and husbands had often found themselves in trouble with the authorities, for no other reason than they happened to be black, the family represented a source of nurturing and support, reinforcinng pride in their cultural identity. For them it acted as a necessary bulwark against the racism which they experienced in a hostile, white-dominated society. Although for many black women the family often signified domestic drudgery, male dominance, economic hardship and subordination of their own needs, in much the same way as it did for white women, their hope for a better future lay not in the abandonment of the family but in its transformation so that it became more receptive to their needs.

At the start of the *The Color Purple*, the family is represented as a relatively uncomplicated patriarchal structure which is dominated by a tyrant who vents his anger on his womenfolk. The person who challenges male tyranny is Sofia ('All my life I had to fight. I had to fight my daddy. I had to fight my brothers' *CP*, p. 38). By the end of the novel, Alphonso has died, and Albert, assisted by his lover and his wife working happily together, has undergone a transformation from a cruel and self-centred egotist to a considerate husband and father who has acquired a new-found respect for women.

What Walker questions in *The Color Purple* is the notion that a child is the exclusive property of the biological mother. Instead, we are offered examples of successful child-rearing which reflect a feminist desire for change as well as the traditional practices of black community. As in *The Bluest Eye*, other women willingly accept responsibility for children whose biological mothers are unable to do so. Thus Sofia's children are cared for by Mary Agnes when Sofia is in gaol. Celie becomes a substitute mother for her husband's children when their mother, Annie Julia, dies. Her own two children are adopted by Corrine, Samuel and Nettie. When Mary Agnes decides to go to Memphis Sofia agrees to look after her daughter. Shug's children become the responsibility of their maternal grandmother. The alternatives to the middle-class norms in childcare are not restricted to black families. As Stanley Earl notes, 'Everyone around here raise by colored. That's how come we turn out so well' (*CP*, p. 222).

As Walker has noted, while many white American writers 'end their books as if there were no better existence for which to struggle', African-American and Third World writers struggle for a 'larger freedom'.[59] The reconstructed families in *The Color Purple* are visionary expressions of human potential. They are at once utopian and pragmatic, utopian because the reality for children growing up is often very different, but attainable precisely because their starting point is already familiar; the extended family which at its best is a tried and tested locus of emotional and practical support within the black community. In *The Color Purple* Walker provides a co-operative and non-hierarchical vision of the reconfigured family, thus enabling her readers to recognise the specificity of their own experience and to imagine how things could be otherwise. Walker demonstrates the alternatives to exclusive one-to-one sexual relationships within marriage through two happy triangular sexual relationships which enhance the well-being of all involved. Jealousy and possessiveness are largely absent in the relationships between Harpo and Sofia and Mary Agnes and also between Albert and Celie and Shug. After Celie nurses Shug back to health, they do not relate to each other as rivals for the attention of the same man but as friends. Shug takes Celie with her to Memphis not to act as her unpaid maid but to love her and to help her to get her back on her feet.

Moreover, *The Color Purple* asserts that women do not have to suffer in silence. Intransigent men can sometimes be shifted by ridicule, verbal resistance or, if all else fails, by a woman's real or threatened departure. *Pace* Trudier Harris, Celie is not passive. To criticise her for passivity is to do so in ignorance of the fear which male violence produces in women – 'I don't know how to fight. All I know how to do is stay alive' (*CP*, p. 17). Years of psychological and physical abuse, first by Alphonso and then by Albert, may well have weakened Celie's spirit but they have not destroyed it. What is surprising is not that the resistance of victims of domestic violence like Celie is slow to develop, but that it ever develops at all, as the experiences of women involved in the refuges for physically abused women in Britain and the United States have amply demonstrated.

What eventually kindles Celie's change of heart is her discovery that she is able to rely unconditionally on the support of the other women around her. After she confesses to Shug that Albert beats her Shug successfully intercedes with him on her behalf. As Linda Abbandonato suggests, in a psychoanalytic reading of *The Color Purple* which underlines the importance of lesbian choices, 'in loving Shug, Celie becomes a desiring subject, and in being loved by Shug, she is made visible to herself as an object of desire. In contrast to the repression that Celie has experienced in accepting her social position as a "mature" woman in a phallocentric culture, her "infantile regression" is an act of radical rebellion.'[60] Breaking the cycle of domestic domination and submission is only possible if women assert their autonomy, thus making it possible for men to relate to them on a basis of equality. From Celie's discovery of sexual pleasure with a woman follows a set of discoveries and demands which diminish the status of men.

The strategies that the women devise to assert their independence in *The Color Purple* include the infectious laughter that deflates the male ego during the anarchic dinner scene in which the women decide to leave their men and go to Memphis: 'Well, say Grady, trying to bring light. A woman can't git a man if peoples talk. Shug look at me and us giggle. Then us laugh sure nuff. Then Squeak start to laugh. Then Sofia. All us laugh and laugh. ... Harpo look at Squeak. Shut up Squeak, he say. It bad luck for women to laugh at men' (*CP*, p. 171). Celie also uses the curse which, as Marjorie Pryse has argued, is one way in which black women have regained their ancient powers, against Albert ('until you do right by me everything you even dream about will fail', *CP*, p. 176).[61]

As Toni Morrison suggested in an interview with Sandy Russell, black women writers are 'writing to repossess, re-name, re-own.'[62] Repossessing and re-owning, in *The Color Purple*, means repossessing and re-owning black men, for, as Walker points out, 'a womanist' like herself is 'not a separatist, except periodically, for health'.[63] White people must take some responsibility for Albert behaving as he does ('the fact is, you got to give 'em something. Either your money, your land, your woman or your ass' (*CP*, p. 155). Like the men in the Olinka tribe ('they not so backward as mens here' (*CP*, p. 230), Albert learns to sew, to do housework and to 'clean that house just like a woman' (*CP*, p. 189). Celie notes with pleasure that 'when you talk to him now he really listen' (*CP*, p. 221). In much the same way, Harpo appears fully human for the first time at the point at which he expresses his love for his ailing father and Sofia is moved by the sight of Harpo holding Albert in his arms: 'After that I start to feel again for Harpo, Sofia say' (*CP*, p. 191).

The symbolic importance of Albert's conversion should not be minimised. It was Virginia Woolf who, flying in the face of the wisdom of her time, argued that public and private struggles against patriarchy should be placed on the same footing. In *Three Guineas* (1938) Woolf contended that the woman who fought domestic tyranny 'was fighting the Fascist or the Nazi' as surely as those who fought him with arms in the limelight of publicity. 'And must not that fight wear down her strength and exhaust her spirit? Should we not help her to crush him in our own country before we ask her to help us to crush him abroad?'[64]

Like Toni Morrison, Walker is committed to the importance of socialisation and education in bringing about change. What *The Color*

Purple explores are changing models of masculinity beginning with the most unpromising of examples. As Albert and Harpo show, it is possible for the most unpromising of men to change the day-to-day behaviour that women feel to be oppressive. But for this to happen men must want to change themselves. Far from being a retreat from the public to the private sphere, as many critics have suggested, *The Color Purple* questions the usefulness of such inscriptions. One important legacy of the women's movement has been the widespread acceptance of the idea that the personal is political. In contrast to the male left, which had traditionally regarded changes in the public arena as being the only changes of any momentum, the women's movement insisted from the beginning that it was in the private sphere that questions of race, gender and sexuality were often experienced most intensely and that it was in their personal lives that women's desire for change was often most passionately felt. The state of peace and harmony which prevails at the end of *The Color Purple* may indeed be utopian. But the history of utopias is that they are rarely free from social and political concerns.

NOTES

1 Alice Walker, *Anything We Love Can Be Saved: A Writer's Activism* (London: The Women's Press, 1997), p. 82.
2 Ibid., pp. xxi, 49, 61, 82.
3 Maria Lauret, *Liberating Literature: Feminist Fiction in America* (London: Routledge, 1994), p. 125.
4 Toni Morrison, *The Bluest Eye* (1970) (London: Triad/Grenada, 1981).
5 Anne Koenen, 'The One Out of Sequence' (1980), in Danille Taylor-Guthrie (ed.), *Conversations with Toni Morrison* (Jackson: University of Mississippi Press, 1994), pp. 67–83, p. 72.
6 Toni Morrison, 'Behind the Making of *The Black Book*', *Black World* February, 1974, pp. 86–90, p. 88.
7 Toni Morrison, 'Rediscovering Black History', *New York Times Magazine*, 11 August 1974, pp. 14–24, p. 14.
8 Gloria Naylor, 'A Conversation: Gloria Naylor and Toni Morrison' (1985), in *Conversations with Toni Morrison*, pp. 188–217, p. 199.
9 Richard Dyer, *White* (London: Routledge, 1997), p. 3.
10 Toni Morrison, 'Behind the Making of *The Black Book*', p. 87.
11 I am indebted to Marion Treby for helpful discussions about Toni Morrison and for bringing *The Black Book* and Morrison's writing about it to my attention.
12 Morrison, 'Rediscovering Black History', p. 14.
13 Morrison, 'Behind the Making of *The Black Book*', p. 89 .
14 Ibid.
15 Toni Morrison, *Playing in the Dark: Whiteness and the Literary Imagination* (Cambridge, MA: Harvard University Press, 1992), p. 9.
16 Ibid., p. 47.
17 Cynthia A. Davis, 'Self, Society and Myth in Toni Morrison's Fiction', in Harold Bloom (ed.), *Toni Morrison* (New York: Chelsea House, 1990), pp. 7–25, p. 7.
18 Karla F.C. Holloway and Stephanie A. Demetrakopoulos, *New Dimensions of Spiri-*

tuality: A Biracial and Bicultural Reading of the Novels of Toni Morrison (New York: Greenwood Press, 1987), p. 38.

19 Dyer, *White*, p. 9.

20 Thomas LeClair, 'The Language Must Not Sweat: A Conversation with Toni Morrison' (1981), in *Conversations with Toni Morrison*, pp. 19–28, p. 127.

21 Barbara T. Christian, *Black Women Novelists: The Development of a Tradition, 1892–1976* (Westport, CT: Greenwood Press, 1980), p. 142.

22 Angela Burton, 'Signifyin(g) Abjection: Narrative Strategies in Toni Morrison's *Jazz*', in Linden Peach (ed.), *Toni Morrison* (Basingstoke: Macmillan, 1998), pp. 170–93, p. 70.

23 Alice Walker, *The Color Purple* (London: The Women's Press, 1982), p. 38. All quotations are from this edition and given parenthetically – (*CP*).

24 LeClair, 'The Language Must Not Sweat: A Conversation with Toni Morrison', p. 125.

25 bel hooks, *Black Looks: Race and Representation* (Boston: South End Press, 1992), p. 166.

26 Melissa Walker, *Down from the Mountaintop: Black Women's Novels in the Wake of the Civil Rights Movement 1966–1989* (New Haven: Yale University Press, 1991), p. 56.

27 Morrison, *Playing in the Dark*, pp. ix–x.

28 LeClair, 'The Language Must Not Sweat: A Conversation with Toni Morrison', p. 204.

29 Kate Davy, 'Outing Whiteness: A Feminist Lesbian Project', in Mike Hill (ed.), *Whiteness: A Critical Reader* (New York: New York University Press, 1998), pp. 204–25, p. 213.

30 Toni Morrison, 'Rootedness: The Ancestor as Foundation', in Mari Evans (ed.), *Black Women Writers 1950–80: A Critical Evaluation* (New York: Anchor-Doubleday, 1984), pp. 339–45, p. 343, p. 344.

31 Trudier Harris, 'Reconnecting Fragments: Afro-American Folk Tradition in *The Bluest Eye*', in Nellie McKay (ed.), *Critical Essays on Toni Morrison* (Boston: G. K. Hall, 1988), pp. 68–76, p. 69

32 Jan Furman, *Toni Morrison's Fiction* (Columbia: University of South Carolina Press, 1996), p. 8.

33 Herbert William Rice, *Toni Morrison and the American Tradition: A Rhetorical Reading* (New York: Peter Lang, 1996).

34 LeClair, 'The Language Must Not Sweat: A Conversation with Toni Morrison', p. 120.

35 Alice Walker, 'Writing *The Color Purple*', in *In Search of our Mothers' Gardens: Womanist Prose by Alice Walker* (London: The Women's Press, 1984), p. 355, p. 354.

36 Alice Walker, interview in *Newsweek*, June 1982. Cited in Mae G. Henderson, '*The Color Purple*: Revisions and Redefinitions', in Harold Bloom (ed.), *Alice Walker* (New York: Chelsea House, 1989), pp. 67–80, p. 67.

37 Alice Walker, *The Same River Twice: Honoring the Difficult, a Meditation on Life, Spirit, Art, and the Making of the Film 'The Color Purple' Ten Years Later* (London: The Women's Press, 1996), p. 171.

38 Walker, 'In Search of our Mothers' Gardens', in *In Search of our Mothers' Gardens*, p. 234.

39 Walker, *The Same River Twice*, p. 170.

40 Walker, 'The Black Woman's Experience', in *In Search of our Mothers' Gardens*, p. 19.

41 Walker, *The Same River Twice*, p. 43.

42 Ibid., p. 29.

43 Ibid., p. 41.
44 Ishmael Reed is the most prominent of a number of black male writers who have condemned *The Color Purple* for perpetuating racist stereotypes and vilifying black men.
45 The introduction of Shug's reconciliation with her father, who is hardly mentioned in the novel, qualifies the devil-may-care rebelliousness which attracts Celie to Shug, and is the one area in which Spielberg is, in my view, seriously open to criticism for departing from the spirit of the original text.
46 Jaqueline Bobo, '*The Color Purple*: Black Women as Cultural Readers', in E. Deidre Pribram (ed.), *Female Spectators* (London: Verso, 1988), pp. 90–109, p. 93, p. 95.
47 Alison Light, 'Fear of the Happy Ending: *The Color Purple*, Reading and Racism', in Linda Anderson (ed.), *Plotting Change: Contemporary Women's Fiction* (London: Edward Arnold, 1990), pp. 85–96, p. 87.
48 LTP (Literature, Teaching Politics), the organisation then representing radical teachers of English literature dedicated a conference to issues raised by *The Color Purple* as an example of a progressive text.
49 *Down from the Mountaintop*.
50 bel hooks, 'Writing the Subject: Reading *The Color Purple*', in Henry Louis Gates, Jr (ed.), *Reading Black, Reading Feminist: A Critical Anthology* (New York: Meridian, 1990), pp. 454–70, p. 456.
51 Trudier Harris, 'On *The Color Purple*: Stereotypes, and Silence', *Black American Literature Forum*, 18, (4) 1984, pp. 55–61, p. 157.
52 Cora Kaplan, 'Keeping the Color in *The Color Purple*', in *Sea Changes: Essays on Culture and Feminism* (London: Verso, 1986), pp. 177–87, p. 185.
53 Ibid., p. 182.
54 Susan Willis, 'I Shop Therefore I Am: Is There a Place for Afro-American Culture in Commodity Culture?', in Cheryl A. Wall (ed.), *Changing Our Own Words: Essays on Criticism, Theory and Writing by Black Women* (London: Routledge, 1989), pp. 173–95, p. 182.
55 Light, 'Fear of the Happy Ending', p. 90.
56 Walker, *In Search of our Mothers' Gardens*, pp. xi, xii.
57 Michèle Barrett and Mary McIntosh, *The Anti-Social Family* (London: Verso, 1982), p. 159.
58 Barrett and McIntosh were later to modify their views in recognition of their earlier Eurocentrism.
59 Mary Helen Washington, 'Teaching Black-Eyed Susans: An Approach to the Study of Black Women Writers', *Black American Literature Forum* 2(1), 1977, pp. 20–4, p. 22.
60 Linda Abbandonato, 'Rewriting the Heroine's Story in *The Color Purple*', in Henry Louis Gates, Jr, and K.A. Appiah (eds), *Alice Walker: Critical Perspectives Past and Future* (New York: Amistad, 1993), pp. 296–308, p. 304
61 Marjorie Pryse, introduction to Marjorie Pryse and Hortense J. Spillers (eds), *Conjuring: Black Women and the Literary Tradition* (Bloomington: Indiana University Press, 1985), p. 2.
62 Sandi Russell, '"It's OK to Say OK"', in Nellie Y. McKay (ed.), *Critical Essays on Toni Morrison* (Boston: G.K. Hall, 1999), pp. 43–7, p. 46.
63 Walker, *In Search of our Mothers' Gardens*, pp. xi, xii.
64 Virginia Woolf, *Three Guineas* (1938) (Harmondsworth: Penguin, 1977), p. 62.

CONCLUSIONS

Re-vision – the act of looking back, of seeing with fresh eyes, of entering an old text from a new critical direction – is for women more than a chapter in cultural history: it is an act of survival.

Adrienne Rich, 'Writing as Re-Vision'

B OTH THE historical period with which this study has been concerned (1962–82) and the fiction written when the ideas of the women's movement were hegemonic, now seem very distant. At a time of increasing fragmentation and uncertainty, the possibility of there ever again being a feminist consensus about what needs to be done and how appears remote and unattainable. As Alison Light has put it, there is now a feeling that 'feminism is now somehow adrift, unanchored and cut off in crucial ways from the everyday texture of women's lives, a sense that the crude but powerful notion of being "post-feminist" may have some real purchase.'[1]

But although the 1960s and 1970s offered women possibilities for change that many who took advantage of such opportunities may regret are no longer available, the temptation to return to that history for templates of political activism should be resisted. As Joan Scanlon, the editor of *Out of the Blue: Growing Up in the Thatcher Decade* states, 'one of the most damaging consequences of this impulse towards nostalgia is the exclusion of younger women's experience in the name of a model which has had its day and cannot be repeated'.[2] Organised feminism exercised the moral and political influence that it did in the 1960s and 1970s because the economic, financial, domestic and legal injustices of which it spoke appeared to be incontrovertible. This is no longer the case. While women on average still earn much less than men, and, usually still expect to find themselves shouldering the bulk of domestic responsibilities, there are many important respects in which women's status and expectations have changed for the better and the gender picture is more complex and variegated than it was.

The principal reason why the feminist models of yesterday are perceived to lack ethical urgency is that the society in which we live is going through an epochal change, and the restructuring in global society requires an equally fundamental restructuring and rethinking of our politics. The most fundamental changes in information technology and microelectronics are taking place on a global scale accompanied by the internationalisation of production, power and politics. At the same time, the chasm in society between the prosperous and the poor, the socially powerful and the excluded, and the rich and impoverished nations of the world is deepening. The transformation of what is political is one of the characteristics of the new times in which we now live. With the urgent need for new modes of politics which reflect the growing recognition of the new global challenges now facing the whole of humanity feminist ideas will have an important part to play in any new transformative political configurations which may emerge. As Jane Miller has stated, women 'have in common the experience of standing in an ambiguous relationship to most forms of authority and of having to internalise the justice of their exclusion'. This experience has 'allowed them to know something, but not everything, about the reality of oppression (and some of the strategies for resisting it) which is the lot of most people in the world'.[3]

The relationship between the literary and the political in the time with which this study is concerned is especially acute and has resulted in the proliferation of voices demanding to be included in the category of the literary, throwing the concept of the literary itself into crisis. The demand to be allowed access to territory that was the exclusive preserve of the privileged few has a long history of representation in women's writing. In 1940 Virginia Woolf had pleaded that 'literature is no one's private ground; literature is common ground. It is not cut up into nations; there are no wars there' and had invited her readers to 'trespass freely and fearlessly and find our own way for ourselves'.[4] What many of the women writers whose work I have discussed – from Alice Walker to Pat Barker, from Marge Piercy to Fay Weldon, from Angela Carter to Buchi Emecheta – have had in common is the desire to speak in a woman's voice about the experience of powerlessness and dispossession and to explore in their writing the subjectivities which have been excluded from the mainstream literary tradition. This does not mean that the experiences of powerlessness and dispossession are the exclusive property of the woman writer nor that the celebratory impulse is not a strong and defining one in women's writing. Alice Walker, for example, celebrates women's creativity at the same time as she laments the physical and sexual abuse of women and girls. Neither does it mean that all the writers whose work I have discusssed are politically or tendentially radical, although we might wish to identify radical elements in their work. Baroness (P.D.) James, as one example, has sat on the Conservative Party benches in the British House of Lords.

While women writers are enriched by being read alongside one another, the very process of situating women's writing within received versions of literary history must challenge those versions themselves as well as the processes whereby they have been constructed. In the words of Adrienne Rich, 'We need to know the writing of the past, and know it differently than we have ever known it; not to pass on a tradition but to break its hold over us.'[5] But the relationship between the male and female writer can be complementary and mutually informing as well as antagonistic. Just as the male chroniclers of working-class life such as Alan Sillitoe and Stan Barstow in the 1960s can be profitably read side by side with the early fiction of Nell Dunn so the writing of James Kelman and William McIlvanney, who have also spoken out in support of sections of the working-class, complements the early fiction of Pat Barker. In much the same way, the work of a black woman immigrant to London like Buchi Emecheta can be usefully compared and contrasted to the first generation of Caribbean men such as George Lamming and Sam Selvon. The concern with a long and vibrant tradition of women's writing, and the insistence that such writing must be viewed in a historical context which has informed this book does not imply that either the woman writer or the woman reader will not enjoy rewarding and stimulating interchanges in her relationships with men, but only that the concerns and experiences of men and women are different, sometimes radically different. The fate of significant groups of women writers – for example the women Romanticists, the women sensation novelists, the women Modernists, and the women writers of the 1930s – at the hands of the literary critics would suggest that if the concerns and experiences of both sexes are not carefully analysed writing by women is more likely to disappear from the literary map than writing by men. Moreover, the concerns and experiences of one sex will in all probability read as being the same as, or be allowed to stand in for, the concerns and experiences of the other, even when their histories and writing would intimate that this is far from the case.

The emphasis on the specificity of women's experience by writers in this period is reflected in the interest in the large number of novels about motherhood by writers including Margaret Drabble, Margaret Forster, Fay Weldon and Lynne Reid Banks which I have discussed. The period also saw imaginative attempts to revitalise popular modes of writing including the fairy tale, the Gothic, science fiction, detective fiction and romance, by Angela Carter, Ursula Le Guin, Joanna Russ, Anita Brookner and others. These updated versions of traditional fictional forms inflected their codes and conventions and on occasion interrogated and destabilised the institutions of heterosexuality and marriage in which such conventions have traditionally been entrenched. Feminist utopias in particular have offered women ethically and ecologically inspired visions of what a feminist future world might be like.

The writings which had the strongest connection to the women's liberation movement in the 1970s were the feminist confessional novels by Erica Jong, Rita Mae Brown and Marilyn French and others. These had a direct relationship to consciousness-raising and were often read in consciousness-raising groups to help women's self-esteem and combat their feelings of isolation. The breakdown of the British Empire and of the traditional working-class communities in Britain provided a rich stimulus to some women novelists. These included Nell Dunn, Pat Barker, Jean Rhys, Ruth Prawer Jhabvala and Buchi Emecheta. In the United States the civil rights movement underpinned the flowering of writing by black women like Alice Walker and Toni Morrison that was to take place in its aftermath.

This study has argued that the knowledge of women's literature cannot be separated from the knowledge of women's history. As Virginia Woolf observed in 'Women and Fiction', it is only when we can measure the way of life and the experience of life made possible to the ordinary woman that we can account for the success and failure of the extraordinary woman as a writer.'[6] In *Sweet Freedom*, their history of the women's liberation movement, Anna Coote and Beatrice Campbell lament 'the generations of girls who have grown up in ignorance of their grandmothers' politics. Only when they reinvent rebellion for themselves do they begin to disinter the buried remains of that knowledge.'[7] In *Only Halfway to Paradise*, Elizabeth Wilson has argued that it is necessary for each generation of feminists to 'go over the same ground, to turn back to history, to literature, and to political economy in order to rediscover women's oppression ... Each succeeding generation of women has to make anew the efforts to retrieve a past that continues to remain hidden ... For this reason alone the existence of a feminist literature is important.'[8]

The reader of women's fiction in the twenty-first century is likely to be faced with a disjunction between a sophisticated and potentially liberating understanding of the unstable nature of all gendered and sexual identities and of the institutions that sustain them, which is offered to her by a combination of poststructuralist ideas and feminist theory, and a desire for more permanent identities and representations to contest the demeaning and restricted view of women which have historically prevailed. She will read fiction searching not only for recognisable pictures of reality but also for ludic elements in the text, alert to its symbolic uses of language, intertextual references, polysemousness and fantasy. The insistence on purely literary criteria for determining which works of fiction should be studied and taught runs the risk of leaving us with only a handful of writers, perhaps Doris Lessing, Toni Morrison and Angela Carter, whose stature as writers of world importance during this time could not be disputed. But the elevation of the political by itself as a criteria of value in opposition to the literary carries the danger of under-valuing the importance of the pleasures of the text and the very reasons why we turn to literary work rather than sociology, politics or history in the first place; i.e. the interaction between ideas, language and imagery which accounts for the pleasure of discovering our feelings, values and beliefs expressed imaginatively in fictional form. I shall allow Toni Morrison to have the last word:

> I am not interested in indulging myself in some private, closed exercise of my imagination that fulfils only the obligation of my personal dreams – which is to say yes, the work must be political. It must have that thrust. That's a pejorative term in critical circles now: If a work of art has any political influence in it, somehow it's tainted.

> My feeling is just the opposite: If it has none it is tainted. The problem comes when you find harangue passing off as art. It seems to me that the best art is political and you ought to be able to make it unquestionably political and irrevocably beautiful at the same time.[9]

NOTES

1 Alison Light, 'Putting on the Style: Feminist Criticism in the 1990s', in Helen Carr (ed.), *From My Guy to Sci-Fi: Genre and Women's Writing in the Postmodern World* (London: Pandora, 1989), pp. 24–35, p. 25.
2 Joan Scanlon (ed.), *Surviving the Blues: Growing Up in the Thatcher Decade* (London: Virago, 1990).
3 Jane Miller, *Women Writing about Men* (London: Virago, 1986), p. 262.
4 Virginia Woolf, 'The Leaning Tower', *A Woman's Essays: Selected Essays*, vol. 1, ed. Rachel Bowlby (London: Penguin, 1992), p. 168.
5 Adrienne Rich, 'When We Dead Awaken: Writing as Re-Vision', in *On Lies, Secrets and Silence: Selected Prose, 1966–1978* (New York: Norton, 1979), pp. 33–49, p. 35.
6 Virginia Woolf, 'Women and Fiction', in Leonard Woolf (ed.), *The Collected Essays of Virginia Woolf*, 4 vols (London: Hogarth, 1966–67), vol. 2, 1966, p. 142.
7 Anna Coote and Beatrix Campbell, *Sweet Freedom: The Struggle for Women's Liberation* (London: Pan, 1982), p. 9.
8 Elizabeth Wilson, *Only Halfway to Paradise: Women in Postwar Britain 1945–1968* (London: Tavistock, 1980), pp. 195–6.
9 Toni Morrison, 'Rootedness: The Ancestor as Foundation', in Mari Evans (ed.), *Black Women Writers: Arguments and Interviews* (London: Pluto Press, 1983), pp. 339–45, pp. 344–5.

SELECTED BIBLIOGRAPHY

PRIMARY READING

Alther, Lisa, *Kinflicks* (Harmondsworth: Penguin, 1977).

Atwood, Margaret, *The Edible Woman* (London: Virago, 1980).

——, *The Handmaid's Tale* (London: Jonathan Cape, 1986).

Barker, Pat, *The Century's Daughter* (London: Virago, 1988).

——, *Union Street* (London: Virago, 1982).

Beal, F.M, *Angel Dance* (New York: Daughters, 1977).

Brookner, Anita, *Hotel du Lac* (London: Jonathan Cape, 1984).

——, *Providence* (London: Jonathan Cape, 1982).

——, *A Start in Life* (London: Jonathan Cape, 1981).

Brown, Rita Mae, *Rubyfruit Jungle* (London: Corgi, 1978).

Bryant, Dorothy, *Ella Price's Journal* (Philadelphia: Lippincote, 1972).

Byatt, A.S., *Shadow of a Sun* (London: Chatto and Windus, 1964), reissued with an introduction by the author as *Shadow of the Sun* (London: Vintage, 1991).

Carter, Angela *The Bloody Chamber and Other Stories* (London: Victor Gollancz, 1979).

——, *Heroes and Villains* (London: Heinemann, 1969).

Dawson, Jennifer, *The Ha-Ha* (London: Anthony Blond, 1961).

Drabble, Margaret, *The Millstone* (London: Weidenfeld and Nicolson, 1965).

Duffy, Maureen, *The Microcosm* (London: Hutchinson, 1966).

——, *That's How it Was* (London: Hutchinson, 1962), reprinted with a preface by the author (London: Virago, 1983).

Dunn, Nell, *Poor Cow* (London: McGibbon and Kee, 1967), reprinted with an introduction by Margaret Drabble (London: Virago, 1988).

——, *Up the Junction* (London: McGibbon and Kee, 1963).

Emecheta, Buchi, *In the Ditch* (London: Barrie and Jenkins, 1972).

——, *Second-Class Citizen* (Allison and Busby, 1974).

Fairbairns, Zoe, *Benefits* (London: Virago, 1979).

Forster, Margaret, *Georgy Girl* (London: Secker and Warburg, 1965).

French, Marilyn, *The Women's Room* (London: André Deutsch, 1977).

Grafton, Sue, *'A' is for Alibi* (New York: Signet, 1984).

James, P.D., *An Unsuitable Job for a Woman* (London: Faber and Faber, 1972).

Jong, Erica, *Fear of Flying* (London: Secker and Warburg, 1974).

Kitchen, Paddy, *Lying-In* (London: Arthur Barker, 1965).

Le Guin, Ursula, *The Left Hand of Darkness* (New York: Ace, 1969 and London: Macdonald, 1969).

Lessing, Doris, *The Golden Notebook* (1962), reprinted with a new preface (1971) by the author (St Albans: Granada, 1972).

Maitland, Sara, *Daughters of Jerusalem* (London: Blond and Biggs, 1978).

Meulenbelt, Anja, *The Shame Is Over* (London: The Women's Press, 1980).

Miner, Valerie, *Murder in the English Department* (London: The Women's Press, 1982).

Morrison, Toni, *The Bluest Eye* (1970) (London: Triad/Grenada, 1981).

Mortimer, Penelope, *The Pumpkin Eater* (London: Hutchinson, 1962).

Muller, Marcia, *Games to Keep the Dark Away* (New York: St. Martin's Press, 1984).

Naylor, Gloria, *The Women of Brewster Place* (New York: Viking Books, 1982).

Paretsky, Sarah, *Killing Orders* (New York: William Morrow, 1985).

Piercy, Marge, *Braided Lives* (New York: Fawcett, 1982).

——, *Woman on the Edge of Time* (New York: Knopf, 1976, and London: The Women's Press, 1979).

Plath, Sylvia, *The Bell Jar* (London: Faber and Faber, 1963).
Prawer Jhabvala, Ruth, *Heat and Dust* (London: John Murray, 1975).
Reid Banks, Lynne, *The L-Shaped Room* (London: Chatto and Windus, 1960).
Rhys, Jean, *Wide Sargasso Sea* (London: André Deutsch, 1966).
Roberts, Michèle, *A Piece of the Night* (London: The Women's Press, 1978).
Russ, Joanna, *The Female Man* (New York: Bantam Books, 1975, and London: The Women's Press, 1985).
Shulman, Alix Kates, *Burning Questions* (New York: Bantam, 1979).
Stefan, Verena, *Shedding* (London: The Women's Press, 1980).
Steiner, Susan, *Murder on her Mind* (New York, Fawcett, 1985).
Walker, Alice, *The Color Purple* (London: The Women's Press, 1982).
——, 'Strong Horse Tea', *In Love and Trouble* (1967) (London: The Women's Press, 1983), pp. 88–98.
Weldon, Fay, *The Fat Woman's Joke* (1967), (London: Sceptre, 1982), p. 9.
——, *Puffball* (London: Hodder and Stoughton, 1980).
Wilson, Barbara, *Murder in the Collective* (London: The Women's Press, 1984).
Winterson, Jeanette, *Oranges Are Not the Only Fruit* (London: Pandora, 1985).
Wynter, Sylvia, *The Hills of Hebron* (London: Jonathan Cape, 1972).

SECONDARY READING

Abbandonato, Linda, 'Rewriting The Heroine's Story in *The Color Purple*', in Henry Louis Gates, Jr., and K.A. Appiah, (eds), *Alice Walker: Critical Perspectives Past and Present* (New York: Amistad, 1993), pp. 296–308.
Agarwal, Ramlal G., *Ruth Prawer Jhabvala: A Study of her Fiction* (New Delhi: Sterling Publishers, 1990).
Albinski, Nan Bowman, *Women's Utopias in British and American Fiction* (London: Routledge, 1988).
Alexander, Flora , *Contemporary Women Novelists* (London: Edward Arnold, 1989).
Allan, Jita Tuzyline, *Womanist and Feminist Aesthetics: A Comparative Review* (Athens: Ohio University Press, 1995).
Allen, Mary, *The Necessary Blankness: Women in Major American Fiction of the Sixties* (Urbana and London: University of Illinois Press, 1976).
Anderson, Benedict, *Imagined Communities* (London: Verso, 1991).
Anderson, Linda (ed.) *Plotting Change: Contemporary Women's Fiction* (London: Edward Arnold, 1990).
——, *Women and Autobiography in the Twentieth-Century: Remembered Futures* (Hemel Hempstead: Harvester Wheatsheaf, 1997).
Andrews, Geoff et al., *The Long 1960s* (London: Macmillan, 1998).
Angier, Carole, *Jean Rhys: Life and Work* (London: André Deutsch, 1990).
Armitt, Lucie, *Where No Man Has Gone Before: Women and Science Fiction* (London: Routledge, 1991).
Armstrong, Isobel (ed.), *New Feminist Discourses: New Critical Essays on Theories and Texts* (London: Routledge, 1992).
——, 'Woolf by the Lake, Woolf at the Circus: Carter and Tradition', in Lorna Sage (ed.), *Flesh and the Mirror: Essays on the Art of Angela Carter* (London: Virago, 1994), pp. 257–79.
Ascher, Carol, Desalvo, Louise, and Ruddick, Sara, *Between Women: Biographers, Novelists, Critics, Teachers and Artists Write about their Work on Women* (Boston: Beacon Press, 1984).
Auerbach, Nina, *Communities of Women: An Idea in Fiction* (Cambridge, MA: Harvard University Press, 1978), p. 4.

Awkward, Michael, *Inspiriting Influences: Tradition, Revision and Afro-American Women's Novels* (New York: Columbia University Press, 1989).

Baker, Niam, *Happily Ever After? Women's Fiction in Postwar Britain 1945–60* (London: Macmillan, 1989).

Barreca, Regina (ed.), *Fay Weldon's Wicked Fictions* (Hanover: University of New England Press, 1994).

Barrett, Michèle and McIntosh, Mary, *The Anti-Social Family* (London: Verso, 1982).

Bartowski, Frances, *Feminist Utopias* (Lincoln and London: University of Nebraska Press, 1989).

Bassnet, Susan, *Feminist Experiences: The Women's Movement in Four Cultures* (London: Allen and Unwin, 1986).

Benn, Melissa, *Madonna and Child: Towards a New Politics of Mothering* (London: Jonathan Cape, 1998).

Berman, Paul, *A Tale of Two Utopias: The Political Journey of the Generation of 1968* (New York: Norton, 1996).

Binyon, T.J., *The Detective in Fiction* (Oxford: Oxford University Press, 1989).

Birch, Helen, 'P.D. James' Stylish Crime', *Women's Review*, 10, 1986, pp. 6–7.

Bjorg, Patrick Bryce, *Toni Morrison: The Search for Self and Place within the Community* (New York: Peter Lang, 1992).

Bloom, Harold (ed.), *Toni Morrison* (New York: Chelsea House, 1990).

——, (ed.), *Alice Walker* (New York: Chelsea House, 1989).

Boone, Joseph Allen, *Libidinal Currents: Sexuality and the Shaping of Modernism* (Chicago: University of Chicago Press, 1998).

Bradbury, Malcolm, *No, Not Bloomsbury* (London: André Deutsch, 1987).

Bristow, Joseph, and Broughton, Trev Lynne (eds), *The Infernal Desires of Angela Carter: Fiction, Femininity, Feminism* (London: Longman, 1997).

Brown, Helen Gurley, *Sex and the Single Girl* (New York: Cardinal, 1962).

Brown, Lloyd W., *Women Writers in Black Africa* (Westport, CT: Greenwood Press, 1981).

Brown, Reva, review of *The Century's Daughter*, *British Book News*, December 1986, pp. 709–10.

Burton, Angela, 'Signifyin(g) Abjection: Narrative Strategies in Toni Morrison's *Jazz*', in Linden Peach (ed.), *Toni Morrison* (Basingstoke: Macmillan, 1998), pp. 170–93.

Byatt, A.S. 'Give Me the Moonlight, Give me the Girl', *The New Review*, 11, 1975, p. 67.

Campbell, Beatrice, *Wigan Pier Revisited: Poverty and Politics in the 80s* (London: Virago, 1984).

Carter, Angela, 'I'm a Socialist, Damn it! How Can You Expect Me to be Interested in Fairies?', interview with Mary Harron, *Guardian*, 15 September 1984, p. 10.

——, 'Notes from the Front Line', in Micheline Wandor (ed.), *On Gender and Writing* (London: Pandora, 1983), pp. 69–77.

——, 'Truly it Felt Like Year One', in Sara Maitland (ed.), *Very Heaven: Looking Back at the 1960s* (London: Virago, 1988), pp. 209–16.

——, *The Sadeian Woman: An Exercise in Cultural History* (London: Virago, 1979).

Chafe, William H., *The Paradox of Change: American Women in the Twentieth Century* (New York and Oxford: Oxford University Press).

Chessler, Phyllis, *Women and Madness* (New York: Avon Books, 1972, reprinted 1991).

Christian, Barbara T., *Black Women Novelists: The Development of a Tradition, 1892–1976* (Westport, CT: Greenwood Press, 1980).

Chodorow, Nancy, *The Reproduction of Mothering* (Berkeley: University of California Press, 1978).

Clarke, Robert, 'Angela Carter's Desire Machine', *Women's Studies*, 14, 1987, pp. 147–61.

Cooper-Clark, Diana, 'Margaret Drabble: Cautious Feminist', *Atlantic Monthly*, 246, November 1980, pp. 69–75.

——, 'Margaret Drabble: Cautious Feminist', in Ellen Rose Cronan (ed.), *Critical Essays on Margaret Drabble* (Boston: G.K. Hall, 1985), pp. 19–30.

Cosslet, Tess, *Women Writing Childbirth: Modern Discourses of Motherhood* (Manchester: Manchester University Press, 1994).

Coward, Rosalind, *Female Desire: Women's Sexuality Today* (London: Paladin, 1984).

——, '"This Novel Changes Lives": Are Women's Novels Feminist Novels? A Response to Rebecca O' Rourke's Article "Summer Reading"', *Feminist Review*, 5, 1980, pp. 53–64.

——, and Semple, Linda , 'Tracking Down the Past: Women and Detective Fiction', in Helen Carr (ed.) *From My Guy to Sci-Fi: Genre and Women's Writing in the Postmodern World* (London: Pandora, 1989), pp. 39–57.

Craig, Patricia and Cadogan, Mary, *The Lady Investigates: Women Detectives and Spies in Fiction* (London: Gollancz, 1981).

Crane, Ralph J., *Ruth Prawer Jhabvala* (New York: Twayne University Press, 1992).

Cranny-Francis, Anne, *Feminist Fiction: Feminist Uses of Generic Fiction* (Cambridge: Polity Press, 1990).

Davy, Kate, 'Outing Whiteness: A Feminist Lesbian Project', in Mike Hill (ed.), *Whiteness: A Critical Reader* (New York: New York University Press, 1998), pp. 204–25.

Davis, Cynthia A., 'Self, Society and Myth in Toni Morrison's Fiction', in Harold Bloom (ed.), *Toni Morrison* (New York: Chelsea House, 1990), pp. 8–25.

Davis, Flora , *Moving the Mountain: The Women's Movement in America Since 1960* (New York and London: Simon and Schuster, 1991).

Davis, Tricia, 'What Kind of a Woman Is She?' Women and Communist Party Politics, 1941–1955', in Rosalind Brunt and Caroline Rowan (eds), *Feminism, Culture and Politics* (London: Lawrence and Wishart, 1982), pp. 85–107.

Day, Aidan, *Angela Carter: The Rational Glass* (Manchester: Manchester University Press, 1998).

de Bolt, Joe, (ed.), *Ursula K. Le Guin: Voyager to Inner Lands and to Outer Space* (Port Washington, NY, and London: Kennikat Press, 1979).

Densmore, Dana, 'Independence from the Sexual Revolution', in Anne Koedt, Ellen Levine and Anita Rapone (eds), *Radical Feminism* (New York: Quadrangle, 1973), pp. 107–18.

Drabble, Margaret, introduction to *Poor Cow* (London: McGibbon and Kee, 1967, reprinted London: Virago, 1988).

DuCille, Ann, *The Coupling Convention: Sex, Text, and Tradition in Black Women's Fiction* (Oxford: Oxford University Press, 1993).

Duncker, Patricia, *Strangers and Sisters: An Introduction to Contemporary Feminist Fiction* (Oxford: Blackwell, 1992).

Duplessis, Rachel Blau, 'The Feminist Apologues of Lessing, Piercey and Russ', *Frontiers*, 4, Spring 1979, pp. 1–8.

Dyer, Richard, *White* (London: Routledge, 1997).

Echols, Alice, *Daring To Be Bad: Radical Feminism in America 1967–1975* (Minneapolis: University of Minneapolis Press, 1989).

Ehrenreich, Barbara, Hess, Elisabeth and Jacobs, Gloria , *Re-Making Love: The Feminisation of Sex* (New York: Doubleday, 1986).

Ellis, John, *Sex, Class and Realism: British Cinema 1956–1963* (London: British Film Institute, 1986).

Emecheta, Buchi, 'It's Me Who's Changed', *Connexion: An International Women's Quarterly*, 4, Spring 1982, pp. 4–5.

Emery, Mary Lou, *Jean Rhys at 'World's End': Novels of Colonial and Sexual Exile* (Austin: University of Austin Press, 1990).

Evans, Sara, *Personal Politics: The Roots of Women's Liberation in The Civil Rights*

Movement and the New Left (New York: Vintage Books, 1980).

Felman, Shoshana, 'Women and Madness: The Critical Fallacy' *Diacritics*, 5(4), Winter 1975, pp. 2–10.

Feminist Anthology Collective, *No Turning Back: Writings from the Women's Liberation Movement 1975–80* (London: The Women's Press, 1981).

Fetterley, Judith, *The Resisting Reader: A Feminist Approach to American Literature* (Bloomington: Indiana University Press, 1978).

Finch, Janet, and Summerfield, Penny, 'Social Reconstruction and the Emergence of Companionate Marriage, 1945–59', in Clarke David (ed.), *Marriage, Domestic Life and Social Change* (London: Routledge, 1991), pp. 7–32.

Flax, Jane, 'Postmodernism and Gender Relations in Feminist Theory', in Linda Nicholson (ed.), *Feminism/Postmodernism* (London: Routledge, 1990), pp. 39–62.

Forma, Aminata, *Mother of All Myths: How Society Moulds and Constrains Mothers* (London: HarperCollins, 1998).

Fox, Pamela, *Class Fictions: Shame and Resistance in the British Working Class Novel 1890–1945* (Durham, NC, and London: Duke University Press, 1994).

French, Marilyn, *Beyond Power: On Women, Men and Morals* (London: Jonathan Cape, 1985).

Frame, Janet, *An Angel at My Table: An Autobiography*, vol. 2 (London: The Women's Press, 1984).

——, *The Envoy from Mirror City: An Autobiography* (1984), vol. 3 (London: The Women's Press, 1985).

Friedman, Susan Stanford, 'Beyond White and Other: Relationality and Narratives of Race in Feminist Discourse', *Signs: Journal of Women in Culture and Society*, 2(1), 1995, pp. 1–49.

Furman, Jan, *Toni Morrison's Fiction* (Columbia: University of South Carolina Press, 1996).

Gamble, Sarah, *Angela Carter: Writing from the Front Line* (Edinburgh: Edinburgh University Press, 1997).

Gardiner, Judith Kegan, *Rhys, Stead, Lessing, and the Politics of Empathy* (Bloomington: Indiana University Press, 1989).

Gasiorek, Andrzej, *Postwar British Fiction: Realism and After* (London: Edward Arnold, 1995).

Gates, Henry Louis, Jr (ed.), *Reading Black, Reading Feminist: A Critical Anthology* (New York: Meridian, 1990).

Gatlin, Rochelle, *American Women Since 1945* (Basingstoke: Macmillan, 1987).

Gavron, Hannah, *The Captive Wife: Conflicts of Housebound Mothers* (London: Routledge and Kegan Paul, 1966).

Gerrard, Nicci, *Into the Mainstream: How Feminism Has Changed Women's Writing* (London: Pandora, 1989).

Giddens, Anthony, *The Transformation of Intimacy; Sexuality, Love and Eroticism in Modern Societies* (Cambridge: Polity/Blackwell, 1992).

Gindin, James, *Postwar British Fiction: New Accents and Attitudes* (Westport, CT: Greenwood Press, 1962).

Giobbi, Guiliana, 'Sisters Beware of Sisters: Sisterhood as a Literary Motif in Jane Austen, A.S. Byatt, and I. Bossi Fedrigotti', *Journal of European Studies*, 87, September 1992, pp. 241–6.

Goldthorpe, J.H. *et al.*, *The Affluent Worker*, 3 vols (Cambridge: Cambridge University Press, 1968–69).

Greene, Gail, *Changing the Story: Feminist Fiction and the Tradition* (Bloomington: Indiana University Press, 1991).

Gregg, Veronica Marie, *Jean Rhys's Historical Imagination: Reading and Writing the Creole* (Chapel Hill: University of North Carolina Press, 1995).

Griffiths, John, *Three Tomorrows: American, British and Soviet Science Fiction* (London: Macmillan, 1980).

Guppy, Shusha, interview with Anita Brookner, *The Paris Review*, Fall 1987, pp. 325–42.

Haffenden, John, 'Playing Straight: Interview with Anita Brookner', *The Literary Review*, September 1984, pp. 25–31.

——, interview with Angela Carter, *Novelists in Interview* (London: Methuen, 1985), pp. 76–97.

Hanscombe, Gilllian E., and Forster, Jackie, *Rocking the Cradle: Lesbian Mothers, a Challenge to Family Living* (London: Peter Owen, 1981).

Harding, Wendy and Martin, Jacky, *A World of Difference: An Intercultural Study of Toni Morrison's Novels* (Westport, CT: Greenwood Press, 1994).

Harris, Trudier, 'Reconnecting Fragments: Afro-American Folk Tradition in *The Bluest Eye*' in Nellie McKay (ed.), *Critical Essays on Toni Morrison* (Boston: G.K. Hall, 1988), pp. 68–76.

Harrison, Nancy R. *Jean Rhys and the Novel as Women's Text* (Chapel Hill: University of North Carolina Press, 1988).

Haywood, Ian, *Working-Class Fiction: From Chartism to Trainspotting* (London: Northcote House, 1997).

—— and Phillips Deborah, *Brave New Causes: Women in British Postwar Fiction* (London: Leicester University Press, 1998).

Heinemann, Margot, '*Burger's Daughter*: The Synthesis of Revelation', in Jefferson Douglas and Martin Graham (eds), *The Uses of Fiction: Essays on the Modern Novel in Honour of Arnold Kettle* (Milton Keynes: Open University Press, 1982), pp. 181–97.

Heinze, Denise, *The Dilemma of 'Double-Consciousness': Toni Morrison's Novels* (Athens: University of Georgia Press, 1993).

Henderson, Mae G., '*The Color Purple*: Revisions and Redefinitions', in Harold Bloom (ed.), *Alice Walker* (New York: Chelsea House, 1989), pp. 67–80.

Henessey, Rosemary, *Materialist Feminism and the Politics of Discourse* (London: Routledge, 1993).

Henri, Adrian, introduction to *Up the Junction* (London: MacGibbon and Kee, 1963, reprinted London: Virago, 1988).

Hirsch, Marianne, *The Mother/Daughter Plot: Narrative, Psychoanalysis, Feminism* (Bloomington: Indiana University Press, 1989).

Hitchcock, Peter, *Dialogics of the Oppressed* (Minneapolis: University of Minnesota Press, 1993).

Hite, Molly, *The Other Side of the Story: Structures and Strategies of Contemporary Feminist Narrative* (Ithaca and London: Cornell University Press, 1989).

Hite, Shere, *The Hite Report* (New York and London: Macmillan, 1976).

Hobsbawm, Eric, 'Address at the Funeral of Margot Heinemann', 19 June 1992, in Margolies, David, and Joannou, Maroula, (eds), *Heart of the Heartless World: Essays in Cultural Resistance in Memory of Margot Heinemann* (London: Pluto Press, 1995), pp. 206–9.

Hogeland, Lisa Maria, *Feminism and its Fictions: The Consciousness-Raising Novel and the Women's Liberation Movement* (Philadelphia: University of Pennysylvania Press, 1998).

Hoggart, Richard, *The Uses of Literacy* (London: Chatto, 1957).

Holloway, Karla F.C. and Stephanie Demetrakopolous, *New Dimensions of Spirituality: A Biracial and Bicultural Reading of the Novels of Toni Morrison* (Westport, CT: Greenwood Press, 1987).

hooks, bel, *Black Looks: Race and Representation* (Boston: South End Press, 1992).

——, *Feminist Theory: From Margin to Centre* (Boston: South End Press, 1984).

——, 'Writing the Subject: Reading *The Color Purple*', in Henry Louis Gates, Jr (ed.),

Reading Black, Reading Feminist: A Critical Anthology (New York: Meridian, 1990), pp. 454–70.

Horowitz, Daniel, *Betty Friedan and the Making of the Feminine Mystique: The American Left, the Cold War and Modern Feminism* (Amherst: Massachusetts University Press, 1999).

Hubbly, Erlene, 'The Formula Challenged: The Novels of P.D. James', *Modern Fiction Studies*, 29(3), 1983, pp. 511–21.

Humm, Maggie, *Border Traffic: Strategies of Contemporary Women Writers* (Manchester: Manchester University Press, 1991).

——, 'Feminist Detective Fiction', in Clive Bloom (ed.), *Twentieth-Century Suspense: The Thriller Comes of Age* (London: Macmillan, 1990), pp. 237–55.

Humphries, Jefferson (ed.), *Southern Literature and Literary Theory* (Athens: University of Georgia Press, 1990).

Irons, Glenwood (ed.) *Feminism in Women's Detective Fiction* (Toronto: University of Toronto Press, 1995).

Jaques, Martin, and Francis Mulhern, (eds), *The Forward March of Labour Halted?* (London: NLB, 1981).

Jezer, Marty, *The Dark Ages: Life in the United States 1945–1960* (Boston: South End Press, 1982).

Jolly, Margaretta, 'After Feminism: Pat Barker, Penelope Lively and the Contemporary Novel', unpublished paper, University of Sussex, 1999.

Jong, Erica, 'Comments on Joan Reardon's *Fear of Flying*: Developing the Feminist Novel: A Letter to the Author', *International Journal of Women's Studies*, 1(6), November–December 1978, pp. 625–6.

Jong, Erica, *Fear of Fifty: A Midlife Memoir* (London: Chatto and Windus, 1994).

Jordan, Elaine, The Dangers of Angela Carter', in Isobel Armstrong (ed.), *New Feminist Discourses: Critical Essays on Theories and Texts* (London: Routledge, 1992), pp. 119–33.

Jouve, Nicole Ward, 'Mother Is a Figure of Speech', in Lorna Sage (ed.), *Flesh and The Mirror: Essays on the Art of Angela Carter*, pp. 136–71.

Kaledin, Eugenia, *American Women in the 1950s: Mothers and More* (Boston: Twayne, 1984).

Kaplan, Carla, *The Erotics of Talk: Women's Writing and Feminist Paradigms* (Oxford: Oxford University Press, 1996).

——, 'Keeping the Color in *The Color Purple*', in *Sea Changes: Essays on Culture and Feminism* (London: Verso, 1986), pp. 177–87.

——, 'Pandora's Box: Subjectivity, Class and Sexuality in Feminist Criticism', in *Sea Changes Culture and Feminism* (London: Verso, 1986), pp. 147–76.

——, 'An Unsuitable Genre for a Feminist', *Women's Review*, 8, 1986, pp. 18–19.

Kaveney, Roz, 'The Science Fictiveness of Women's Science Fiction', in Helen Carr (ed.) *From My Guy to Sci-Fi: Genre and Women's Writing in the Postmodern World* (London: Pandora, 1989), pp. 78–97.

Kelly, Kathleen Coyne, *A.S. Byatt* (New York: Twayne, 1996).

Kenyon, Olga, *Women Novelists Today: A Survey of English Women's Writing in the Seventies and Eighties* (Brighton: Harvester, 1988).

Kenny, Michael, 'Communism and the New Left', in Geoff Andrews et al. (eds), *Opening the Books: Essays on the Social and Cultural History of the British Communist Party* (London: Pluto Press, 1995), pp. 195–209.

Kiernan, Kathleen, Land, Hilary, and Lewis, Jane, *Lone Motherhood in Twentieth-Century Britain: From Footnote to Front Page* (Oxford: Clarendon Press, 1998).

Klein, Kathleen Gregory, *The Woman Detective: Gender and Genre* (Urbana: University of Illinois Press, 1988).

Koenen, Anne, 'The One Out of Sequence' (1980) in Danille Taylor-Guthrie (ed.),

Conversations with Toni Morrison (Jackson: University of Mississippi Press, 1994), pp. 67–83.

Koedt, Anne, 'The Myth of the Vaginal Orgasm', in Ellen Levine and Anita Rapone (eds), *Radical Feminism* (New York: Quadrangle, The New York Times Book Company, 1973), pp. 198–207.

Kristeva, Julia, 'Women's Time' (1979), trans. 1981, in Toril Moi (ed.), *The Kristeva Reader* (Oxford: Basil Blackwell, 1986), pp. 187–213.

Laing, Stuart, *Representations of Working-Class Life 1957–1964* (Basingstoke: Macmillan, 1984).

Lauret, Maria, *Liberating Literature: Feminist Fiction in America* (London: Routledge, 1994).

——, 'Seizing Time and Making New: Feminist Criticism, Politics and Contemporary Feminist Fiction', *Feminist Review*, 31, Spring 1989, pp. 94–106.

LeClair, Thomas, 'The Language Must Not Sweat: A Conversation with Toni Morrison' (1981), in Danille Taylor-Guthrie (ed.), *Conversations with Toni Morrison*, pp. 119–37.

LeFanu, Sarah, *In the Chinks of the World Machine: Feminism and Science Fiction* (London: The Women's Press, 1988.

—— 'Sex, Sub-Atomic Particles and Sociology', in Lucie Armitt (ed.), *Where No Man Has Gone Before* (London: Routledge, 1990), pp. 178–86.

Le Guin, Ursula, 'Is Gender Necessary? Redux' (1976/1987), in *Dancing on the Edge of the World: Thoughts on Words, Women, Places* (London: Gollancz, 1989).

Lessing, Doris, 'Profile', *New Review*, 1(8), (November 1974), pp. 17–23.

——, 'The Small Personal Voice', in *A Small Personal Voice: Essays, Reviews Interviews*, ed. Paul Schlueter (New York: Alfed A. Knopf, 1974).

Lewis, Jane, 'From Equality to Liberation: Contextualising the Emergence of the Women's Liberation Movement', in Bart Moore-Gilbert and John Seed (eds), *Cultural Revolution? The Challenge of the Arts in the 1960s* (London: Routledge, 1992), pp. 96–118.

——, *Women in Britain Since 1945: Women, Family, Work and the State in the Post-War Years* (Oxford: Blackwell, 1992).

Lewis, Peter, *The Fifties* (London: Heinemann, 1978).

Light, Alison, 'Fear of the Happy Ending: *The Color Purple*: Reading and Racism', in Linda Williams (ed.), *Plotting Change: Contemporary Women's Fiction* (London: Edward Arnold, 1990), pp. 85–99.

Lorde, Audre, 'The Master's Tools Will Never Dismantle The Master's House', in Cherry Moraga and Gloria Anzaldua (eds), *This Bridge Called My Back: Writings by Radical Women of Color* (New York: Women of Color Press, 1991), pp. 98–101.

Lovell, Terry, 'Ideology and Coronation Street', in Richard Dyer (ed.), *Coronation Street* (London: British Film Institute, 1981).

Lovenduski, Joni and Randall, Vicky, *Contemporary Feminist Politics* (Oxford: Oxford University Press, 1993).

Lyndon, Neil, *No More Sex Wars: The Failures of Feminism* (London: Sinclair-Stevenson, 1992).

Maslen, Elizabeth, *Doris Lessing* (Plymouth: Northcote House, 1994).

Matus, Jill, *Toni Morrison* (Manchester: Manchester University Press, 1998).

McKay, Nellie (ed.), *Critical Essays on Toni Morrison* (Boston: G.K. Hall, 1988).

Macedo, Stephen (ed.), *Reassessing the Sixties: Debating the Political and Cultural Legacy* (New York: Norton, 1997).

Makinen, Merja, 'Angela Carter's *The Bloody Chamber* and the Decolonization of Feminine Sexuality', *Feminist Review*, 42, Autumn 1992, pp. 2–15.

Mann, Jessica, *Deadlier than the Male: An Investigation into Feminine Crime Writing* (Newton Abbot and London: David and Charles, 1981).

Massie, Alan, *The Novel Today: A Critical Guide to the British Novel 1970–89* (London: Longman, 1990).

May, Elaine Tyler, 'Explosive Issues: Sex, Woman and the Bomb', in Lary May (ed.), *Recasting America: Culture and Politics in the Age of the Cold War* (Chicago: University of Chicago Press, 1988), pp. 154–70.

——, *Homeward Bound: American Families in the Cold War* (New York: Basic Books, 1988).

Mickelson, Anne Z. , *Reaching Out: Sensitivity and Order in Recent American Fiction by Women* (Metuchen, NJ, and London: Scarecrow Press, 1979).

Miles, Rosalind, *The Female Form: Women Writers and the Conquest of the Novel* (London: Routledge, Kegan and Paul, 1987).

Miller, Douglas T. and Nowak Marion, *The Fifties: The Way We Really Were* (New York: Doubleday, 1977).

Millett, Kate, 'The Shame Is Over', *MS*, January, 1975, pp. 25–7.

Monteith, Sharon, 'Warring Fictions: Reading Pat Barker', *Moderne Sprake*, 1(1), 1997, pp. 124–9.

Moore-Gilbert, Bart, and Seed, John (eds), *Cultural Revolution: The Challenge of the Arts in the 1960s* (London: Routledge, 1992).

Morgan, Ellen, 'Humanbeing: Form and Focus in the Neo-Feminist Novel', in Cheryl L. Brown and Karen Olson (eds), *Feminist Criticism: Essays on Theory, Poetry and Prose* (Metuchen, NJ, and London: The Scarecrow Press, 1978), pp. 272–8.

Morris, Pam, *Literature and Feminism: An Introduction* (Oxford: Blackwell 1993).

Morrison, Toni, 'Behind the Making of *The Black Book*', *Black World*, February 1974, pp. 86–90.

——, *Playing in the Dark: Whiteness and the Literary Imagination* (Cambridge, MA: Harvard University Press, 1992).

——, 'Rediscovering Black History', *New York Times Magazine*, 11 August 1974, pp. 14–24.

——, 'Rootedness: The Ancestor as Foundation', in Mari Evans (ed.), *Black Women Writers 1950–80: A Critical Evaluation* (New York: Anchor-Doubleday, 1984), pp. 339–45.

Mortimer, John, 'The Stylish Prime of Miss Carter', *Sunday Times*, 24 January 1982, p. 36.

Moylan, Tom *Demand the Impossible: Science Fiction and the Utopian Imagination* (London: Methuen, 1986).

Munt, Sally, 'The Investigators: Lesbian Crime Fiction', in Susannah Radstone (ed.), *Sweet Dreams: Sexuality, Gender and Popular Fiction* (London: Lawrence and Wishart, 1988), pp. 91–119.

——, *Murder by the Book? Feminism and the Crime Novel* (London: Routledge, 1994).

Myrdal, Alva, and Klein, Viola, *Women's Two Roles* (London: Routledge, Kegan and Paul, 1956).

Naylor, Gloria, 'A Conversation: Gloria Naylor and Toni Morrison' (1985), in Danille Taylor-Guthrie (ed.), *Conversations with Toni Morrison* (Jackson: University of Mississippi Press, 1994), pp. 188–217.

Ohmann, Richard, *Politics of Letters* (Middletown, CT: Wesleyan University Press, 1987).

Orr, Peter, *The Poet Speaks* (London: Routledge and Kegan Paul, 1966).

Page, Philip, *Dangerous Freedom: Fusion and Fragmentation in Toni Morrison's Novels* (Jackson: University of Mississippi Press, 1995).

Palmer, Paulina, *Contemporary Women's Fiction: Narrative Practice and Theory* (Hemel Hempstead: Harvester, 1989).

——, 'Gender as Performance in the Fiction of Angela Carter and Margaret Atwood', in Joseph Bristow and Trev Broughton (eds), *The Infernal Desires of Angela Carter:*

Fiction, Femininity, Feminism (London: Longman, 1997), pp. 24–43.

Parrinder, Patrick, *Science Fiction: Its Criticism and Teaching* (London: Methuen, 1980).

Parry, Benita, 'Problems in Current Theories of Colonial Discourse', *Oxford Literary Review*, 9, 1988, pp. 27–58.

Patterson, Sheila, *Immigration and Race Relations in Britain 1960–67* (London and Oxford: Oxford University Press, 1969).

Peach, Linden, *Angela Carter* (London: Macmillan, 1998).

——, (ed.), *Toni Morrison: Contemporary Critical Essays* (London: Macmillan, 1998).

Pearce, Lynne, and Wisker, Gina (eds), Introduction, *Fatal Attractions: Rescripting Romance in Contemporary Literature and Film* (London: Pluto, 1988).

Peterson, Nancy C, *Toni Morrison: Critical and Theoretical Approaches* (Baltimore: Johns Hopkins University Press, 1997).

Phoenix, Ann, Woollett, Anne and Lloyd, Eva (eds), *Motherhood: Meanings, Practices and Ideologies* (London: Sage, 1991).

Plath, Sylvia, *Letters Home: Correspondence 1950–61*, ed. Amelia Schober Plath (London: Faber and Faber, 1975).

——, *The Journals of Sylvia Plath 1950–1962* ed. Ted Hughes and Frances McCullough (New York: The Dial Press, 1982).

Porter, Dennis, 'Detection and Ethics: The Case of P.D. James', in Barbara A. Rader and Howard G. Zettler (eds), *The Sleuth and the Scholar: Origins, Evolution, and Current Trends in Detective Fiction* (New York: Greenwood Press, 1988), pp. 11–18.

Preussner, Dee, 'Talking with Margaret Drabble', *Modern Fiction Studies*, 25, 1979–80, pp. 563–77

Pryse, Marjorie and Spillers, Hortense J. (eds), *Conjuring: Black Women and the Literary Tradition* (Bloomington: Indiana University Press, 1985).

Reisman, David, Nathan Glazer, and Ruel Denny, *The Lonely Crowd* (New Haven: Yale University Press, 1950).

Randall, Vicky, *Women and Politics* (London: Macmillan, 1987).

Reddy, Maureen, *Sisters in Crime: Feminism and the Crime Novel* (New York: Frederick Ungar), 1988.

Rice, Herbert William, *Toni Morrison and the American Tradition* (New York: Peter Lang, 1996).

Rich, Adrienne, *Of Woman Born: Motherhood as Experience and Institution* (New York: W.W. Norton, reprinted London: Virago, 1986).

——, 'When We Dead Awaken: Writing as Re-Vision' (1971), in *On Lies, Secrets and Silence* (New York: Norton, 1979), pp. 33–49.

Richardson, Sarah (ed.), *Writing on the Line: Twentieth Century Working-Class Women Writers* (London: The Working Press, 1996).

Riley, Denise, *War in the Nursery: Theories of the Child and Mother* (London: Virago, 1983).

Roberts, Elizabeth, *Women and Families: An Oral History, 1940–1970* (Oxford: Basil Blackwell, 1995).

Roberts, Robert, *The Classic Slum: Salford Life in the First Quarter of the Century* (Manchester: Manchester University Press, 1971).

Robertson, Grace, *Grace Robertson: Photojournalist of the 50s* (London: Virago, 1989).

Robinson, Sally, *Engendering the Subject: Gender and Self-Representation in Contemporary Women's Fiction* (Albany: State University of New York Press, 1991).

Rose, Ellen Cronan, 'Review Essay: American Feminist Criticism of Contemporary Women's Fiction', *Signs*, 18(12), 1993, pp. 246–75,

Rose, Mark, *Alien Encounters: Anatomy of Science Fiction* (Cambridge, MA: Harvard University Press, 1981).

Rosinksy, Natalie M., *Feminist Futures: Contemporary Women's Speculative Fiction* (Ann Arbor, Michigan: UMI Research Press, 1984).

Rowbottom, Sheila, 'To Be Or Not To Be: The Dilemma of Mothering', *Feminist Review*, 31, 1989, pp. 82–93.

Rubenstein, Roberta, *The Novelistic Vision of Doris Lessing* (Urbana, University of Illinois Press, 1979).

Russell, Sandi, 'It's Ok to Say Ok', in Nellie Y. McKay (ed.), *Critical Essays on Toni Morrison* (Boston: G.K. Hall, 1999), pp. 43–7.

Sage, Lorna, *Angela Carter* (London: Northcote House, 1994).

——, (ed.), *Flesh and the Mirror: Essays in the Art of Angela Carter* (London: Virago, 1994).

——, *Women in the House of Fiction: Postwar Women Novelists* (London: Routledge, 1992).

Samuel, Raphael, 'The Lost World of British Communism', parts 1–3, *New Left Review*, 154, 155, 156, 1985–87.

Seabrook, Jeremy, *What Went Wrong? Working People and the Ideals of the Labour Movement* (London: Gollancz, 1978).

Sedgwick, Eve Kosofsky, *Epistemology of the Closet*, (Hemel Hempstead: Harvester, 1990).

Sayers, Sonya, *et al.* (eds), *The 60s Without Apology* (Minneapolis: University of Minnesota Press, 1984).

Scarry, Elaine, *The Body in Pain: The Making and Unmaking of the World* (Oxford: Oxford University Press, 1985).

Shaw, Marion, and Vanacker, Sabine, *Reflecting on Miss Marple* (London: Routledge, 1991).

Showalter, Elaine, *The Female Malady: Women, Madness and Culture, 1830–1980* (London: Virago, 1987).

——, *A Literature of their Own: British Women Writers from Charlotte Bronte to Doris Lessing* (London: Virago, 1978).

Siebenheller, Norma, *P.D. James* (New York: Frederick Ungar, 1981).

Skinner John, *The Fictions of Anita Brookner: Illusions of Romance* (Basingstoke: Macmillan, 1992).

Sinfield, Alan (ed.), *Literature, Politics and Culture in Postwar Britain* (Oxford: Blackwell, 1989).

Smith P.J., *Lesbian Panic: Homoeroticism in Modern British Women's Fiction* (New York: Columbia University Press, 1997).

Steedman, Carolyn, *Landscape for a Good Woman: A Story of Two Lives* (London: Virago, 1986).

Steinem, Gloria, *Outrageous Acts and Everyday Rebellions* (New York: Holt, Rinehart and Winston, 1983).

Spitzer, Susan, 'Fantasy and Femaleness in Margaret Drabble's *The Millstone*', *Novel*, 11, Spring 1978, pp. 227–45.

Spivack, Gayatari, 'Three Women's Texts and a Critique of Imperialism', *Critical Inquiry*, 12 Autumn, 1985.

Stuart, Andrea, '*The Color Purple*: In Defence of Happy Endings', in Lorraine Gamman and Margaret Marshment (ed.), *The Female Gaze: Women as Viewers of Popular Culture* (London: The Women's Press, 1988), pp. 60–75.

Stewart, Grace, *A New Mythos: The Novel of the Artist as Heroine 1877–1977* (Montreal: Eden Press, 1981).

Suleiman, Susan Rubin, *Subversive Intent: Gender, Politics and the Avant-Garde* (Cambridge, MA: Harvard University Press, 1980).

Sucher, Laurie, *The Fiction of Ruth Prawer Jhabvala: The Politics of Passion* (London: Macmillan, 1989).

Sutherland, John, *Best Sellers: Popular Fiction of the 1970s* (London: Routledge and Kegan Paul, 1981).

Stewart, Albert, and Albert, Judith Clavir (eds), *The Sixties: Documents of a Rebellious Decade* (New York: Praegar, 1984).

Swinden, Patrick, *The English Novel of History and Society, 1940–80* (London: Macmillan, 1984).

Taylor, D.J. *After the War: The Novel and English Society since 1945* (London: Chatto, 1993).

Taylor, Jenny (ed.), *Notebooks/Memoirs/Archives, Reading and Rereading Doris Lessing* (London: Routledge and Kegan Paul, 1982).

Taylor-Guthrie, Danille (ed.), *Conversations with Toni Morrison* (Jackson: University of Mississippi Press, 1994).

Templin, Charlotte, *Feminism and the Politics of Literary Reputation: The Example of Erica Jong* (Lawrence: University Press of Kansas, 1995).

Thompson, E.P., *William Morris: Romantic to Revolutionary* (1961) (revised edition London: Merlin Press, 1977).

Todd, Janet, *Women Writers Talking* (New York: Holmes and Meier, 1983).

Todd, Richard, *A.S. Byatt* (London: Northcote House, 1997).

Tyler, Anne, 'Starting out Submissive: Review of *The Women's Room* by Marilyn French', *New York Times Book Review*, 16 October 1977, p. 7, p. 38.

Uglow, Jenny (ed.), *Shaking a Leg: Journalism and Writings, The Collected Angela Carter* (London: Chatto and Windus, 1997).

Updike, John, 'Jong: Love', Review of *Fear of Flying* by Erica Jong, *New Yorker*, 17 December, 1973, pp. 149–51.

Wagner-Martin, Linda W., *Sylvia Plath* (London: Chatto and Windus, 1988).

Walker, Alice, *In Search of our Mothers' Gardens: Womanist Prose by Alice Walker* (London: The Women's Press, 1984), pp. 66–70.

——, *Anything We Love Can Be Saved: A Writer's Activism* (New York: Random House, 1997).

——, *The Same River Twice: Honouring the Difficult, a Meditation on Life, Spirit, Art, and the Making of the Film 'The Color Purple' Ten Years Later* (London: The Women's Press, 1996).

Walker, Melissa, *Down from the Mountain: Black Women's Novels in the Wake of the Civil Rights Movement 1966–1989* (New Haven: Yale University Press, 1991).

Wall, Cheryl A. (ed.), *Changing our Own Words: Essays on Criticism, Theory and Writing by Black Women* (London: Routledge, 1989).

Wandor, Micheline, *Once a Feminist: Stories of a Generation* (London: Virago, 1990).

Warner, Marina, *From the Beast to the Blonde: On Fairy Tales and their Tellers* (London: Chatto and Windus, 1994).

Waugh, Patricia, *Feminine Fictions: Revisiting the Postmodern* (London: Routledge, 1989).

Williams, Raymond, 'Region and Class in the Novel', in Douglas Jefferson and Graham Martin (eds), *The Uses of Fiction: Essays on the Novel in Honour of Arnold Kettle* (Milton Keynes: Open University Press, 1982), pp. 59–69.

——, *Politics and Letters: Interview with New Left Review* (London: NLB, 1979).

Willis, Susan, 'I Shop Therefore I Am: Is There a Place for Afro-American Culture in Commodity Culture?', in Cheryl A. Wall (ed.), *Changing our Own Words: Essays on Criticism, Theory and Writing by Black Women* (London: Routledge, 1989).

Wilson, Elizabeth, *Only Halfway to Paradise: Women in Postwar Britain 1945–1968* (London: Tavistock, 1980).

——, 'Tell It Like It Is': Women and Confessional Writing', in Susannah Radstone (ed.), *Sweet Dreams: Sexuality, Gender and Popular Fiction* (London: Lawrence and Wishart, 1988), pp. 21–45.

——, 'Yesterday's Heroines: On Rereading Lessing and de Beauvoir', in Jenny Taylor (ed.), *Notebooks/Memoirs/Archives, Reading and Rereading Doris Lessing* (London:

Routledge and Kegan Paul, 1982), pp. 57–75.

Wisker, Gina, *It's My Party: Reading Twentieth Century Women's Writing* (London: Pluto Press, 1994).

Woolf, Virginia, 'The Leaning Tower', in Rachel Bowlby, *A Woman's Essays* (London: Penguin, 1992), pp. 154–78.

——, *A Room of One's Own* (London: Hogarth, 1928).

——, 'Women and Fiction', in Leonard Woolf (ed.), *The Collected Essays of Virginia Woolf*, 4 vols (London: Hogarth, 1966–67), vol. 2, 1966, pp. 141–52.

Walter, Natasha, *The New Feminism* (London: Little Brown, 1998).

Zeman, Anthea, *Presumptious Girls: Women and their World in the Serious Woman's Novel* (London: Weidenfeld and Nicolson, 1977).

INDEX

Note: literary works can be found under authors' names.